Jackson vs. Biddle's Bank

PROBLEMS IN AMERICAN CIVILIZATION

Under the editorial direction of
Edwin C. Rozwenc
Amherst College

Jackson vs. Biddle's Bank

The Struggle Over the Second Bank of the United States

Second Edition

Edited and with an introduction by

George Rogers Taylor

Amherst College

D. C. HEATH AND COMPANY
Lexington, Massachusetts   Toronto   London

International Standard Book Number: 0-669-84491-8

Library of Congress Catalog Card Number: 72-3835

CONTENTS

Classic Accounts of the Controversy

More Recent Analyses

INTRODUCTION

Alone among the great nations of the world the United States still lacks a highly centralized banking system. The reasons for this are largely historical; they stem from the struggle over the attempt to recharter the second Bank of the United States. The bitterness of that controversy and the fear and hatred of the second Bank were such that only very slowly and with the greatest reluctance has this country permitted the creation of something approaching a central banking institution.

Following the expiration of the charter of the second Bank of the United States in 1836 the state banks were entirely on their own. The Independent Treasury System of the federal government, established in 1846 (it also existed for a brief period in 1840–1841), was little more than a receiving and disbursing instrument for the federal treasury. But in connection with the need for funds during the Civil War, and also to bring about a safer and more uniform currency, the National Banking System was inaugurated in 1864. Particularistic and without central direction, this system, though it brought about improved currency conditions, proved inadequate to meet those situations which required financial leadership and concerted action. Only after fifty years and a succession of serious financial crises were old prejudices against central direction sufficiently overcome to permit the establishment of the Federal Reserve System in 1914. And even then the arrangement adopted was not *unitary* but *federal*, and a serious attempt was made to avoid giving complete power over its operations either to private business or to the federal government.

The beginnings of this struggle which has had such a lasting effect on our financial institutions go back to the first years of our national history, when the Federalists under the leadership of Hamilton secured the chartering of the first Bank of the United States. This institution, modeled after the Bank of England, was regarded by the dominant merchant class of that time as a financial institution necessary to the orderly and efficient functioning of both public and private business. To the agrarians led by Jefferson and to their chief spokesman, John Taylor of Caroline, it was an instrument of concentrated power threatening the interests of farmers and planters. Alarm over the threat of the Bank died down somewhat after the Anti-Federalists came into power, but when the charter expired in 1811 it was not renewed.

The history of the second Bank of the United States is briefly traced in the first of the readings contained in this volume. This is followed by the text of Jackson's veto message. As the best-known presidential veto in American history, it merits careful study.

The Philadelphia Resolutions and the editorial reprinted in the *National Intelligencer* provide contemporary evidence of the bitter reaction to the veto message. And the Senate speech by Daniel Webster makes available the well-considered view of the chief spokesman for the forces favoring the recharter of the Bank. Thomas Hart Benton, leader for Jackson in the Senate, answers the critics in the next section, as also do the editorial from the Washington *Globe* and the letter from the Democratic historian, George Bancroft which follow. The trend of these contemporary items, it will be observed, reflects rather less concern with the issues involved than with the coming presidential election.

Far from ending in the 1830s, the Bank War has continued down to the present day, resulting in an ever-growing volume of writing not unevenly balanced between the defenders and the attackers. The former are given their day in court by the inclusion of two items: the first is from the pen of the able historian of the Bank, Ralph C. H. Catterall, who fifty years ago wrote what is still recognized as the most detailed and authoritative study of that institution, and the second is an article by Bray Hammond, perhaps the most able and vigorous of recent defenders of the second Bank. Opposed to these stands the work of Arthur M. Schlesinger, Jr., from whose Pulitzer Prize-winning book, *The Age of Jackson,* four chapters have been included. Many of the reviews of this book were very favorable indeed, but a dissenting one, a critical composition by Hammond, has been included because it specifically raises the bank issue and permits a brief, last word to the proponents of the Bank in this more than a century of controversy. Finally, the student may well suspend judgment on the merits of the problem until he has considered the factual and analytical material contained in the excerpts from the writings of Jean Alexander Wilburn and Peter Temin, two younger scholars who have recently investigated the subject.

In the choice of these readings one issue, the constitutionality of the institution, has been slighted. Though regarded as of the greatest moment at the time, this aspect of the problem has declined in interest for modern readers. One issue has been stressed, the danger believed by many to result from the concentration of great economic power in the hands of a few men not directly responsible to the people for their behavior. The problems arising in this connection—especially those having to do with the relations of private finance and business to the state—are as contemporary as today and tomorrow and as fiercely debated now as they were one hundred years ago when Old Hickory threw down the gage of battle to Nicholas Biddle.

Note: The statement by Claude G. Bowers in the Clash of Issues is quoted from *The Party Battles of the Jackson Period* (Boston, 1922), p. 318.

The Clash of Issues

Jackson's Veto Message:

It is to be regretted that the rich and powerful too often bend the acts of Government to their selfish purposes. . . . In the full enjoyment of the gifts of Heaven and the fruits of superior industry, economy, and virtue, every man is equally entitled to protection by law; but when the laws undertake to add to these natural and just advantages artificial distinctions, to grant titles, gratuities, and exclusive privileges, to make the rich richer and the potent more powerful, the humble members of society—the farmers, mechanics, and laborers—who have neither the time nor the means of securing like favors to themselves, have a right to complain of the injustice of their Government. . . . In the act before me there seems to be a wide and unnecessary departure from . . . just principles.

Daniel Webster, Jackson's political opponent:

This message . . . manifestly seeks to inflame the poor against the rich; it wantonly attacks whole classes of the people, for the purpose of turning against them the prejudices and the resentments of other classes. It is a state paper which finds no topic too exciting for its use, no passion too inflammable for its address and its solicitation.

Ralph C. H. Catterall, the historian of the Bank:

Jackson and his supporters committed an offense against the nation when they destroyed the bank. The magnitude and enormity of that offense can only be faintly realized, but one is certainly justified in saying that few greater enormities are chargeable to politicians than the destruction of the Bank of the United States.

Claude G. Bowers, a historian sympathetic to Jackson:

Even among the ultra-conservatives of business, the feeling was germinating that Jackson was not far wrong in the conclusion that a moneyed institution possessing the power to precipitate panics to influence governmental action, was dangerous to the peace, prosperity, and liberty of the people.

George Rogers Taylor

A BRIEF HISTORY OF THE SECOND BANK OF THE UNITED STATES

George Rogers Taylor, editor of this volume and a student of American economic history, is professor emeritus from Amherst College.

Early in January 1817 the second Bank of the United States opened for business in Carpenter's Hall, Philadelphia. In this building the first Bank of the United States had wound up its affairs six years before. It was appropriate that the second Bank should begin at the old stand, for, although considerably larger, it was organized along lines substantially similar to those of its predecessor. And it was an augury of its future financial power that in 1821 it should move from the modest quarters where the old bank had quietly performed its functions to a sumptuous temple built for its occupancy and designed by William Strickland on lines of the Parthenon in Athens.

Why should the same political party and even many of the same persons who had refused to recharter the Bank of the United States in 1811 have voted to establish an even larger institution in 1816? The chief reason was the war, a war which had been fought on the military front with an inefficiency and ineptness rivaled only in the administration of the government's finances. Without strong leadership and beset by partisan strife, Congress failed to make a beginning toward the passage of vital taxation measures until the war was nearly over, and the administration of the treasury under William Jones and George W. Campbell proved almost incredibly bad. By the beginning of 1815 the credit of the United States had fallen to its lowest ebb since the founding of the federal government. The war department was pressed to find enough money to pay a bill for $30, and the treasury could not secure funds to meet the interest on that part of the public debt held in New England. Banks had multiplied during the war and greatly extended their note issues. By the fall of 1814 most banks outside New

Adapted from George Rogers Taylor, *The Transportation Revolution,* Vol. IV of *Economic History of the United States* (New York, 1951), pp. 301–309. Used by permission of Holt, Rinehart & Winston.

FIGURE 1. The Second Bank of the United States, Philadelphia. (Historical Pictures Service, Chicago)

England had been forced to suspend specie payments. The currency consisted of a flood of bank notes circulating at varying discounts and increasing quantities of United States Treasury notes also of fluctuating value. Prices had risen to the highest point for the whole nineteenth century.

As one means of bringing some order out of this chaos and assisting the government in financing the war, sentiment grew for the reestablishment of a national bank. Leaders in promoting this movement were John Jacob Astor, David Parish, Stephen Girard, and other wealthy merchants. Their patriotic sentiments were in happy accord with their personal financial interests. They believed the establishment of a national bank would aid the government to finance the war and would also raise the price of government stock in which they were heavy investors. With their approval President Madison appointed and the Senate confirmed, October 1814, Alexander Dallas as Secretary of the Treasury. An able Philadelphia lawyer known to favor the establishment of a national bank, he and Senator John C. Calhoun were most active in drawing up plans for a new bank charter. After prolonged debate extending over more than two years a bill acceptable to the administration emerged. President Madison overcame his constitutional scruples and, despite the efforts of Daniel Webster and John Randolph, who led two opposition groups, the act was passed and approved by the President on April 10, 1816.

The charter provided that the capital of the second Bank of the United States should be $35 million, of which one fifth was to be subscribed by the federal government. The shareholders were to elect twenty directors of the Bank and the President of the United States was to appoint five. The new institution could issue notes in denominations of not less than $5 which would be accepted by the government in payment for taxes; the total value of notes issued must not exceed $35 million. Notes must be redeemed in specie or the Bank was to forfeit 12 percent per annum on any part of its circulation not so honored. The federal government was to receive $1.5 million from the Bank in return for the charter privilege.

Although earlier proponents had looked upon the Bank mainly as a means for aiding the treasury in financing the war, the chief objects sought by the Bank's sponsors in 1816 were to force the state banks to resume specie payments and to establish a satisfactory national currency. In view of later controversies as to its function it is worth noting that Secretary Dallas regarded it as much more than merely a giant commercial bank. Thus he wrote to Calhoun, December 24, 1815: ". . . it is not an institution created for the purposes of commerce and profit alone, but more for the purposes of national policy, as an auxiliary in the exercise of some of the highest powers of the Government." Nevertheless many, including some government officials and officers of the Bank, did not hold this broad view but appear to have regarded the Bank as merely a great financial institution chiefly obligated to make profits for its stockholders.

Unfortunately, the Bank got off to a bad start and soon headed into serious trouble. President Madison and Secretary Dallas had agreed

that the Bank should be under strong Republican influence and succeeded in having William Jones, an ardent Republican politician of
Philadelphia, elected as the first president. Why this man who during
the war had shown notorious incompetence as Secretary of Navy and
Acting Secretary of Treasury should have been chosen for this key
position is difficult to understand. Apparently his contemporaries regarded him as a loyal political follower and a trustworthy individual.
At any rate he at once adopted a loose, expansionist policy for the
Bank, seemingly with the purpose of maximizing profits for stockholders. Branches were promptly opened in the more important
commercial cities of the country and loans and discounts rapidly
expanded, especially in these branch offices.

Trouble first developed in the branches, which were subjected to
little or no control by the parent institution. The Baltimore branch
from the beginning was in the hands of a ring of unscrupulous opera-
tors who easily robbed it of more than a million dollars before they
were exposed and the branch forced into the hands of a receiver.
Most of the members of the board of directors of the parent bank
speculated in the Bank's own stock, and Jones himself accepted a
present of $18,000 which his officers "earned" for him by this kind of
speculation. Whether in the branches or in the main office in Philadelphia, wherever one might look, there was malfeasance, misfeasance,
or merely administrative incompetence. In January 1819, President
Jones was permitted to resign. After less than two years under his
guidance, the greatest financial institution in the country had been
brought perilously close to bankruptcy.

Yet beyond matters of internal management Jones should not be
held solely or indeed chiefly responsible for the ineffectiveness of
the Bank. William H. Crawford, who became Secretary of the Treasury in October 1816, soon went along with the inflationary policy of
the state banks, thus making corrective action by the Bank of the
United States virtually impossible. In order to accommodate the state
banks the Bank of the United States had no option but to extend its
credit to them and so could not put effective pressure on them to pay
off the loans extended to them by the Bank. Unable to force the state
banks to remit specie, the Bank of the United States was helpless to
obtain more than nominal resumption of specie payments. Confusion
in the currency continued unabated and, with the tremendous expan-

sion of credit, the specie holdings of the banks, including the Bank of the United States, reached levels clearly inadequate to cope with any substantial shock to business confidence. With prices of exports remaining high and business booming well into 1818, neither Secretary Crawford nor President Jones had the wisdom or the political courage to put effective brakes on the inflation. This is, of course, hardly surprising. For when in our checkered monetary history has the public in the midst of a boom welcomed the imposition of anti-inflationary measures?

The Bank was saved by Langdon Cheves, a respected South Carolina lawyer who became president in 1819 and remained in that position until 1823. Brought in to restore the financial soundness of the institution, he promptly and decisively tightened the administration, for the first time brought the branches under control, sharply reduced the loans outstanding, and began action to collect on the defaulted debts of both state banks and individuals. By 1820 the notes of the Bank in circulation had been reduced to about $3.5 million from over $8 million in 1818 and loans to $31,401,000 from $41,181,000. Cheves's methods promptly returned the Bank to financial soundness but his conservative policies resulted in reduced dividends to stockholders, who soon became restive and began to demand more creative leadership. Cheves resigned in the fall of 1823 to be succeeded by Nicholas Biddle, a brilliant, strong-willed man of 37, who had already made a favorable reputation for himself as a writer, as a member of the Pennsylvania senate, and as one of the government directors of the second Bank of the United States.

Long before Biddle took over, the Bank had acquired the bitter hostility of the state banks. In fact, the Bank of the United States could do little which did not evoke the jealousy of these local institutions. When Jones, following a policy of expansion, had established branches in western and southern cities, the local banks had protested against such competition and secured state legislation designed to curtail the operations of the branches. Two states, Indiana (1816) and Illinois (1818), prohibited by provisions in their state constitutions the establishment within their borders of any but state banks. Other states, including Maryland, Tennessee, Georgia, North Carolina, Kentucky, and Ohio, levied taxes upon the branches of the Bank of the United States which would have driven the Bank from the states imposing them had it not been for favorable action by the United States Supreme Court. In one of his most famous decisions, *M'Culloch v. Maryland,* Chief Justice Marshall in 1819 declared that the second Bank of the United States was a necessary and proper instrument of the United States government for carrying out its fiscal operations and was therefore constitutional. Moreover, he found the attempt of the state of Maryland to tax the Bank unconstitutional because, said he, if this were permitted then a state might ". . . tax all the means employed by the government, to an excess which would defeat all the ends of government."

When under Cheves the Bank reversed its expansionist policy and called in its loans, the hostility of state banks was even greater than when circulation was being extended. The drastic contraction was accompanied by a wave of bank failures which meant bankruptcy for business firms and financial institutions, especially in the West and South. With many of the state banks which survived this debacle the second Bank of the United States was often on bad terms, chiefly because it reasonably enough insisted that the state banks should not remain for long periods indebted to it for huge sums. Under Jones the branch of the Bank of the United States in Savannah, Georgia, had extended credits of about $200,000 to the state banks of that city. The Bank of the United States under Cheves tried to reduce this debt and made an extremely liberal offer permitting the state banks to use $100,000 without interest if they paid all in excess of that amount. The state banks in rejecting this offer attacked the Bank of the United States as a "mammoth" come to destroy them. Not until the dispute had gone to the Supreme Court was the Bank of the United States able to enforce its claims against the Savannah banks.

Under Biddle the Bank soon began cautiously to expand its operations and to assume a position of strength and prosperity. Growth, relatively moderate through 1828, accelerated thereafter. Bank notes issued averaged $1.5 million in 1823, $11 million in 1828, and $19 million in 1831. Emphasis was placed on commercial loans of short maturity, and transactions in domestic bills of exchange greatly increased. These latter totaled nearly $9 million in 1823, rose to $21.4 million in 1828, and reached $49.5 million by 1831. At the same time earnings increased greatly. By 1828 a surplus of $1.5 million had been accumulated and in the latter half of that year the Bank began paying dividends at the rate of 7 percent per annum, a rate which it continued as long as it retained its charter.

The operations of the Bank had at last reached a scale sufficient to permit it to perform the dominant role for which it had been originally cast. From the beginning it had proved an efficient fiscal agent for the federal government, not only acting as a safe depository for treasury funds but also successfully transferring these funds from one part of the country to another and meeting government drafts for disbursement at each of its branches. For the years 1816–1827, the Bank transferred funds for the United States Treasury averaging about $28 million per year at a saving estimated at more than $1 million. Moreover, the government secured necessary funds quickly and economically from the Bank of the United States whenever borrowing was necessary.

In the second place, the Bank of the United States helped to create a sound national currency both by maintaining specie payments on its own notes and by bringing pressure on the state banks to do the same. During Jones's presidency the Bank had attempted to accept the notes of all its branches at face value whenever they were presented at any of its offices. This could not be continued, for western branches expanded their note issues to meet the need for exchange on the East with the result that the eastern branches accepting these notes were stripped of their specie. The policy was therefore changed to one which honored bank notes at face value in specie only at Philadelphia and at the branch of issue; at a distance from the place of issue notes circulated at a small discount, usually less than 1 percent. This discount was much less than it had ordinarily been before the Bank was established, but it nevertheless gave critics of the Bank an opportunity to accuse it of not maintaining a uniform currency.

In the third place, the Bank of the United States helped to make credit and currency more abundant in the West and South. To a very considerable extent the Bank of the United States built up its business outside the eastern states on the basis of capital raised in those states. In doing this it aided the frontier areas by helping to provide both the capital and currency needed for their development.

Especially after 1823 when, under Biddle's strong direction, the Bank operated effectively to provide a uniform currency and to restrain the state banks from over-issue by regularly presenting their notes for specie. But the contention of Bray Hammond and those who have followed him that Biddle, at least up to his deliberate contraction of 1832, directed the institution effectively as a central bank can no longer be accepted.[1] The distinguishing function of a central bank is to act as a bankers' bank, guiding its activities not for the purpose of making a profit but so as to forward the public good by discouraging tendencies to over-expansion in the economy and giving prompt relief to banks and business in times of crisis. This central banking function insofar as it was carried out after 1815 was performed not by the Bank of the United States but by the United States Treasury; and in periods of severe liquidation it was the United States Treasury, not the Bank of the United States, which through specie deposits went to the aid of hard-pressed state banks and helped them to weather the storm.

Unwisely, as later events proved, Biddle applied for recharter of the second Bank of the United States in January 1832, four years before the existing charter expired. He thus threw down the gage of battle to Andrew Jackson in an election year. Congress passed a bill to continue the Bank with little change and President Jackson vetoed it, July 10, 1832. The veto message declared the Bank unconstitutional and condemned it as a device for giving financial advantage and power to a small and irresponsible group of wealthy persons living in eastern cities and even in foreign countries. Biddle threw the whole influence of the Bank against the election of Jackson, who as we know was reelected by an overwhelming vote, though by a smaller proportion of the total vote than in 1828.

But this did not end the Bank War. Suspicious of the Bank and vindictive as well, Jackson believed that the government should promptly begin to remove its deposits in the Bank and force it to prepare for the winding up of its affairs. William J. Duane had been made Secretary of the Treasury early in 1833, soon after McLane left that position to head the State Department. When Duane, a stooge for McLane, who was very close to the Bank group, refused to accept the removal policy, Jackson forced his resignation and appointed in his

---

[1] Bray Hammond, *Banks and Politics in America* (Princeton, 1957), pp. 286–287, 300–312, 323–325. For the contrary position, see Peter Temin, *The Jacksonian Economy* (New York, 1969), pp. 53–58.

place his Attorney General, Roger B. Taney. Taney definitely opposed the Bank; he had been one of those assisting the President in drafting the veto message on the bill to recharter. Actually no appreciable shift of existing deposits took place but as new government receipts came in they were simply placed on deposit in state banks.

Nicholas Biddle, no less headstrong than Jackson and still hoping to force the recharter of the Bank, fought back, not scrupling to utilize the full resources of his institution. Believing that only a drastic credit contraction would convince the administration and the country of the folly of permitting the Bank to go out of existence, he began in August 1833 to curtail credit, and despite growing protests even from favorably disposed business and banking leaders continued the curtailment to September 1834. To William Appleton, president of the Boston branch of the Bank, he wrote in January 1834: "Nothing but the evidence of suffering abroad will produce any effect in Congress." And early in the next month he wrote to another correspondent: ". . . all the other Banks and all the merchants may break, but the Bank of the United States shall not break." Biddle succeeded in precipitating a crisis which in 1834 forced discount rates as high as 18 to 36 percent and brought great distress to the business community. But by this display of power he ruined whatever chances the Bank may have had for recharter. Many business leaders, even those of conservative tendencies, now turned against that institution. Biddle had demonstrated what his enemies had charged: the ability of the Bank to affect the whole course of business of the country and his willingness to use that power to the public detriment and his own personal advantage.

The subsequent history of the Bank is quickly told. Having failed in 1834 to frighten the government into giving it a new charter, the Bank reversed its policy and greatly expanded its operations. On the expiration of its United States charter in 1836 it secured a new one from the state of Pennsylvania and continued in business until October 1839 when, caught with greatly over-extended loans, it found itself in serious financial straits and forced to suspend specie payments. It never really recovered and was forced into liquidation in 1841.

President Andrew Jackson

VETO MESSAGE, JULY 10, 1832

Andrew Jackson's veto of the bill to recharter the second Bank of the United States is one of the best-known presidential vetoes in American history. Several of Jackson's aides assisted in drafting the veto message, but Amos Kendall, a leading member of the Kitchen Cabinet, appears to have been chiefly responsible. Though the rhetoric is Kendall's, the sentiments expressed are the strongly held views of Old Hickory.

The bill "to modify and continue" the act entitled "An act to incorporate the subscribers to the Bank of the United States" was presented to me on the 4th July instant. Having considered it with the solemn regard to the principles of the Constitution which the day was calculated to inspire, and come to the conclusion that it ought not to become a law, I herewith return it to the Senate, in which it originated, with my objections.

A bank of the United States is in many respects convenient for the Government and useful to the people. Entertaining this opinion, and deeply impressed with the belief that some of the powers and privileges possessed by the existing bank are unauthorized by the Constitution, subversive of the rights of the States, and dangerous to the liberties of the people, I felt it my duty at an early period of my Administration to call the attention of Congress to the practicability of organizing an institution combining all its advantages and obviating these objections. I sincerely regret that in the act before me I can perceive none of those modifications of the bank charter which are necessary, in my opinion, to make it compatible with justice, with sound policy, or with the Constitution of our country.

The present corporate body, denominated the president, directors, and company of the Bank of the United States, will have existed at the time this act is intended to take effect twenty years. It enjoys an exclusive privilege of banking under the authority of the General Government, a monopoly of its favor and support, and, as a necessary consequence, almost a monopoly of the foreign and domestic ex-

Reprinted from *House Miscellaneous Documents*, 53rd Congress, 2d Session, 1893–1894, II, 576–591.

change. The powers, privileges, and favors bestowed upon it in the original charter, by increasing the value of the stock far above its par value, operated as a gratuity of many millions to the stockholders.

An apology may be found for the failure to guard against this result in the consideration that the effect of the original act of incorporation could not be certainly foreseen at the time of its passage. The act before me proposes another gratuity to the holders of the same stock, and in many cases to the same men, of at least seven millions more. This donation finds no apology in any uncertainty as to the effect of the act. On all hands it is conceded that its passage will increase at least 20 or 30 percent more the market price of the stock, subject to the payment of the annuity of $200,000 per year secured by the act, thus adding in a moment one-fourth to its par value. It is not our own citizens only who are to receive the bounty of our Government. More than eight millions of the stock of this bank are held by foreigners. By this act the American Republic proposes virtually to make them a present of some millions of dollars. For these gratuities to foreigners and to some of our own opulent citizens the act secures no equivalent whatever. They are the certain gains of the present stockholders under the operation of this act, after making full allowance for the payment of the bonus.

Every monopoly and all exclusive privileges are granted at the expense of the public, which ought to receive a fair equivalent. The many millions which this act proposes to bestow on the stockholders of the existing bank must come directly or indirectly out of the earnings of the American people. It is due to them, therefore, if their Government sell monopolies and exclusive privileges, that they should at least exact for them as much as they are worth in open market. The value of the monopoly in this case may be correctly ascertained. The twenty-eight millions of stock would probably be at an advance of 50 percent, and command in market at least $42 million subject to the payment of the present bonus. The present value of the monopoly, therefore, is $17 million and this the act proposes to sell for three millions, payable in fifteen annual installments of $200,000 each.

It is not conceivable how the present stockholders can have any claim to the special favor of the Government. The present corporation has enjoyed its monopoly during the period stipulated in the original contract. If we must have such a corporation, why should not the Government sell out the whole stock and thus secure to the people the full market value of the privileges granted? Why should not Congress create and sell twenty-eight millions of stock, incorporating the purchasers with all the powers and privileges secured in this act and putting the premium upon the sales into the Treasury?

But this act does not permit competition in the purchase of this monopoly. It seems to be predicated on the erroneous idea that the present stockholders have a prescriptive right not only to the favor but to the bounty of Government. It appears that more than a fourth part of the stock is held by foreigners and the residue is held by a few hundred of our own citizens, chiefly of the richest class. For their benefit does this act exclude the whole American people from competition in the purchase of this monopoly and dispose of it for many millions less than it is worth. This seems the less excusable because some of our citizens not now stockholders petitioned that the door of competition might be opened, and offered to take a charter on terms much more favorable to the Government and country.

But this proposition, although made by men whose aggregate wealth is believed to be equal to all the private stock in the existing bank, has been set aside, and the bounty of our Government is proposed to be again bestowed on the few who have been fortunate enough to secure the stock and at this moment wield the power of the existing institution. I can not perceive the justice or policy of this course. If our Government must sell monopolies, it would seem to be its duty to take nothing less than their full value, and if gratuities must be made once in fifteen or twenty years let them not be bestowed on the subjects of a foreign government nor upon a designated and favored class of men in our own country. It is but justice and good policy, as far as the nature of the case will admit, to confine our favors to own own fellow-citizens, and let each in his turn enjoy an opportunity to profit by our bounty. In the bearings of the act before me upon these points I find ample reasons why it should not become a law.

It has been urged as an argument in favor of rechartering the present bank that the calling in of its loans will produce great embarrassment and distress. The time allowed to close its concerns is ample, and if it has been well managed its pressure will be light, and heavy only in case its management has been bad. If, therefore, it shall produce distress, the fault will be its own, and it would furnish a reason against renewing a power which has been so obviously abused. But will there ever be a time when this reason will be less powerful? To acknowledge its force is to admit that the bank ought to be perpetual, and as a consequence the present stockholders and those inheriting their rights as successors be established a privileged order, clothed both with great political power and enjoying immense pecuniary advantages from their connection with the Government.

The modifications of the existing charter proposed by this act are not such, in my view, as make it consistent with the rights of the States or the liberties of the people. The qualification of the right of the bank to hold real estate, the limitation of its power to establish branches, and the power reserved to Congress to forbid the circulation of small notes are restrictions comparatively of little value or importance. All the objectionable principles of the existing corporation, and most of its odious features, are retained without alleviation.

The fourth section provides

> *that the notes or bills of the said corporation, although the same be, on the faces thereof, respectively made payable at one place only, shall nevertheless be received by the said corporation at the bank or at any of the offices of discount and deposit thereof if tendered in liquidation or payment of any balance or balances due to said corporation or to such office of discount and deposit from any other incorporated bank.*

This provision secures to the State banks a legal privilege in the Bank of the United States which is withheld from all private citizens. If a State bank in Philadelphia owe the Bank of the United States and have notes issued by the St. Louis branch, it can pay the debt with those notes, but if a merchant, mechanic, or other private citizen be in like circumstances he can not by law pay his debt with those notes, but must sell them at a discount or send them to St. Louis to be cashed. This boon conceded to the State banks, though not unjust in itself, is most odious because it does not measure out equal justice to the high and the low, the rich and the poor. To the extent of its practical effect it is a bond of union among the banking establishments of the nation, erecting them into an interest separate from that of the people, and its necessary tendency is to unite the Bank of the

United States and the State banks in any measure which may be thought conducive to their common interest.

The ninth section of the act recognizes principles of worse tendency than any provision of the present charter.

It enacts that "the cashier of the bank shall annually report to the Secretary of Treasury the names of all stockholders who are not resident citizens of the United States, and on the application of the treasurer of any State shall make out and transmit to such treasurer a list of stockholders residing in or citizens of such State, with the amount of stock owned by each." Although this provision, taken in connection with a decision of the Supreme Court, surrenders, by its silence, the right of the States to tax the banking institutions created by this corporation under the name of branches throughout the Union, it is evidently intended to be construed as a concession of their right to tax that portion of the stock which may be held by their own citizens and residents. In this light, if the act becomes a law, it will be understood by the States, who will probably proceed to levy a tax equal to that paid upon the stock of banks incorporated by themselves. In some States that tax is now 1 percent, either on the capital or on the shares, and that may be assumed as the amount which all citizen or resident stockholders would be taxed under the operation of this act. As it is only the stock *held* in the States and not that *employed* within them which would be subject to taxation, and as the names of foreign stockholders are not to be reported to the treasurers of the States, it is obvious that the stock held by them will be exempt from this burden. Their annual profits will therefore be 1 percent more than the citizen stockholders, and as the annual dividends of the bank may be safely estimated at 7 percent, the stock will be worth 10 or 15 percent more to foreigners than to citizens of the United States. To appreciate the effects which this state of things will produce, we must take a brief review of the operations and present condition of the Bank of the United States.

By documents submitted to Congress at the present session it appears that on the 1st of January 1832, of the twenty-eight millions of private stock in the corporation, $8,405,500 were held by foreigners, mostly of Great Britain. The amount of stock held in the nine Western and Southwestern States is $140,200, and in the four Southern States is $5,623,100, and in the Middle and Eastern States is about

$13,522,000. The profits of the bank in 1831, as shown in a statement to Congress, were about $3,455,598; of this there accrued in the nine Western States about $1,640,048; in the four Southern States about $352,507, and in the Middle and Eastern States about $1,463,041. As little stock is held in the West, it is obvious that the debt of the people in that section to the bank is principally a debt to the Eastern and foreign stockholders; that the interest they pay upon it is carried into the Eastern States and into Europe, and that it is a burden upon their industry and a drain of their currency, which no country can bear without inconvenience and occasional distress. To meet this burden and equalize the exchange operations of the bank, the amount of specie drawn from those States through its branches within the last two years, as shown by its official reports, was about $6 million. More than half a million of this amount does not stop in the Eastern States, but passes on to Europe to pay the dividends of the foreign stockholders. In the principle of taxation recognized by this act the Western States find no adequate compensation for this perpetual burden on their industry and drain of their currency. The branch bank at Mobile made last year $95,140, yet under the provisions of this act the State of Alabama can raise no revenue from these profitable operations, because not a share of the stock is held by any of her citizens. Mississippi and Missouri are in the same condition in relation to the branches at Natchez and St. Louis, and such, in a greater or less degree, is the condition of every Western State. The tendency of the plan of taxation which this act proposes will be to place the whole United States in the same relation to foreign countries which the Western States now bear to the Eastern. When by a tax on resident stockholders the stock of this bank is made worth 10 or 15 percent more to foreigners than to residents, most of it will inevitably leave the country.

Thus will this provision in its practical effect deprive the Eastern as well as the Southern and Western States of the means of raising a revenue from the extension of business and great profits of this institution. It will make the American people debtors to aliens in nearly the whole amount due to this bank, and send across the Atlantic from two to five millions of specie every year to pay the bank dividends.

In another of its bearings this provision is fraught with danger. Of the twenty-five directors of this bank five are chosen by the Government and twenty by the citizen stockholders. From all voice in these elections the foreign stockholders are excluded by the charter. In proportion, therefore, as the stock is transferred to foreign holders the extent of suffrage in the choice of directors is curtailed. Already is almost a third of the stock in foreign hands and not represented in elections. It is constantly passing out of the country, and this act will accelerate its departure. The entire control of the institution would necessarily fall into the hands of a few citizen stockholders, and the ease with which the object would be accomplished would be a temptation to designing men to secure that control in their own hands by monopolizing the remaining stock. There is danger that a president and directors would then be able to elect themselves from year to year, and without responsibility or control manage the whole concerns of the bank during the existence of its charter. It is easy to conceive that great evils to our country and its institutions might flow from such a concentration of power in the hands of a few men irresponsible to the people.

Is there no danger to our liberty and independence in a bank that in its nature has so little to bind it to our country? The president of the bank has told us that most of the State banks exist by its forbearance. Should its influence become concentered, as it may under the operation of such an act as this, in the hands of a self-elected directory whose interests are identified with those of the foreign stockholders, will there not be cause to tremble for the purity of our elections in peace and for the independence of our country in war? Their power would be great whenever they might choose to exert it; but if this monopoly were regularly renewed every fifteen or twenty years on terms proposed by themselves, they might seldom in peace put forth their strength to influence elections or control the affairs of the nation. But if any private citizen or public functionary should interpose to curtail its powers or prevent a renewal of its privileges, it can not be doubted that he would be made to feel its influence.

Should the stock of the bank principally pass into the hands of the subjects of a foreign country, and we should unfortunately become involved in a war with that country, what would be our condition? Of the course which would be pursued by a bank almost wholly owned by the subjects of a foreign power, and managed by those whose interests, if not affections, would run in the same direction there can be no doubt. All its operations within would be in aid of the hostile fleets and armies without. Controlling our currency, receiving our public moneys, and holding thousands of our citizens in dependence, it would be more formidable and dangerous than the naval and military power of the enemy.

If we must have a bank with private stockholders, every consideration of sound policy and every impulse of American feeling admonishes that it should be *purely American.* Its stockholders should be composed exclusively of our own citizens, who at least ought to be friendly to our Government and willing to support it in times of difficulty and danger. So abundant is domestic capital that competition in subscribing for the stock of local banks has recently led almost to riots. To a bank exclusively of American stockholders, possessing the powers and privileges granted by this act, subscriptions for $200 million could be readily obtained. Instead of sending abroad the stock of the bank in which the Government must deposit its funds and on which it must rely to sustain its credit in times of emergency, it would rather seem to be expedient to prohibit its sale to aliens under penalty of absolute forfeiture.

It is maintained by the advocates of the bank that its constitutionality in all its features ought to be considered as settled by precedent and by the decision of the Supreme Court. To this conclusion I can not assent. Mere precedent is a dangerous source of authority, and should not be regarded as deciding questions of constitutional power except where the acquiescence of the people and the States can be considered as well settled. So far from this being the case on this subject, an argument against the bank might be based on precedent. One Congress, in 1791, decided in favor of a bank; another, in 1811, decided against it. One Congress, in 1815, decided against a bank; another, in 1816, decided in its favor. Prior to the present Congress, therefore, the precedents drawn from that source were equal. If we resort to the States, the expressions of legislative, judicial, and executive opinions against the bank have been probably to those in its favor as 4 to 1. There is nothing in precedent, therefore, which, if its authority were admitted, ought to weigh in favor of the act before me.

If the opinion of the Supreme Court covered the whole ground of this act, it ought not to control the coordinate authorities of this

Government. The Congress, the Executive, and the Court must each for itself be guided by its own opinion of the Constitution. Each public officer who takes an oath to support the Constitution swears that he will support it as he understands it, and not as it is understood by others. It is as much the duty of the House of Representatives, of the Senate, and of the President to decide upon the constitutionality of any bill or resolution which may be presented to them for passage or approval as it is of the supreme judges when it may be brought before them for judicial decision. The opinion of the judges has no more authority over Congress than the opinion of Congress has over the judges, and on that point the President is independent of both. The authority of the Supreme Court must not, therefore, be permitted to control the Congress or the Executive when acting in their legislative capacities, but to have only such influence as the force of their reasoning may deserve.

But in the case relied upon the Supreme Court have not decided that all the features of this corporation are compatible with the Constitution. It is true that the court have said that the law incorporating the bank is a constitutional exercise of power by Congress; but taking into view the whole opinion of the court and the reasoning by which they have come to that conclusion, I understand them to have decided that inasmuch as a bank is an appropriate means for carrying into effect the enumerating powers of the General Government, therefore the law incorporating it is in accordance with that provision of the Constitution which declares that Congress shall have power "to make all laws which shall be necessary and proper for carrying those powers into execution." Having satisfied themselves that the word *"necessary"* in the Constitution means *"needful," "requisite," "essential," "conducive to,"* and that "a bank" is a convenient, a useful, and essential instrument in the prosecution of the Government's "fiscal operations," they conclude that to "use one must be within the discretion of Congress" and that "the act to incorporate the Bank of the United States is a law made in pursuance of the Constitution"; "but," say they, *where the law is not prohibited and is really calculated to effect any of the objects intrusted to the Government, to undertake here to inquire into the degree of its necessity would be to pass the line which circumscribes the judicial department and to tread on legislative ground."*

The principle here affirmed is that the "degree of its necessity," involving all the details of a banking institution, is a question exclusively for legislative consideration. A bank is constitutional, but it is the province of the Legislature to determine whether this or that particular power, privilege, or exemption is "necessary and proper" to enable the bank to discharge its duties to the Government, and from their decision there is no appeal to the courts of justice. Under the decision of the Supreme Court, therefore, it is the exclusive province of Congress and the President to decide whether the particular features of this act are *necessary* and *proper* in order to enable the bank to perform conveniently and efficiently the public duties assigned to it as a fiscal agent, and therefore constitutional, or *unnecessary* and *improper,* and therefore unconstitutional.

Without commenting on the general principle affirmed by the Supreme Court, let us examine the details of this act in accordance with the rule of legislative action which they have laid down. It will be found that many of the powers and privileges conferred on it can not be supposed necessary for the purpose for which it is proposed to be created, and are not, therefore, means necessary to attain the end in view, and consequently not justified by the Constitution.

The original act of incorporation, section 21, enacts "that no other bank shall be established by any future law of the United States during the continuance of the corporation hereby created, for which the faith of the United States is hereby pledged: *Provided,* Congress may renew existing charters for banks within the District of Columbia not increasing the capital thereof, and may also establish any other bank or banks in said District with capitals not exceeding in the whole $6 million if they shall deem it expedient." This provision is continued in force by the act before me fifteen years from the 3d of March 1836.

If Congress possessed the power to establish one bank, they had power to establish more than one if in their opinion two or more banks had been "necessary" to facilitate the execution of the powers delegated to them in the Constitution. If they possessed the power to establish a second bank, it was a power derived from the Constitution to be exercised from time to time, and at any time when the interests of the country or the emergencies of the Government might make it expedient. It was possessed by one Congress as well as another, and by all Congresses alike, and alike at every session. But the

Congress of 1816 have taken it away from their successors for twenty years, and the Congress of 1832 proposes to abolish it for fifteen years more. It can not be *"necessary"* or *"proper"* for Congress to barter away or divest themselves of any of the powers vested in them by the Constitution to be exercised for the public good. It is not *"necessary"* to the efficiency of the bank, nor is it *"proper"* in relation to themselves and their successors. They may *properly* use the discretion vested in them, but they may not limit the discretion of their successors. This restriction on themselves and grant of a monopoly to the bank is therefore unconstitutional.

In another point of view this provision is a palpable attempt to amend the Constitution by an act of legislation. The Constitution declares that "the Congress shall have power to exercise exclusive legislation in all cases whatsoever" over the District of Columbia. Its constitutional power, therefore, to establish banks in the District of Columbia and increase their capital at will is unlimited and uncontrollable by any other power than that which gave authority to the Constitution. Yet this act declares that Congress shall *not* increase the capital of existing banks, nor create other banks with capitals exceeding in the whole $6 million. The Constitution declares that Congress *shall* have power to exercise exclusive legislation over this District *"in all cases whatsoever,"* and this act declares they shall not. Which is the supreme law of the land? This provision can not be *"necessary"* or *"proper"* or *constitutional* unless the absurdity be admitted that whenever it be "necessary and proper" in the opinion of Congress they have a right to barter away one portion of the powers vested in them by the Constitution as a means of executing the rest.

On two subjects only does the Constitution recognize in Congress the power to grant exclusive privileges or monopolies. It declares that "Congress shall have power to promote the progress of science and useful arts by securing for limited times to authors and inventors the exclusive right to their respective writings and discoveries." Out of this express delegation of power have grown our laws of patents and copyrights. As the Constitution expressly delegates to Congress the power to grant exclusive privileges in these cases as the means of executing the substantive power "to promote the progress of science and useful arts," it is consistent with the fair rules of construction to conclude that such a power was not intended to be granted as a means of accomplishing any other end. On every other subject which comes within the scope of Congressional power there is an ever-living discretion in the use of proper means, which can not be restricted or abolished without an amendment of the Constitution. Every act of Congress, therefore, which attempts by grants of monopolies or sale of exclusive privileges for a limited time, or a time without limit, to restrict or extinguish its own discretion in the choice of means to execute its delegated powers is equivalent to a legislative amendment of the Constitution, and palpably unconstitutional.

This act authorizes and encourages transfers of its stock to foreigners and grants them an exemption from all State and national taxation. So far from being *"necessary and proper"* that the bank should possess this power to make it a safe and efficient agent of the Government in its fiscal operations, it is calculated to convert the Bank of the United States into a foreign bank, to impoverish our people in time of peace, to disseminate a foreign influence through every section of the Republic, and in war to endanger our independence.

The several States reserved the power at the formation of the Constitution to regulate and control titles and transfers of real property, and most, if not all, of them have laws disqualifying aliens from acquiring or holding lands within their limits. But this act, in disregard of the undoubted right of the States to prescribe such disqualifications, gives to alien stockholders in this bank an interest and title, as members of the corporation, to all the real property it may acquire within any of the States of this Union. This privilege granted to aliens is not *"necessary"* to enable the bank to perform its public duties, nor in any sense *"proper,"* because it is vitally subversive of the rights of the States.

The Government of the United States have no constitutional power to purchase lands within the States except "for the erection of forts, magazines, arsenals, dockyards, and other needful buildings," and even for these objects only "by the consent of the legislature of the State in which the same shall be." By making themselves stockholders in the bank and granting to the corporation the power to purchase lands for other purposes they assume a power not granted in the Constitution and grant to others what they do not themselves possess. It is not *"necessary"* to the receiving, safe-keeping, or transmission of the funds of the Government that the bank should possess this power, and it is not *"proper"* that Congress should thus enlarge the powers delegated to them in the Constitution.

The old Bank of the United States possessed a capital of only $11 million, which was found fully sufficient to enable it with dispatch and safety to perform all the functions required of it by the Government. The capital of the present bank is $35 million—at least twenty-four more than experience has proved to be *necessary* to enable a bank to perform its public functions. The public debt which existed during the period of the old bank and on the establishment of the new has been nearly paid off, and our revenue will soon be reduced. This increase of capital is therefore not for public but for private purposes.

The Government is the only *"proper"* judge where its agents should reside and keep their offices, because it best knows where their presence will be *"necessary."* It can not, therefore, be *"necessary"* or *"proper"* to authorize the bank to locate branches where it pleases to perform the public service, without consulting the Government, and contrary to its will. The principle laid down by the Supreme Court concedes that Congress can not establish a bank for purposes of private speculation and gain, but only as a means of executing the delegated powers of the General Government. By the same principle a branch bank can not constitutionally be established for other than public purposes. The power which this act gives to establish two branches in any State, without the injunction or request of the Government and for other than public purposes, is not *"necessary"* to the due *execution* of the powers delegated to Congress.

The bonus which is exacted from the bank is a confession upon the face of the act that the powers granted by it are greater than are *"necessary"* to its character of a fiscal agent. The Government does not tax its officers and agents for the privilege of serving it. The bonus of a million and a half required by the original charter and that of three millions proposed by this act are not exacted for the privilege of granting "the necessary facilities for transferring the public funds from place to place within the United States or the Territories thereof, and for distributing the same in payment of the public creditors without charging commission or claiming allowance on account of the difference of exchange," as required by the act of incorporation, but for something more beneficial to the stockholders. The original act declares that it (the bonus) is granted "in consideration of the exclusive privileges and benefits conferred by this act upon the said bank," and the act before me declares it to be "in consideration of the exclusive benefits and privileges continued by this act to the said corporation for fifteen years, as aforesaid." It is therefore for "exclusive privileges and benefits" conferred for their own use and emolument, and not for the advantage of the Government, that a bonus is exacted. These surplus powers for which the bank is required to pay can not surely be *"necessary"* to make it the fiscal agent of the Treasury. If they were, the exaction of a bonus for them would not be *"proper."*

It is maintained by some that the bank is a means of executing the constitutional power "to coin money and regulate the value thereof." Congress have established a mint to coin money and passed laws to regulate the value thereof. The money so coined, with its value so regulated, and such foreign coins as Congress may adopt are the only currency known to the Constitution. But if they have other power to regulate the currency, it was conferred to be exercised by themselves, and not to be transferred to a corporation. If the bank be established for that purpose, with a charter unalterable without its consent, Congress have parted with their power for a term of years, during which the Constitution is a dead letter. It is neither necessary nor proper to transfer its legislative power to such a bank, and therefore unconstitutional.

By its silence, considered in connection with the decision of the Supreme Court in the case of McCulloch against the State of Maryland, this act takes from the States the power to tax a portion of the banking business carried on within their limits, in subversion of one of the strongest barriers which secured them against Federal encroachments. Banking, like farming, manufacturing, or any other occupation or profession, is *a business,* the right to follow which is not originally derived from the laws. Every citizen and every company of citizens in all of our States possessed the right until the State legislatures deemed it good policy to prohibit private banking by law. If the prohibitory State laws were now repealed, every citizen would again possess the right. The State banks are a qualified restoration of the right which has been taken away by the laws against banking, guarded by such provisions and limitations as in the opinion of the State legislatures the public interest requires. These corporations, unless there be an exemption in their charter, are, like private bankers and banking companies, subject to State taxation. The manner in which these taxes shall be laid depends wholly on legislative discretion. It may be upon the bank, upon the stock, upon the profits, or in any other mode which the sovereign power shall will.

Upon the formation of the Constitution the States guarded their taxing power with peculiar jealousy. They surrendered it only as it regards imports and exports. In relation to every other object within their jurisdiction, whether persons, property, business, or professions, it was secured in as ample a manner as it was before possessed. All persons, though United States officers, are liable to a poll tax by the States within which they reside. The lands of the United States are liable to the usual land tax, except in the new States, from whom agreements that they will not tax unsold lands are exacted when they are admitted into the Union. Horses, wagons, any beasts or vehicles, tools, or property belonging to private citizens, though employed in the service of the United States, are subject to State taxation. Every private business, whether carried on by an officer of the General Government or not, whether it be mixed with public concerns or not, even if it be carried on by the Government of the United States itself, separately or in partnership, falls within the scope of the taxing power of the State. Nothing comes more fully within it than banks and the business of banking, by whomsoever instituted and carried on. Over this whole subject-matter it is just as absolute, unlimited, and uncontrollable as if the Constitution had never been adopted, because in the formation of that instrument it was reserved without qualification.

The principle is conceded that the States can not rightfully tax the operations of the General Government. They can not tax the money of the Government deposited in the State banks, nor the agency of those banks in remitting it; but will any man maintain that their mere selection to perform this public service for the General Government would exempt the State banks and their ordinary business from State taxation? Had the United States, instead of establishing a bank at Philadelphia, employed a private banker to keep and transmit their funds, would it have deprived Pennsylvania of the right to tax his bank and his usual banking operations? It will not be pretended.

Upon what principle, then, are the banking establishments of the Bank of the United States and their usual banking operations to be exempted from taxation? It is not their public agency or the deposits of the Government which the States claim a right to tax, but their banks and their banking powers, instituted and exercised within State jurisdiction for their private emolument—those powers and privileges for which they pay a bonus, and which the States tax in their own banks. The exercise of these powers within a State, no matter by whom or under what authority, whether by private citizens in their original right, by corporate bodies created by the States, by foreigners or the agents of foreign governments located within their limits, forms a legitimate object of State taxation. From this and like sources, from the persons, property, and business that are found residing, located, or carried on under their jurisdiction, must the States, since the surrender of their right to raise a revenue from imports and exports, draw all the money necessary for the support of their governments and the maintenance of their independence. There is no more appropriate subject of taxation than banks, banking, and bank stocks, and none to which the States ought more pertinaciously to cling.

It can not be *necessary* to the character of the bank as a fiscal agent of the Government that its private business should be exempted from that taxation to which all the State banks are liable, nor can I conceive it *"proper"* that the substantive and most essential powers reserved by the States shall be thus attacked and annihilated as a means of executing the powers delegated to the General Government. It may be safely assumed that none of those sages who had an agency in forming or adopting our Constitution ever imagined that any portion of the taxing power of the States not prohibited to them nor delegated to Congress was to be swept away and annihilated as a means of executing certain powers delegated to Congress.

If our power over means is so absolute that the Supreme Court will not call in question the constitutionality of an act of Congress the subject of which "is not prohibited, and is really calculated to effect any of the objects intrusted to the Government," although, as in the case before me, it takes away powers expressly granted to Congress and rights scrupulously reserved to the States, it becomes us to proceed in our legislation with the utmost caution. Though not directly, our own powers and the rights of the States may be indirectly legislated away in the use of means to execute substantive powers. We may not enact that Congress shall not have the power of exclusive legislation over the District of Columbia, but we may pledge the faith of the United States that as a means of executing other powers it shall not be exercised for twenty years or forever. We may not pass an act prohibiting the States to tax the banking business carried on within their limits, but we may, as a means of executing our powers over other objects, place that business in the hands of our agents and then declare it exempt from State taxation in their hands. Thus may our own powers and the rights of the States, which we can not directly curtail or invade, be frittered away and extinguished in the use of means employed by us to execute other powers. That a bank of the United States, competent to all the duties which may be required by the Government, might be so organized as not to infringe on our own delegated powers or the reserved rights of the States I do not entertain a doubt. Had the Executive been called upon to furnish the project of such an institution, the duty would have been cheerfully performed. In the absence of such a call it was obviously proper that he should confine himself to pointing out those prominent features in the act presented which in his opinion make it incompatible with the Constitution and sound policy. A general discussion will now take place, eliciting new light and settling important principles; and a new Congress, elected in the midst of such discussion, and furnishing an equal representation of the people according to the last census, will bear to the Capitol the verdict of public opinion, and, I doubt not, bring this important question to a satisfactory result.

Under such circumstances the bank comes forward and asks a renewal of its charter for a term of fifteen years upon conditions which not only operate as a gratuity to the stockholders of many millions of dollars, but will sanction any abuses and legalize any encroachments.

Suspicions are entertained and charges are made of gross abuse and violation of its charter. An investigation unwillingly conceded and so restricted in time as necessarily to make it incomplete and unsatisfactory discloses enough to excite suspicion and alarm. In the practices of the principal bank partially unveiled, in the absence of important witnesses, and in numerous charges confidently made and as yet wholly uninvestigated there was enough to induce a majority of the committee of investigation—a committee which was selected from the most able and honorable members of the House of Representatives—to recommend a suspension of further action upon the bill and a prosecution of the inquiry. As the charter had yet four years to run, and as a renewal now was not necessary to the successful prosecution of its business, it was to have been expected that the bank itself, conscious of its purity and proud of its character, would have withdrawn its application for the present, and demanded the severest scrutiny into all its transactions. In their declining to do so there seems to be an additional reason why the functionaries of the Government should proceed with less haste and more caution in the renewal of their monopoly.

The bank is professedly established as an agent of the executive branch of the Government, and its constitutionality is maintained on that ground. Neither upon the propriety of present action nor upon the provisions of this act was the Executive consulted. It has had no opportunity to say that it neither needs nor wants an agent clothed with such powers and favored by such exemptions. There is nothing in its legitimate functions which makes it necessary or proper. Whatever interest or influence, whether public or private, has given birth to this act, it can not be found either in the wishes or necessities of the executive department, by which present action is deemed premature, and the powers conferred upon its agent not only unnecessary, but dangerous to the Government and country.

It is to be regretted that the rich and powerful too often bend the acts of Government to their selfish purposes. Distinctions in society will always exist under every just government. Equality of talents, of education, or of wealth can not be produced by human institutions. In the full enjoyment of the gifts of Heaven and the fruits of superior industry, economy, and virtue, every man is equally entitled to protection by law; but when the laws undertake to add to these natural and just advantages artificial distinctions, to grant titles, gratuities, and exclusive privileges, to make the rich richer and the potent more powerful, the humble members of society—the farmers, mechanics, and laborers—who have neither the time nor the means of securing like favors to themselves, have a right to complain of the injustice of their Government. There are no necessary evils in government. Its evils exist only in its abuses. If it would confine itself to equal protection, and, as Heaven does its rains, shower its favors alike on the high and the low, the rich and the poor, it would be an unqualified blessing. In the act before me there seems to be a wide and unnecessary departure from these just principles.

Nor is our Government to be maintained or our Union preserved by invasions of the rights and powers of the several States. In thus attempting to make our General Government strong we make it weak. Its true strength consists in leaving individuals and States as much as possible to themselves—in making itself felt, not in its power, but in its beneficence; not in its control, but in its protection; not in binding the States more closely to the center, but leaving each to move unobstructed in its proper orbit.

Experience should teach us wisdom. Most of the difficulties our Government now encounters and most of the dangers which impend over our Union have sprung from an abandonment of the legitimate objects of Government by our national legislation, and the adoption of such principles as are embodied in this act. Many of our rich men have not been content with equal protection and equal benefits, but have besought us to make them richer by act of Congress. By attempting to gratify their desires we have in the results of our legislation arrayed section against section, interest against interest, and man against man, in a fearful commotion which threatens to shake the foundations of our Union. It is time to pause in our career to review our principles, and if possible revive that devoted patriotism and spirit of compromise which distinguished the sages of the Revolution and the fathers of our Union. If we can not at once, in justice to interests vested under improvident legislation, make our Government what it ought to be, we can at least take a stand against all new grants of monopolies and exclusive privileges, against any prostitution of our Government to the advancement of the few at the expense of the many, and in favor of compromise and gradual reform in our code of laws and system of political economy.

I have now done my duty to my country. If sustained by my fellow-citizens, I shall be grateful and happy; if not, I shall find in the motives which impel me ample grounds for contentment and peace. In the difficulties which surround us and the dangers which threaten our institutions there is cause for neither dismay nor alarm. For relief and deliverance let us firmly rely on that kind Providence which I am sure watches with peculiar care over the destinies of our Republic, and on the intelligence and wisdom of our countrymen. Through *His* abundant goodness and *their* patriotic devotion our liberty and Union will be preserved.

Unfavorable Contemporary Reactions to the Veto

Niles' Weekly Register
RESOLUTIONS ADOPTED AT A PUBLIC MEETING AT PHILADELPHIA, JULY 16, 1832

"*Resolved,* That we have read with astonishment, indignation and alarm, the message of the president of the United States, accompanying his return of the bill for rechartering the bank of the United States. With astonishment, that the highest officer of the government should wantonly trifle with the best interests of the country, and reject the expressed wishes of a majority of the people. With indignation, at the injustice which distinguishes every line of that discreditable document. And with alarm, at the unconstitutional and disorganizing doctrines, which have for the first time prevailed in the proceedings of our government.

"*Resolved,* That in the language, doctrines, temper and purposes of that message, we perceive additional and incontrovertible evidence, that the opinions and actions of the president, are controlled by the influence of factious and designing men, who seek their own continuance in power, even at the sacrifice of the country, the constitution, and the union.

"*Resolved,* That the principles of that message, if carried into practice, as they are sure to be upon the reelection of Jackson, would leave no man safe in the enjoyment of his property; would place the honest earnings of the industrious citizen at the disposal of the idle, the profligate and the vicious, would subvert every pillar of the constitution, and remove every landmark of the law, and would substitute for a government of perfect freedom and perfect equality, a system of

From *Niles' Weekly Register,* July 21, 1832, p. 375.

Methought the souls of all that I had murder'd came to my tent. Act. 5. Sc. 3.

RICHARD III.

FIGURE 2. Andrew Jackson, "Hero of New Orleans," portrayed as the despotic and cruel King Richard III. (Courtesy of the Print Department, Boston Public Library)

anarchy, corruption and misrule, naturally terminating in absolute despotism.

"*Resolved,* That in the tone and language of that message, we recognize a determination on the part of general Jackson, to be the dictator of a submissive, not the president of a free people—a determination to strike down every other department of the government, and to arrogate to himself the high functions which the constitution has wisely entrusted to other hands.

"*Resolved,* That the rejection of the bank of the United States, the repeated assaults of president Jackson upon the principles of protection to American industry, upon the authority of the supreme court, and upon the independence of both houses of congress, have severed every just and honorable tie by which the people of Pennsylvania were connected with him.

"*Resolved,* That the reelection of a president whose official path has been literally strewed with his own violated pledges, and with the disappointed hopes of his patriotic friends, who has thus wantonly trampled upon the interests of his fellow citizens, and upon the constitution of his country, would, in the estimation of this meeting, be a national calamity, the consequences of which we cannot contemplate without a shudder.

"*Resolved,* That we will use all lawful and honorable means by opposing the reelection of Andrew Jackson to avert this calamity—and we solemnly call upon our fellow citizens of Pennsylvania and of the union, heartily and manfully to contend at the approaching election for the maintenance of those principles, and the promotion of those rights, which the patriots of our revolution sealed with their blood."

The Portland Maine Daily Advertiser

A TYPICAL NEWSPAPER EDITORIAL

There is no part of the Veto Message more deservedly reprobated, and more reprehensible, than that part which attempts to array the poor against the rich, and thus to set in opposition the prejudices which one class may have against another. The object of all banks, it is more than insinuated, is to make the rich richer and the poor poorer. We will not dwell upon the refutation of so unworthy an insinuation. But we ask the property-holders, if they are willing to lend a hand for some new Agrarian project, which shall upset all the rights of property, and establish an equal division of estates and chattels. A more deranging, radical, law-upsetting document was never promulgated by the wildest Roman fanatic. The revolutionists of France went but little further. But how undignified, how disreputable is it, in the President of a constitutional republic to lay his blows not only upon the laws and upon the Judiciary, but even to degrade his station by insinuations, which would do discredit to Cromwell or the *people-loving* Robespierre. Is the President preparing for a crown by cajoling us with the prospect of an equal division of goods—by offering his aid to overturn the rights of property, to humble the wealthy, and to put down the exalted? If so, we ask, which is worth the most, monarchy, despotism, the tyranny of one man—or, honorable poverty, and the present enjoyment of a constitution and laws which throw the field of exertion wide open to industry, energy, and economy? Let it be remembered that every military chieftain, Sylla, Caesar, Cromwell, all have obtained unlimited and despotic power by pretending to be the sole friends of the People and often by denouncing the rich, and by cajoling the poor with prospects, which they never intended to be realized, or only realized with chains and slavery, and dungeons, or enrollment in the legions assembled to add to the power of the tyrant.

Reprinted from the *National Intelligencer* (Washington, D.C.), August 9, 1832.

Daniel Webster

SPEECH IN THE UNITED STATES SENATE, JULY 11, 1832

Daniel Webster, a senator from Massachusetts and the leading orator of the day, made the opening speech in the Senate for those who condemned Jackson's veto. Formerly a Federalist, he was a friend of Biddle and a retainer of the Bank who had become a bitter foe of President Jackson.

Mr. President, I will not conceal my opinion that the affairs of the country are approaching an important and dangerous crisis. At the very moment of almost unparalleled general prosperity, there appears an unaccountable disposition to destroy the most useful and most approved institutions of the government. Indeed, it seems to be in the midst of all this national happiness that some are found openly to question the advantages of the Constitution itself; and many more ready to embarrass the exercise of its just power, weaken its authority, and undermine its foundations. How far these notions may be carried, it is impossible yet to say. We have before us the practical result of one of them. The bank has fallen, or is to fall.

It is now certain, that, without a change in our public counsels, this bank will not be continued, nor will any other be established, which, according to the general sense and language of mankind, can be entitled to the name. Within three years and nine months from the present moment, the charter of the bank expires; within that period, therefore, it must wind up its concerns. It must call in its debts, withdraw its bills from circulation, and cease from all its ordinary operations. All this is to be done in three years and nine months; because, although there is a provision in the charter rendering it lawful to use the corporate name for two years after the expiration of the charter, yet this is allowed only for the purpose of suits and for the sale of the estate belonging to the bank, and for no other purpose whatever. The whole active business of the bank, its custody of public deposits, its transfer of public moneys, its dealing in exchange, all its loans and discounts, and all its issues of bills for circulation, must cease and

Part of a speech by Daniel Webster delivered to Congress, in *Register of Debates in Congress,* 1831–1832, VIII, pt. 1, pp. 1221–1223, 1225–1229, 1239–1240.

determine on or before the third day of March 1836; and within the same period its debts must be collected, as no new contract can be made with it, as a corporation, for the renewal of loans, or discount of notes or bills, after that time.

The President is of opinion, that this time is long enough to close the concerns of the institution without inconvenience. His language is, "The time allowed the bank to close its concerns is ample, and if it has been well managed, its pressure will be light, and heavy only in case its management has been bad. If, therefore, it shall produce distress, the fault will be its own." Sir, this is all no more than general statement, without fact or argument to support it. We know what the management of the bank has been, and we know the present state of its affairs. We can judge, therefore, whether it be probable that its capital can be all called in, and the circulation of its bills withdrawn, in three years and nine months, by any discretion or prudence in management, without producing distress. The bank has discounted liberally, in compliance with the wants of the community. The amount due to it on loans and discounts, in certain large divisions of the country, is great; so great, that I do not perceive how any man can believe that it can be paid, within the time now limited, without distress.

. . . A great majority of the people are satisfied with the bank as it is, and desirous that it should be continued. They wished no change. The strength of this public sentiment has carried the bill through Congress, against all the influence of the administration, and all the power of organized party. But the President has undertaken, on his own responsibility, to arrest the measure, by refusing his assent to the bill. He is answerable for the consequences, therefore, which necessarily follow the change which the expiration of the bank charter may produce; and if these consequences shall prove disastrous, they can fairly be ascribed to his policy only, and the policy of his administration.

Although, Sir, I have spoken of the effects of this *veto* in the Western country, it has not been because I considered that part of the United States exclusively affected by it. Some of the Atlantic States may feel its consequences, perhaps, as sensibly as those of the West, though not for the same reasons. The concern manifested by Pennsylvania for the renewal of the charter shows her sense of the importance of the bank to her own interest, and that of the nation. That great and enterprising State has entered into an extensive system of internal improvements, which necessarily makes heavy demands on her credit and her resources; and by the sound and acceptable currency which the bank affords, by the stability which it gives to private credit, and by occasional advances, made in anticipation of her revenues, and in aid of her great objects, she has found herself benefited, doubtless, in no inconsiderable degree. Her legislature has instructed her Senators here to advocate the renewal of the charter at this session. They have obeyed her voice, and yet they have the misfortune to find that, in the judgment of the President, *the measure is unconstitutional, unnecessary, dangerous to liberty, and is, moreover, ill-timed.*

But, Mr. President, it is not the local interest of the West, nor the particular interest of Pennsylvania, or any other State, which has influenced Congress in passing this bill. It has been governed by a wise foresight, and by a desire to avoid embarrassment in the pecuniary concerns of the country, to secure the safe collection and convenient transmission of public moneys, to maintain the circulation of the country, sound and safe as it now happily is, against the possible effects of a wild spirit of speculation. Finding the bank highly useful, Congress has thought fit to provide for its continuance.

. . . There are some other topics, treated in the message, which ought to be noticed. It commences by an inflamed statement of what it calls the "favor" bestowed upon the original bank by the government, or, indeed, as it is phrased, the "monopoly of its favor and support"; and through the whole message all possible changes are rung on the "gratuity," the "exclusive privileges," and "monopoly," of the bank charter. Now, Sir, the truth is, that the powers conferred on the bank are such, and no others, as are usually conferred on similar institutions. They constitute no monopoly, although some of them are of necessity, and with propriety, exclusive privileges. "The original act," says the message, "operated as a gratuity of many millions to the stockholders." What fair foundation is there for this remark? The stockholders received their charter, not gratuitously, but for a valuable consideration in money, prescribed by Congress, and actually paid. At some times the stock has been above *par,* at other times below *par,* according to prudence in management, or according to commercial occurrences. But if, by a judicious administration of its affairs, it had kept its stock always above *par,* what pretence would there be, nevertheless, for saying that such augmentation of its value was a "gratuity" from government? The message proceeds to declare, that the present act proposes another donation, another gratuity, to the same men, of at least seven millions more. It seems to me that this is an extraordinary statement, and an extraordinary style of argument, for such a subject and on such an occasion. In the first place, the facts are all assumed; they are taken for true without evidence. There are no proofs that any benefit to that amount will accrue to the stockholders, nor any experience to justify the expectation of it. It rests on random estimates, or mere conjecture. But suppose the continuance of the charter should prove beneficial to the stockholders: do they not pay for it? They give twice as much for a charter of fifteen years, as was given before for one of twenty. And if the proposed *bonus,* or premium, be not, in the President's judgment, large enough, would he, nevertheless, on such a mere matter of opinion as that, negative the whole bill? May not Congress be trusted to decide even on such a subject as the amount of the money premium to be received by government for a charter of this kind?

But, Sir, there is a larger and a much more just view of this subject. The bill was not passed for the purpose of benefiting the present stockholders. Their benefit, if any, is incidental and collateral. Nor was it passed on any idea that they had a *right* to a renewed charter, although the message argues against such right, as if it had been somewhere set up and asserted. No such right has been asserted by any body. Congress passed the bill, not as a bounty or a favor to the present stockholders, nor to comply with any demand of right on their part; but to promote great public interests, for great public objects. Every bank must have some stockholders, unless it be such a bank as the President has recommended, and in regard to which he seems not likely to find much concurrence of other men's opinions; and if the stockholders, whoever they may be, conduct the affairs of the bank prudently, the expectation is always, of course, that they will make it profitable to themselves, as well as useful to the public. If a bank charter is not to be granted, because, to some extent, it may be profitable to the stockholders, no charter can be granted. The objection lies against all banks.

Sir, the object aimed at by such institutions is to connect the public safety and convenience with private interests. It has been found by experience, that banks are safest under private management, and that government banks are among the most dangerous of all inventions. Now, Sir, the whole drift of the message is to reverse the settled judgment of all the civilized world, and to set up government banks, independent of private interest or private control. For this purpose the message labors, even beyond the measure of all its other labors, to create jealousies and prejudices, on the ground of the alleged benefit which individuals will derive from the renewal of this charter. Much less effort is made to show that government, or the public, will be injured by the bill, than that individuals will profit by it. Following up the impulses of the same spirit, the message goes on gravely to allege, that the act, as passed by Congress, proposes to make a *present* of some millions of dollars to foreigners, because a portion of the stock is held by foreigners. Sir, how would this sort of argument apply to other cases? The President has shown himself not only willing, but anxious, to pay off the 3 percent stock of the United States at *par*, notwithstanding that it is notorious that foreigners are owners of the greater part of it. Why should he not call that a donation to foreigners of many millions?

I will not dwell particularly on this part of the message. Its tone and its arguments are all in the same strain. It speaks of the certain gain of the present stockholders, of the value of the monopoly; it says that all monopolies are granted at the expense of the public; that the many millions which this bill bestows on the stockholders come out of the earnings of the people; that, if government sells monopolies, it ought to sell them in open market; that it is an erroneous idea, that the present stockholders have a prescriptive right either to the favor or the bounty of government; that the stock is in the hands of a few, and that the whole American people are excluded from competition in the purchase of the monopoly. To all this I say, again, that much of it is assumption without proof; much of it is an argument against that which nobody has maintained or asserted; and the rest of it would be equally strong against any charter, at any time. These objections existed in their full strength, whatever that was, against the first bank. They existed, in like manner, against the present bank at its creation, and will always exist against all banks. Indeed, all the fault found with the bill now before us is, that it proposes to continue the bank substantially as it now exists. "All the objectionable principles of the existing corporation," says the message, "and most of its odious features, are retained without alleviation"; so that the message is aimed against the bank, as it has existed from the first, and against any and all others resembling it in its general features.

Allow me, now, Sir, to take notice of an argument founded on the practical operation of the bank. That argument is this. Little of the stock of the bank is held in the West, the capital being chiefly owned by citizens of the Southern and Eastern States, and by foreigners. But the Western and Southwestern States owe the bank a heavy debt, so heavy that the interest amounts to a million six hundred thousand a year. This interest is carried to the Eastern States, or to Europe, annually, and its payment is a burden on the people of the West, and a drain of their currency, which no country can bear without inconvenience and distress. The true character and the whole value of this argument are manifest by the mere statement of it. The people of the West are, from their situation, necessarily large borrowers. They need money, capital, and they borrow it, because they can derive a benefit from its use, much beyond the interest which they pay. They borrow at 6 percent of the bank, although the value of money with them is at least as high as eight. Nevertheless, although they borrow at this low rate of interest, and although they use all they borrow thus profitably, yet they cannot pay the interest without "inconvenience and distress"; and then, Sir, follows the logical conclusion, that, although they cannot pay even the interest without inconvenience and distress, yet less than four years is ample time for the bank to call in the whole, both principal and interest, without causing more than a light pressure. This is the argument.

Then follows another, which may be thus stated. It is competent to the States to tax the property of their citizens vested in the stock of this bank; but the power is denied of taxing the stock of foreigners; therefore the stock will be worth 10 or 15 percent more to foreigners than to residents, and will of course inevitably leave the country and make the American people debtors to aliens in nearly the whole amount due the bank, and send across the Atlantic from two to five millions of specie every year, to pay the bank dividends.

Mr. President, arguments like these might be more readily disposed of, were it not that the high and official source from which they proceed imposes the necessity of treating them with respect. In the first place, it may safely be denied that the stock of the bank is any more valuable to foreigners than to our own citizens, or an object of greater desire to them, except in so far as capital may be more abundant in the foreign country, and therefore its owners more in want of opportunity of investment. The foreign stockholder enjoys no exemption from taxation. He is, of course, taxed by his own government for his incomes, derived from this as well as other property; and this is a full answer to the whole statement. But it may be added, in the second place, that it is not the practice of civilized states to tax the property of foreigners under such circumstances. Do we tax, or did we ever tax, the foreign holders of our public debt? Does Pennsylvania, New York, or Ohio tax the foreign holders of stock in the loans contracted by either of these States? Certainly not. Sir, I must confess I had little expected to see, on such an occasion as the present, a labored and repeated attempt to produce an impression on the public opinion unfavorable to the bank, from the circumstance that foreigners are among its stockholders. I have no hesitation in saying, that I deem such a train of remark as the message contains on this point, coming from the President of the United States, to be injurious to the credit and character of the country abroad; because it manifests a jealousy, a lurking disposition not to respect the property, of foreigners invited hither by our own laws. And, Sir, what is its tendency but to excite this jealousy, and create groundless prejudices?

From the commencement of the government, it has been thought desirable to invite, rather than to repel, the introduction of foreign capital. Our stocks have all been open to foreign subscriptions; and the State banks, in like manner, are free to foreign ownership. Whatever State has created a debt has been willing that foreigners should become purchasers, and desirous of it. How long is it, Sir, since Congress itself passed a law vesting new powers in the President of the United States over the cities in this District, for the very purpose of increasing their credit abroad, the better to enable them to borrow money to pay their subscriptions to the Chesapeake and Ohio Canal? It is easy to say that there is danger to liberty, danger to independence, in a bank open to foreign stockholders, because it is easy to say any thing. But neither reason nor experience proves any such danger. The foreign stockholder cannot be a director. He has no voice even in the choice of directors. His money is placed entirely in the management of the directors appointed by the President and Senate and by the American stockholders. So far as there is dependence or influence either way, it is to the disadvantage of the foreign stockholder. He has parted with the control over his own property, instead of exercising control over the property or over the actions of others. And, Sir, let it now be added, in further answer to this class of objections, that experience has abundantly confuted them all. This government has existed forty-three years, and has maintained, in full being and operation, a bank, such as is now proposed to be renewed, for thirty-six years out of the forty-three. We have never for a moment had a bank not subject to every one of these objections. Always, foreigners might be stockholders; always, foreign stock has been exempt from State taxation, as much as at present; always the same power and privileges; always, all that which is now called a "monopoly," a "gratuity," a "present," has been possessed by the bank. And yet there has been found no danger to liberty, no introduction of foreign influence, and no accumulation of irresponsible power in a few hands. I cannot but hope, therefore, that the people of the United States will not now yield up their judgment to those notions which would reverse all our best experience, and persuade us to discontinue a useful institution from the influence of vague and unfounded declamation against its danger to the public liberties. Our liberties, indeed, must stand upon very frail foundations, if the government cannot, without endangering them, avail itself of those common facilities, in the collection of its revenues and the management of its finances, which all other governments, in commercial countries, find useful and necessary.

In order to justify its alarm for the security of our independence, the message supposes a case. It supposes that the bank should pass principally into the hands of the subjects of a foreign country, and that we should be involved in war with that country, and then it exclaims, "What would be our condition?" Why, Sir, it is plain that all the advantages would be on our side. The bank would still be our institution, subject to our own laws, and all its directors elected by ourselves; and our means would be enhanced, not by the confiscation and plunder, but by the proper use, of the foreign capital in our hands. And, Sir, it is singular enough, that this very state of war, from which this argument against a bank is drawn, is the very thing which, more than all others, convinced the country and the government of the necessity of a national bank. So much was the want of such an institution felt in the late war, that the subject engaged the attention of Congress, constantly, from the declaration of that war down to the time when the existing bank was actually established; so that in this respect, as well as in others, the argument of the message is directly opposed to the whole experience of the government, and to the general and long-settled convictions of the country. . . .

Mr. President, we have arrived at a new epoch. We are entering on experiments, with the government and the Constitution of the country, hitherto untried, and of fearful and appalling aspect. This message calls us to the contemplation of a future which little resembles the past. Its principles are at war with all that public opinion has sustained, and all which the experience of the government has sanctioned. It denies first principles; it contradicts truths, heretofore received as indisputable. It denies to the judiciary the interpretation of law, and claims to divide with Congress the power of originating statutes. It extends the grasp of executive pretension over every power of the government. But this is not all. It presents the chief magistrate of the Union in the attitude of arguing away the powers of that government over which he has been chosen to preside; and adopting for this purpose modes of reasoning which, even under the influence of all proper feeling towards high official station, it is difficult to regard as respectable. It appeals to every prejudice which may betray men into a mistaken view of their own interests, and to every passion which may lead them to disobey the impulses of their understanding. It urges all the specious topics of State rights and national encroachment against that which a great majority of the States have affirmed to be rightful, and in which all of them have acquiesced. It sows, in an unsparing manner, the seeds of jealousy and ill-will against that government of which its author is the official head. It raises a cry, that liberty is in danger, at the very moment when it puts forth claims to powers heretofore unknown and unheard of. It effects alarm for the public freedom, when nothing endangers that freedom so much as its own unparalleled pretenses. This, even, is not all. It manifestly seeks to inflame the poor against the rich; it

Race over Uncle Sam's Course.
4ᵗʰ March 1833

FIGURE 3. President Andrew Jackson uses his executive power to veto rechartering of the Second United States Bank, and in the eyes of many threatens the American system of government. (Courtesy of the Print Department, Boston Public Library)

wantonly attacks whole classes of the people, for the purpose of turning against them the prejudices and the resentments of other classes. It is a state paper which finds no topic too exciting for its use, no passion too inflammable for its address and its solicitation.

Such is this message. It remains now for the people of the United States to choose between the principles here avowed and their government. These cannot subsist together. The one or the other must be rejected. If the sentiments of the message shall receive general approbation, the Constitution will have perished even earlier than the moment which its enemies originally allowed for the termination of its existence. It will not have survived to its fiftieth year.

Favorable Contemporary Reactions to the Veto

Thomas Hart Benton
SPEECH IN THE UNITED STATES SENATE, JULY 13, 1832

Senator Thomas Hart Benton led the Jackson forces in Congress on the struggle over the rechartering of the second Bank. Known as "Old Bullion Benton," he condemned the use of small bank notes and pressed for dependence upon gold and silver money. His shooting brawl with Jackson in 1813 was now overlooked as he threw his support to Jackson in the election of 1832. What is included here is a portion of a Senate speech by Benton as reported in a contemporary newspaper and reproduced in his book.

Why debate the bank question now, and not debate it before? Then was the time to make converts; now, none can be expected. Why are lips unsealed now, which were silent as the grave when this act was on its passage through the Senate? The senator from Kentucky himself, at the end of one of his numerous perorations, declared that he expected to make no converts. Then, why speak three hours? And other gentlemen speak a whole day? Why this post facto—post mortem—this posthumous—debate?—The deed is done. The bank bill is finished. Speaking cannot change the minds of senators, and make them reverse their votes; still less can it change the President, and make him recall his veto. Then why speak? To whom do they speak? With what object do they speak? Sir! this post facto debate is not for the Senate, nor the President, not to alter the fate of the bank bill. It is to rouse the officers of the bank—to direct the efforts of its mercenaries in their designs upon the people—to bring out its stream of corrupting influence, by inspiring hope, and to embody all its recruits at the polls to vote against President Jackson. Without an avowal we would all know this; but we have not been left without

Thomas Hart Benton, *Thirty Years' View* (New York, 1854) I: 257, 260, 261–263.

an avowal. The senator from Massachusetts (Mr. Webster), who opened yesterday, commenced his speech with showing that Jackson must be put down; that he stood as an impassable barrier between the bank and a new charter; and that the road to success was through the ballot boxes at the presidential election. The object of this debate is then known, confessed, declared, avowed; the bank is in the field; enlisted for the war; a battering ram—the *catapulta,* not of the Romans, but of the National Republicans; not to beat down the walls of hostile cities, but to beat down the citadel of American liberty; to batter down the rights of the people; to destroy a hero and patriot; to command the elections, and to elect a Bank President by dint of bank power.

The bank is in the field, a combatant, and a fearful and tremendous one, in the presidential election. If she succeeds, there is an end of American liberty—an end of the republic. The forms of election may be permitted for a while, as the forms of the consular elections were permitted in Rome, during the last years of republic; but it will be for a while, only. The President of the bank, and the President of the United States, will be cousins, and cousins in the royal sense of the word. They will elect each other. They will elect their successors; they will transmit their thrones to their descendants, and that by legislative construction. The great Napoleon was decreed to be hereditary emperor by virtue of the 22d article of the constitution of the republic. The conservative Senate and the Tribunitial Assembly made him emperor by construction; and the same construction which was put upon the 22d article of the French constitution of the year VIII may be as easily placed upon the "general welfare" clause in the constitution of these United States.

The Bank is in the field, and the West—the Great West, is the selected theater of her operations. There her terrors, her seductions, her energies, her rewards and her punishments, are to be directed. The senator from Massachusetts opened yesterday with a picture of the ruin in the West, if the bank were not rechartered; and the senator from Kentucky, Mr. Clay, wound up with a retouch of the same picture today, with a closeness of coincidence which showed that this part of the battle ground had been reviewed in company by the associate generals and duplicate senators. Both agree that the West is to be ruined if the bank be not rechartered; and rechartered it cannot be, unless the *veto* President is himself vetoed. This is certainly candid. But the gentlemen's candor did not stop there. They went on to show the *modus operandi;* to show how the ruin would be worked, how the country would be devastated—if Jackson was not put down, and the bank rechartered.

(Mr. Clay and Mr. Webster had rebuked the President for his allusion to the manner in which the bank charter had been pushed through Congress, pending an unfinished investigation, reluctantly conceded.) . . . [but was that] not true? . . . [was it not] wrong to push the charter through in that manner, and . . . [had not] the President . . . done right to stop it, to balk this hurried process, and to give the people time for consideration and [to] enable them to act? He had only brought the subject to the notice of the Congress and the people, but had not recommended immediate legislation, before the subject had been canvassed before the nation. It was a gross perversion of his messages to quote them in favor of immediate decision without previous investigation. He was not evading the question. The veto message proved that. He sought time for the people, not for himself, and in that he coincided with a sentiment lately expressed by the senator himself (from Kentucky) at Cincinnati; he was coinciding with the example of the British parliament, which had not yet decided the question of rechartering the Bank of England, and which had just raised an extraordinary committee of thirty-one members to examine the bank through all her departments; and, what was much more material, he had coincided with the spirit of our constitution, and the rights of the people, in preventing an expiring minority Congress from usurping the powers and rights of their successors. The President had not evaded the question. He had met it fully. He might have said nothing about it in his messages of 1829, 1830, and 1831. He might have remained silent, and had the support of both parties; but the safety and interest of the country required the people to be awakened to the consideration of the subject. He had waked them up; and now that they are awake, he has secured them time for consideration. Is this evasion?

(Messrs. C. and W. had attacked the President for objecting to foreign stockholders in the Bank of the United States.) . . . yes! but these road and canal companies did not happen to be the bankers of the United States! The foreign stockholders in this bank were the bankers of the United States. They held its money; they collected its revenues; they almost controlled its finances; they were to give or withhold aid in war as well as peace, and, it might be, against their own government. Was the United States to depend upon foreigners in a point so material to our existence? The bank was a national institution. Ought a national institution to be the private property of aliens? It was called the Bank of the United States, and ought it to be the bank of the nobility and gentry of Great Britain? The senator from Kentucky had once objected to foreign stockholders himself. He did this in his speech against the bank in 1811; and although he had revoked the constitutional doctrines of that speech, he (Mr. B.) never understood that he had revoked the sentiments then expressed of the danger of corruption in our councils and elections, if foreigners wielded the moneyed power of the purse commanded that of the sword—and would he commit both to the hands of foreigners? All the lessons of history admonish us to keep clear of foreign influence. The most dangerous influence from foreigners is through money. The corruption of orators and statesmen, is the ready way to poison the councils, and to betray the interest of a country. Foreigners now own one fourth of this bank; they may own the whole of it! What a temptation to them to engage in our elections! By carrying a President, and a majority of Congress, to suit themselves, they not only become masters of the moneyed power, but also of the political power, of this republic. And can it be supposed that the British stockholders are indifferent to the issue of this election? That they, and their agents, can see with indifference the reelection of a man who may disappoint their hopes of fortune, and whose achievement at New Orleans is a continued memento of the most signal defeat the arms of England ever sustained?

(Mr. B. addressed himself to the Jackson bank men, present and absent. They might continue to be for a bank and for Jackson; but they could not be for *this* bank, and for Jackson.) This bank is now the open, as it long has been the secret, enemy of Jackson. It is now in the hands of his enemies, wielding all its own money—wielding even the revenues and the credit of the Union—wielding twelve millions of dollars, half of which were intended to be paid to the public creditors on the first day of July, but which the bank has retained to itself by a false representation in the pretended behalf of the merchants. All this moneyed power, with an organization which pervades the continent, working every where with unseen hands, is now operating against the President; and it is impossible to be in favor of this power and also in favor of him at the same time. Choose ye between them! To those who think a bank to be indispensable, other alternatives present themselves. They are not bound nor wedded to this. New American banks may be created. Read, sir, Henry Parnell. See his invincible reasoning, and indisputable facts, to show that the Bank of England is too powerful for the monarchy of Great Britain! Study his plan for breaking up that gigantic institution, and establishing three or four independent banks in its place, which would be so much less dangerous to liberty, and so much safer and better for the people. In these alternatives, the friends of Jackson, who are in favor of national banks, may find the accomplishment of their wishes without a sacrifice of their principles, and without committing the suicidal solecism of fighting against him while professing to be for him.

(Mr. B. addressed himself to the West—the great, the generous, the brave, the patriotic, the devoted West.) It was the selected field of battle. There the combined forces, the national republicans, and the national republican bank, were to work together, and to fight together. The holy allies understand each other. They are able to speak in each other's names, and to promise and threaten in each other's behalf. For this campaign the bank created its debt of thirty millions in the West; in this campaign the associate leaders use that debt for their own purposes. Vote for Jackson! and suits, judgments, and executions shall sweep, like the besom of destruction, throughout the vast region of the West! Vote against him! and indefinite indulgence is basely promised! The debt itself, it is pretended, will, perhaps, be forgiven; or, at all events, hardly ever collected! Thus, an open bribe of thirty millions is virtually offered to the West; and, lest the seductions of the bribe may not be sufficient on one hand, the terrors of destruction are brandished on the other! Wretched, infatuated men! Do they think the West is to be bought? Little do they know of the generous sons of that magnificent region! poor, indeed, in point of money, but rich in all the treasures of the heart! rich in all the qualities of freemen and republicans! rich in all the noble feelings which look with equal scorn upon a bribe or a threat. The hunter of the West, with moccasins on his feet, and a hunting shirt drawn around him, would repel with indignation the highest bribe that the bank could offer him. The wretch who dared to offer it, would expiate the insult with his blood.

(Mr. B. rapidly summed up with a view of the dangerous power of the bank, and the present audacity of her conduct.) She wielded a debt of seventy millions of dollars, with an organization which extended to every part of the Union, and she was sole mistress of the moneyed power of the republic. She had thrown herself into the political arena, to control and govern the presidential election. If she succeeded in that election, she would wish to consolidate her power by getting control of all other elections. Governors of States, judges of the courts, representatives and senators in Congress, all must belong to her. The Senate especially must belong to her; for, there lay the power to confirm nominations and to try impeachments; and, to get possession of the Senate, the legislatures of a majority of the States would have to be acquired. The war is now upon Jackson, and if he is defeated, all the rest will fall an easy prey. What individual could stand in the States against the power of the bank, and that bank flushed with a victory over the conqueror of the conquerors of Bonaparte? The whole government would fall into the hands of this moneyed power. An oligarchy would be immediately established; and that oligarchy, in a few generations, would ripen into a monarchy. All governments must have their end; in the lapse of time, this republic must perish; but that time, he now trusted, was far distant; and when it comes, it should come in glory, and not in shame. Rome had her Pharsalia, and Greece her Chaeronea; and this republic, more illustrious in her birth than Greece or Rome, was entitled to a death as glorious as theirs. She would not die by poison—perish in corruption—no! A field of arms, and of glory, should be her end. She had a right to a battle—a great, immortal battle—where heroes and patriots could die with the liberty which they scorned to survive, and consecrate, with their blood, the spot which marked a nation's fall.

The Pittsburgh (Pennsylvania) Manufacturer

A NEWSPAPER EDITORIAL

. . . We turn with hope, with something more than hope, with confidence, entire confidence, to the patriot Andrew Jackson. Well it is for the people that they have him at their head, at this crisis of their political destinies, and well it is for the principles of republicanism and "equal rights," that he now controls the helm of government, in these United States. His veto on this bill will open the eyes of thousands to the awful precipice over which they were tottering, with utter indifference. It will show to those who have heretofore viewed the subject with apathy, how necessary it is for Freemen to watch the insidious movements, of a monied aristocracy—who with peculiar subtlety, are ever ready to rise, grapple with, overpower, and bind the liberties of any people. We repeat, in unvarnished language, the monied aristocracies, above all others, are most inimical to "liberty and equality," and most prone to favor the principles of despotism and slavery, in our country, such an aristocracy has risen, with the institution misnamed the United States Bank. So powerful and audacious has it already become, that it maintains its political party— cherishes its political favorites, bribes and corrupts the public press, and unfeelingly crushes all within its reach, who may be so honest and fearless as to express disapprobation at its course and character. But its days are numbered. It will receive its death-blow from the patriotic Jackson, the man of the People. He has watched its corrupting power, its unwarrantable abuses, and now when called on to act, he will consistent with his emphatic sentiments, made heretofore, through his messages and conversations, put a period to its existence.

We call on the people to be "up and doing." A crisis has arrived in their political destinies. Wealth and corruption are attempting an ascendancy over the liberties purchased by the blood of our forefathers. With one voice, with one arm, mighty and just as that which placed the Hero of Orleans in the Presidential Chair, let us rise in our might, and sustain his veto, on this vampire (misnomered the U.S. Bank) of our country's prosperity.

Reprinted from the *Globe* (Washington, D.C.), July 20, 1832.

George Bancroft

A LETTER

By 1834 George Bancroft was already becoming a leading spokesman for the Democratic Party. In an era when support of Andrew Jackson brought social ostracism in his native Massachusetts, Bancroft came out boldly for Jacksonian measures. As a national party the Democrats suffered from a dearth of intellectual leaders—a deficiency which Bancroft with his unusual natural ability, his Harvard training, and his background of study and travel in Europe was uniquely qualified to fill. The first volume of his justly famous ten-volume History of the United States *was published in 1834. On almost every page this work reflects the nationalistic spirit of the time, as well as the author's enthusiasm for Jacksonian Democracy.*

Northhampton, October 1, 1834

The United States Bank, as at present constituted, ought never to be renewed. The reasons are obvious.

1. The capital is too vast. In proportion to the wealth of the country, it is the largest moneyed monopoly in the world. Not England with its hundred millions of subjects, and its aristocratic factions for leaders, not the France of Napoleon, nor the legitimacy, nor of Louis Phillippe, not Russia with its despotic government and its millions of serfs, has ever created a moneyed institution with resources comparatively so great. Republican America, the Virgin of the New World, the government which is especially charged by wholesome legislation to prevent all extreme inequalities of fortune, has surpassed every country in Europe in the lavish concession of influence and privileges to a moneyed corporation.

2. There is equal room for objection to the power of the United States Bank to accumulate and retain real estate under the form of mortgages; a power as durable as its charter, equal to that of the Massachusetts General Hospital in its character, and coextensive with the Union; a feature in the bank, so offensive, that it is now condemned even by its friends.

3. The power of establishing branches at its will in any portion

This selection is part of a letter addressed to Messrs. S. Judd, J. H. Flint, S. Parsons, C. Clark, C. P. Huntington, and J. Wright, printed in the *Boston Courier*, October 23, 1834.

of the Union, is another too lavish concession. An institution, lifted above the local laws, and defying the powers of state legislation, by which it can never be taxed, can offer no just motive for a branch, except where it may be required as an organ of the treasury.

4. The power of the bank to supply the currency with bills of a small denomination, is, in a national point of view, too little restricted. Under its operation and the rivalry of the state banks, specie is almost entirely withdrawn from the hands of the people; and credit, which is so fluctuating and so delicate, has been pushed to such an excess, that every little scarcity in the money market is felt throughout the country with fourfold severity. The excessive use of credit and frequent ruinous pressures are inseparable.

5. The power of the bank to resist inquiry is too great. I hold to the republican doctrine of strict accountability. Every organ of the government, and every corporation that lives by the favor of the government, should be exposed to the searching influence of a "roving hunt" and a diligent inquiry. The severer the scrutiny, the better. . . .

Of these objectives against the United States Bank, the one, relating to its immense capital, is the most weighty. I have been surprised at the apathy of the people on this subject. . . . [We must try to] sink deep in the hearts of the people the conviction, that vast associations of wealth are never to be tolerated. No matter what are the details of the grant, these immense moneyed combinations, whether they present themselves in the shape of a Life and Trust company, with power vast enough to convert the yeomanry of whole countries into a dependant tenantry, or a mammoth State Bank of many millions, or a United States Bank with a capital disproportioned to the wealth and industry of the country, should always be resisted.

The evils of these associations of boundless wealth are of the most deadly kind.

A Bank of thirty-five millions, under a charter like that of the existing bank, may attain an immense political influence, present in every part of the union, blindly following the impulse of one mind, and reckless of consequences in zeal of political ambition. Next to the national executive, the direction of the United States Bank is the most powerful body in the republic. Let the farmers of Massachusetts attempt by a healthful combination to produce an impression on the public mind, and they will learn from the experiment, how feeble and disjoined and ill-continued are their efforts in comparison with that of an association, which controls all the credit than can rest on a capital of thirty-five millions. The gross revenues of the bank may easily be made to amount to five millions of dollars, the net revenue to more than two and a half millions. The state of Massachusetts is also a corporation, with a revenue less than one twelfth part of the actual revenue of the United States Bank. The patronage of the government of Massachusetts is hardly fifty thousand dollars, the patronage of the direction of the United States Bank is between one and two millions, besides the very great influence which comes from the loan of sixty or seventy millions.

Another and a powerful reason against so great a capital, lies in the control of commercial operations, which is thus secured to a single company, and exercised by a single mind; an objection which would apply with still greater force to any bank; to be managed by the executive or its subservient instruments. No man or body of men ought ever to be invested with such exorbitant powers that, in case of misdemeanor, the guilty cannot be arraigned without plunging the country in distress. . . .

But the great objection in my mind to the continuance of the present United States Bank, lies in its tendency to promote extreme inequalities in point of fortune. It forms a part of a system of deadly hostility to the policy which the country should pursue. The Bank is possessed of immense resources and commanding influence; its sympathies, its prejudices, are all on the side of wealth; and its existence has a steady and evident tendency to conciliate for capital a controlling influence on legislation.

Of all political heresies the most baleful is that, which would base political power on wealth. It is too late to invent theories on the subject; history has solved the question. Where the people possess no authority, their rights obtain no respect. Their political degradation is followed by insult and misery; and the gulf between the rich man and Lazarus perpetually grows wider and deeper. . . . [Examples are cited from Roman, English, and French history.] Show me one instance where popular institutions have violated the rights of property, and I will show you a hundred, nay a thousand instances, where the people have been pillaged by the greedy cupidity of a privileged class. There is more danger from monopolies than from combinations of workmen. There is more danger that capital will swallow up the profits of labor, than that labor will confiscate capital.

Political influence is steadily tending to the summit level of property; and this political influence of wealth must be balanced by the political power of numbers. Even then this political influence often controls elections, and often with a giant's tread, stalks into the halls of legislation.

When the merchant demands that his interests should prevail over those of liberty, it is the clamor of capital. The flag of the United States should protect every bale of goods over which it waves, and carry its guardian influence even to the Falkland Islands or the harbors of Sumatra; to the Antipodes or the Poles; but the control of legislation is too sacred a trust to be surrendered. We tolerate no commercial aristocracy like that of Tyre or Florence, of Carthage or Venice. Here merchants are never to be princes.

When a life and trust company ask for privileges, which enable capital to consume the moderate profits of the farmer by tempting him to incur the hazards of debt, it is the clamor of capital, deafening the voice of benevolence and legislative wisdom.

When the creditor demands that the debtor may once more be allowed to pledge his body and his personal freedom, it is the clamor of capital.

When "vested rights" claim a veto on legislation, and assert themselves as the law paramount in defiance of the constitution which makes the common good the supreme rule, it is the clamor of capital, desiring to renew one of the abuses of feudal institutions.

When the usurer invokes the aid of society to enforce the contracts, which he has wrung without mercy from the feverish hopes of pressing necessity, it is the clamor of capital, which like the grave, never says, It is enough.

When employers combine to reduce the wages of labor, and at the same time threaten an indictment for conspiracy against the combinations of workmen, it is the clamor of capital.

The feud between the capitalist and the laborer, the house of Have and the house of Want, is as old as social union, and can never be entirely quieted; but he who will act with moderation, prefer facts to theories, and remember that every thing in this world is relative and not absolute, will see that the violence of the contest may be stilled, if the unreasonable demands of personal interests are subjected to the decisions of evenhanded justice. . . .

National happiness is not always increased by the increase of national wealth; a state may be excessively opulent, and its people be wretched, the influence of wealth on happiness depends on the mode of its acquisition and the mode of its distribution. But labor, as it has just been defined, is always a source of happiness. Its object is always good; its healthy abundance is the most cheering spectacle that civilization can offer. Labor should enjoy the happiness which it creates. . . .

Classic Accounts of the Controversy

Ralph C. H. Catterall
THE BANK AT BAY

Ralph C. H. Catterall taught history at the University of Chicago and went on to become head of the history department at Cornell University. His classic study entitled The Second Bank of the United States *was published in 1902. Though superseded by many specialized studies, it has retained over the years both a solid usefulness and a remarkable freshness.*

The Bank and the Democracy

The opinion prevailed in 1829 that the bank was almost impregnable in popular favor, a conviction which was not confined to its friends but found voice in the expressed fear of its enemies. How mistaken it was the consideration of the influences at work against the continuance of the bank will reveal. These influences may all be reduced to five heads: the widespread belief that the bank was unconstitutional, the hostility of the states, the opposition of state banks, the rise of the Democracy, and the envy and hatred which the poor always feel for the rich.

Sumner considers the constitutional question as having no vitality when Jackson's first message was delivered, and it must be conceded that it had less vitality at this moment than ever before. Nevertheless, the belief in the bank's unconstitutionality was still vigorous, and was extremely prevalent in Virginia, Georgia, Ohio, Kentucky, Tennessee, and South Carolina, and only less so in the other southern and western states. Though it had been quiescent for years, the discussion of the constitutional question was certain to arise as soon as the proposition to recharter was broached.

The undying hostility of the states, which believed their rights

From Ralph C. H. Catterall, *The Second Bank of the United States* (Chicago: University of Chicago Press, 1902), pp. 164–185, 243–284, 476–477.

infringed and feared the centralizing tendencies of the bank, was intimately connected with the constitutional question. In South Carolina and Georgia the "states'-rights" party opposed the bank almost exclusively for the latter reason, though they were also influenced by the conviction that it was injurious to the material welfare of the state. In the West similar objections were offered; in Kentucky the struggle over the "relief system" involved the bank and made it very unpopular; in 1825 Governor Desha, of that state, bitterly denounced it in his annual message; in Tennessee the state law imposing a tax upon any branch established there was not repealed until 1827; in Ohio the commonwealth persisted in opposition until 1824; in Alabama the governor and legislature protested against the establishment of a branch in 1827; in Connecticut an attempt was made in 1829 to tax the stock held by its citizens; and in 1830 South Carolina imposed a tax of 1 percent upon the dividends of stockholders resident in that state. In New York, state pride was offended because Philadelphia and not New York City was the location of the bank; while of still deadlier import was the struggle for commercial supremacy between the two cities, to secure which the bank was of great importance. The situation was further complicated by the political rivalry between the two states. In the scramble for national honors Pennsylvania politicians were forced to support, New York politicians to oppose, the bank. It was of fatal import to the institution that at this juncture the Democracy of New York was headed by Martin Van Buren, the acutest politician of his day and an enemy of the bank. The hostility of the states as a whole, however, was less pronounced in 1829 than at any other period of the bank's existence.

The opposition of state banks whose interests were involved arrayed a powerful party against the bank. It had forced many of them to restrict their business by compelling payment for their notes in specie, and it had been particularly active and particularly offensive in this respect in the South and West. Consequently it could count upon opposition from most of these corporations. Other reasons were operative also, as a review of the situation in New York will show. Here, as elsewhere, the bank reduced the profits of the state banks, because it loaned at 6 percent, being compelled to do so by its charter, while the New York banks, which might legally have charged 7 percent, were compelled to loan at the lower rate because the big bank did so; another reason for hostility was found in the safety-fund system which bound the politicians and the bankers in a common union. The politicians expected to control the New York banks through this system, but could not reach the Bank of the United States; while the bankers felt that they were subjected to restraints not imposed upon the national bank, and cherished the dislike which the members of one system are apt to feel for those under another and unfriendly system. These remarks relative to New York will show how the conflict of interests was likely to be united with the opposition of politicians. Yet it is true that, as in the case of constitutional objections and state opposition, the local institutions were distinctly more friendly to the national bank in 1829 than at any other time. Many of them petitioned that it might be rechartered.

Democracy, devoted to the principle of equality, is opposed to all forms of privilege, and to none more than to a monetary monopoly. When it is recollected that the Bank of the United States was at that time the one great monopoly in the country, and that against it were directed all the passionate opposition and fear which today fall upon banks, railroad companies, and trusts, its danger from the rising power of that fierce Democracy which with Andrew Jackson swept over the country may be faintly measured. The Democracy was positive that the bank was a menace to the political and social interests of the United States; that it made "the rich richer and the poor poorer"; that it depressed the weak and made "the potent more powerful"; that it accentuated the differences of society, creating on the one hand a powerful aristocracy and on the other hand an impotent and beggarly proletariat. These opinions were especially prevalent in the West, where Democracy was most powerful. While the other factors in the determination of the bank's fate had been diminishing in potency, this had increased with every year since the granting of the charter.

Inextricably linked with the Democratic opposition was the ceaseless hostility between rich and poor, the envy and hatred of the man who has nothing for the man who has much, the ill-will which the debtor eternally cherishes for the creditor; all the social arguments directed against the bank gathered force and passion from this feeling and at the same time added to it.

These were the forces which worked toward the destruction of the bank. What were the conserving forces? For the most part persons interested in the bank and conscious that they were so: its employees, its debtors, its stockholders; enlightened businessmen who understood the value of the bank; statesmen of the nationalizing school, who would uphold the bank because they believed it to be in accordance with the political principles they professed; and finally a motley crowd of noisy politicians and newspaper men. These factors of strength could not be very important. The employees could have no weight in politics; the debtors were only a few thousands; politicians would inevitably follow the majority; the statesmen would be compelled to yield principle to expediency; while the enlightened businessmen would be of more injury than assistance to any cause they supported, for they belonged to that intelligent class whose influence upon American affairs has always been inconsiderable, partly because they are themselves objects of suspicion to the democratic masses. There remained the stockholders. The distribution of the stock was consequently of some moment in determining the strength of the bank. In July 1831, there were 4,145 stockholders, of whom 466 were foreigners. This small number of people, and mostly people who took little or no interest in politics, could give the bank no popular strength, and the dreadful fact that foreigners held stock, and that among these were English lords and ladies, was a source of positive weakness to it. Add to this that the bulk of the domestic stock was localized in the states of Massachusetts, Pennsylvania, New York, Maryland, Virginia, and South Carolina, and it is plain that the bank could derive little assistance from the distribution of its stock.

Any additional support of the bank would spring from the realization of its usefulness to the general public: its services in supplying a sound currency, in managing the business of the treasury efficiently and cheaply, and in furnishing banking accommodations at a reasonable rate. But these were virtues hidden from the vulgar and could never be made apparent to them because of the abstruseness and involved nature of financial discussions. The bank's hold on popular favor was consequently of the most tenuous kind; as Webster said, popular prejudice once aroused was "more than a match for ten banks"; and it was certain that in a conflict with a popular president the bank had not the faintest hope of success. That it failed to realize this was its error and its misfortune.

The beginning of the bank struggle may be dated from December 13, 1827, on which day P. P. Barbour, of Virginia, introduced in the House of Representatives a resolution directing the sale of the bank stock owned by the government. It was suspected that this movement portended "the beginning of an attack" which would "lead to permanent distrust in the stability of the institution," and the price of the stock immediately fell. It was also believed that the act indicated the hostility of Jackson politicians to the bank. The motion to adopt the resolution was lost by the overwhelming vote of 174 to 9, a result which caused the stock to recover its standing in the market and convinced many that the bank would be rechartered.

The next attack was made incidentally by Senator Benton in February 1828, in a series of resolutions relative to the sinking fund. Though there was no direct reference to the bank in the resolutions, yet the senator's speech in support of them reveals a purpose to attack it as an institution enjoying undemocratic privileges at the expense of the people; for he constantly refers to the balances of public money in the bank as "the gratuitous deposites," and the whole purpose of his resolutions was to reduce these deposits. In December 1828, Benton pertinaciously resumed the aggressive in a series of resolutions, one of which declared that the Bank of the United States "ought to be required to make a compensation . . . or the use of the balances of public money on its hands." On the 6th of January he spoke to his resolutions, devoting considerable attention to the sums of public money in the keeping of the bank and advancing the astonishing argument that the provision in the charter which permitted the secretary of the treasury to remove the deposits "included the right to make terms for letting them remain." This was far from being the opinion of the Committee on Finance, which reported on the 20th of February, controverting Benton's arguments and asserting that the bonus had been paid in consideration of the privilege of holding the deposits. But Benton's attack upon the privileges of the bank had its effect upon popular opinion, and later he asserted that the attempt to secure compensation for the balances was the actual beginning of the struggle with the bank.

The next act of opposition grew out of circumstances attending the election of Jackson in 1828. Complaints were made that the branches at Lexington, Charleston, Portsmouth, and New Orleans had attempted to secure Jackson's defeat. At this time Amos Kendall, who was just beginning to assert his dominance of Jackson's political thinking, Isaac Hill, a pettifogging politician and newspaper editor of New Hampshire, and Francis P. Blair, of Kentucky, an editor who had borrowed from the bank and had apparently settled his account at a loss to the institution, were the principal authors of these charges. Kendall and Blair were infected with the monetary heresies which then raged in Kentucky, and both believed that the bank had participated in campaigns for the purpose of overthrowing the "old court" party. The complaints against the Kentucky branches were communicated to Biddle as early as January 1829, coming from the Democratic congressmen of that state through Postmaster McLean, who suggested the selection of directors "from both political parties." He also furnished from Colonel R. M. Johnson a list of members of the Jackson party in Kentucky who were considered eligible and fit for such positions. Biddle, in reply, repelled the insinuation that the bank's appointments were dictated by political considerations, and repudiated the suggestion of "a system of political balance" as resulting in "almost inevitably" forcing upon the bank "incompetent or inferior persons." He then forwarded the charges to the Kentucky branches, with a request for information and a warning to avoid all political action. The officers of the branches replied, denying the charges and demonstrating to Biddle's satisfaction that the nominations made by the congressmen were unfit and designed to transform the offices into political machines, while the cashier at Louisville declared that there was a scheme to make a Jackson partisan president of that branch. These explanations did not satisfy the plotters against the bank, who continued to insinuate charges to Jackson, filling his mind with suspicions to which he gave free expression.

Under these circumstances Secretary Ingham, of the treasury, was persuaded by Senator Woodbury of New Hampshire to make complaint to Biddle of the noxious activity of Jeremiah Mason, president of the Portsmouth branch. Woodbury wished that Ingham should use his "influence at the mother bank in producing a change." Ingham requested that the charges be investigated, intimating that Mason was using his place for political purposes. Two weeks earlier Biddle had received a letter of a similar tenor from Woodbury, and, almost simultaneously with Ingham's, one written by Isaac Hill to two gentlemen in Philadelphia, intended for his perusal and containing two memorials. The first of these was from a number of merchants at Portsmouth complaining of the business methods of the branch, and the second was from the Jackson members of the New Hampshire legislature, uttering similar complaints and containing a list of names for directors, four of which were those of Jackson men. This cumulative attack from the secretary, the senator, the second comptroller of the treasury, the New Hampshire legislature, and the merchants of Portsmouth, added to the action in regard to the Kentucky branches and the charges against the branch at New Orleans, convinced the board of directors that there was an organized attempt to convert the bank into a Democratic party machine. The animus of the attacks was revealed, they thought, in a sentence in Woodbury's letter declaring that Mason was "a particular friend of Mr. Webster, and his political character is doubtless well known to you," and another sentence in Hill's letter which asserted that "the friends of General Jackson in New Hampshire have had but too much reason to complain of the management of the branch at Portsmouth." The opinion of the directors has been adopted by most historians, who believe that Jackson's hostility is to be dated from the repulse of the attempt. This opinion has the corroborative weight of assertions made by Daniel Webster, John C. Calhoun, and John Quincy Adams. It is, however, only partially true. In so far as it involves Hill and Woodbury, it may be accepted, but the implication of Jackson and the bulk of the party is demonstrably false. Ingham also disclaimed any such purpose both in his letters to Biddle in 1829, and again in 1832, asserting that he acted as a friend in order "to avert the meditated destruction of the bank." His disclaimer is strengthened by the fact that he was ignorant of the action of his subordinate, Hill, who was behind the whole affair.

Ingham's letters, therefore, as showing an intention to make a party machine out of the bank on the part of the administration, or as revealing the source of Jackson's enmity to it, may be safely neglected. On the other hand, they prove that Democratic politicians believed that they had ground for complaining of the bank. The truth is that the vast majority of the bank's officers and directors were drawn from the ranks of the party hostile to Jackson, not because the bank supported this party, but because most of the businessmen were unfriendly to Jackson, and the officers and directors had to be selected from the ranks of the businessmen. Yet this result, so simple and obvious, naturally appeared to Jackson and his supporters exceedingly hostile. By the Jackson Democrats the opinion was firmly held that the branch at Portsmouth was a political engine; that Mason, an aggressive and influential politician and the close personal friend of Webster, owed his appointment to these circumstances, and especially to Webster's influence—in which latter surmise they were quite correct—and that Mason then "undertook to establish" the bank's "absolute control over both parties." Hill, in his letter of July 17, 1829, asserted that all now asked was that it should "not continue to be an engine of political oppression by any party"; while in 1832 he declared that the branch "was made a party engine previous to the last Presidential election—its directors were exclusively of one political party—its favors were dispensed with a view to affect that election; and it was the principal instrument to give, in the choice of electors of President in 1828, a small majority to the party in that State which has ever since been in a minority."

The Ingham correspondence is of still greater import as revealing the attitude of the Jackson Democracy toward questions of privilege and monopoly, and consequently toward the bank. It shows that the party from its political principles was necessarily hostile to the bank, and that Ingham believed, as did McLean, the Kentucky congressmen, Kendall and Hill, Woodbury, and Major Lewis, that only "checks and counterpoises" would provide "a just equilibrium"; in other words, that only by having an equal number of directors from both parties could the bank be kept out of politics. This was absurd, since the bank's interests could only be injured by adopting any such principle for the selection of its directors. On the other hand, it was a great privileged monopoly, and therefore justly obnoxious to the democratic theory of equality. Ingham pointed this out by asserting that two opposing principles struggled for control in the management of the bank: the democratic, which held "that the bank ought to exist exclusively for national purposes, and for the common benefit of all," and the aristocratic, which held that it was the "prominent use" of the bank "to strengthen the arm of wealth, and counterpoise the influence of extended suffrage in the disposition of public affairs." Whatever may be said about the first principle, it is manifestly false to assert that anyone supported the second. The stockholders of the bank certainly did not invest their funds with the purpose of counterpoising "the influence of extended suffrage" or for any other political purpose. It was enough, however, that the Democracy believed that they did, and that it was correct in considering the bank as enjoying exclusive privileges in which the masses could not participate.

The political charges against the bank were rendered effective by the complaints of the merchants that Mason's course was offensive to them. The truth is that the office at Portsmouth had been too free with its accommodations, and had consequently fallen into difficulties during the pressure of 1828. Hereupon the board had elected Jeremiah Mason president, and that gentleman proceeded rigorously to cut off accommodations and collect the debts of the branch. In this he had been eminently successful. He had reduced the time of the renewal of accommodation loans from 120 to 60 days, and had insisted on the payment of 20 percent of the notes before renewing them, instead of 10 percent as previously. In pursuing these measures Mason acted only as a businessman, but his acts were excessively irritating to debtors and gave an opportunity to the politicians.

Biddle, whose apprehensions had been keenly excited by the similar complaints about the Kentucky offices, immediately replied to both Woodbury and Ingham, repelling the charges, and, incited by his suspicions, wrote a second letter to Ingham showing a spirit of uncompromising hostility both to what he considered an attempt to involve the bank in politics, and to the "official lecture," which he thought the secretary was not justified in delivering. Ingham believed himself unjustly treated and retorted sharply in a letter which, according to General Cadwalader, revealed "the writhing of the scotched snake." In Biddle's opinion it revealed far more than this: it announced relations between the bank and the administration which he was not inclined to admit. "The Secretary of the Treasury believes," said Biddle, "1st: That the 'relations between the Government and the bank' confer some supervision of the choice of the officers of the bank, ... 2d: That there is some 'action of the Government on the bank' not precisely explained, but in which he is the proper agent; and, finally, 3d: That it is his right and his duty to suggest the views of the administration as to the political opinions and conduct of the officers of the bank." Ingham had not said as much as this, but he had talked of suggesting the government's views as to the "proper management" of the bank. His letter certainly did not tend to change Biddle's opinion of the motive behind it, nor his desire to teach the secretary to mind his own business, and he wrote Cadwalader outlining a reply, which should be sent by the latter, as it "would come better from you and would annoy the individual more." He was glad, he said, that they had withstood him.

Biddle had scarcely dispatched this letter to Cadwalader when he was still further confirmed in his conviction that the real battle was with the administration for the bank's integrity, by the receipt of a letter from Mason stating that at Hill's instigation an attempt was being made to remove the pension funds of the government from the Portsmouth branch to a state bank in Concord, of which Hill had formerly been president. Immediately afterward the secretary of war ordered the removal of the funds to the Concord bank. "It requires little prescience," wrote Cadwalader, "to see in these disgusting developments the germ of a course of systematic hostility against the Bank. In the hands of impartial and independent men the institution is not what they wish to make it—an engine of subserviency to their political objects." Nor was this the only added complication. Secretary Ingham objected to paying the commission charged by the bank for transferring government funds abroad, asserted that he could procure the service elsewhere at a cheaper rate, and threatened to place part of the public deposits with a state bank, which would oblige the administration by making the transfers for 1 percent commission instead of for 3½.

Ingham was now thoroughly exasperated, Biddle only less so: "If we must fight," exclaimed the latter, "I want no fairer battle ground." After investigating the Portsmouth affair, he wrote to Cadwalader: "I can now say with the utmost confidence that the whole is a party intrigue got up by a combination of small bankrupts and smaller Demagogues." The business opposition to Mason melted completely away in the face of investigation. Indignant at the attempts which he believed were being made upon the bank's independence, Biddle returned to Philadelphia and wrote a withering reply to Ingham, in which he took the liberty of inferring the three points already noted as involved in Ingham's earlier letter. This action was "altogether unexpected" by the guileless secretary, and "created a strong impression"; in fact, he was deeply incensed that these meanings should have been read into his letter, and indignantly repudiated them, at the same time asserting that the administration did have power over the bank by its authority to appoint five directors and the secretary's right to remove the government deposits. The whole letter, along with Asbury Dickins's comments to Biddle on his letter of the 15th of September, leaves no doubt that the secretary was much more ingenuous in his correspondence than Biddle and most historians have supposed. Dickins's regretful warnings and pleadings for conciliation convinced Biddle that he had possibly misjudged the secretary, and in answer to Ingham's letter, spun out to a prodigious length and full of the sputterings of inappeasable and helpless wrath, he returned a good-tempered reply closing the correspondence. "You shall not complain of me now," he wrote to Dickins, "for I have written as conciliatory as possible an answer to the voluminous and belligerent epistle of your chief." It is evident that Biddle had mistaken the purpose and temper of the secretary, who had blundered into a position favorable to Hill, but resented with indignation the imputation of "a connection with the movements of these other people," the Hills and Kendalls, whose tool he was, but not their conscious coadjutor.

What effect did this *contretemps* have upon Jackson? If his own word can be credited, little or none. He wrote to Biddle:

> *I feel very sensibly the services rendered by the Bank at the last payment of the national debt and shall take an opportunity of declaring it publicly in my message to Congress. That is my own feeling to the Bank— and Mr. Ingham's also—He and you got into a difficulty thro' the foolishness —if I may use the term of Mr. Hill. Observing he was a little embarrassed I said Oh that has all passed now. He said with the Parent Board and myself [yourself?] he had ever[y] reason to be satisfied—that he had heard complaints and then mentioned a case at Louisville—of which he promised to give me the particulars.*
>
> *I said Well I am very much gratified at this frank explanation. We shall all be proud of any kind mention in the message—for we should feel like soldiers after an action commenced by their General. Sir said he it would be only an act of justice to mention it [i.e., the bank's services to the government].*

This extract shows Jackson amused, indifferent, and open in his attitude, perhaps a little contemptuous as regards poor Ingham, whom

he certainly did not like, and whose discomfiture was in all proba-
bility more pleasing to him than otherwise.

The next movement against the bank foreshadowed Jackson's
attack in his first message. On the 30th of November Amos Kendall
informed James Watson Webb, editor of the New York *Courier and
Enquirer,* that the president would take ground against the bank in
his message, and furnished Webb with a number of queries for publication, in which a scheme of a substitute for the bank was outlined:
Would the state banks "take measures to satisfy the general government of their safety in receiving deposits of the revenue; and trans-
acting the banking concerns of the United States?" Would "the
Legislatures of the several states adopt resolutions on the subject
and instruct their senators how to vote?" Would "a proposition be
made to authorize the government to issue exchequer bills, to the
amount of the annual revenue, redeemable at pleasure, to constitute
a circulating medium equivalent to the notes issued by the United
States Bank?" These queries appeared in the *Courier and Enquirer*
embodied in an editorial article, with no intimation that they came
from the administration. In them is to be found the suggestion of the
removal of the deposits, of the experiment of using the state banks as
places of deposit, of an attack by the state legislatures upon the
bank, and of a substitute for the bank's currency supported later by
Jackson. That the act of Kendall was not an isolated one is shown by
the response of the South Carolina legislature. Resolutions were introduced there requesting their representatives in Congress and in-
structing the senators of South Carolina to oppose the recharter of
the bank unless it were to be confined to the District of Columbia,
declaring for a bank without foreign stockholders, and requesting that
the Senate Committee on Finance should be asked to report on the
feasibility of a national bank without private stockholders.

To Nicholas Biddle these cumulative assaults were a revelation. He
believed it necessary to meet the attempts to overthrow the bank
which he clearly saw were already making. His method of doing this,
after his first ebullition of anger and indignation expressed in the
Ingham correspondence, was to adopt the means of conciliation suggested by McLean and Ingham, namely, to appoint friends of the
administration to seats at the boards of the bank and the branches.

This was indeed a lame and impotent conclusion after his brave challenge to the secretary, his bold declaration that "for the bank . . .
there is but one course of honor or of safety. Whenever its duties
come in conflict with the spirit of party, it should not compromise
with it, nor capitulate to it, but resist it—resist it openly and fear-
lessly." To mitigate the wrath of his enemies and deprive them of
their weapon of attack he appointed men who were friendly to the
administration as directors at Baltimore, New York, Utica, Portsmouth, New Orleans, and the western offices. He tried to put himself
in touch with the administration, opening a correspondence with
Major Lewis, Jackson's most intimate and confidential adviser; and
he expressed himself "desirous of treating Major Barry with great
kindness and liberality"—Major Barry owing money to the bank and
being unable to pay it when due.

There has been much conjecture as to the origin and nature of
Jackson's opposition to the bank. Historians in general believe that
he did not contemplate action in regard to it when he first came to
Washington as president. His relations with it, they think, conclu-
sively prove this. It is true that he had been offended by the refusal
of the New Orleans branch to cash his drafts on the secretary of state,
but he would hardly remember this trivial annoyance. On the other
hand, declare Parton and von Holst, he had recommended in 1821 the
establishment of a branch at Pensacola, and so late as 1828 the appointment of certain officers at the Nashville branch. Now there is no
doubt that Jackson had done both of these things, but they have little
significance, since nothing is easier than to secure signatures to a
petition, which was all that either act amounted to. Moreover, the
letter recommending officers for the Nashville branch was not written
in 1828, but in 1818. With this correction of dates, the whole weight
of the argument is removed, and Jackson's act loses all significance
in the determination of his attitude in 1829. Of his opposition to the
bank before coming to Washington there exists, moreover, incontrovertible proof. In 1827 Biddle was warned that Jackson had opposed
the repeal of the Tennessee law taxing branches established in that
state. James A. Hamilton, writing of an interview with Jackson in
December 1827, says that "he expressed strong opinions against the
Bank of the United States." He had undoubtedly wished to insert a
paragraph attacking the bank in his first inaugural, but had been dis-

suaded by politicians wiser than himself. Again in 1829 Lewis wrote that Jackson had certainly been led to believe "during the *pendency* of the presidential election" that the Lexington branch had acted toward his candidacy in an unfriendly manner, loaning money with the object of defeating him. This conviction gave a personal flavor to Jackson's opposition, yet that opposition was at bottom not personal, but based upon constitutional and social opinions. The bank was in Jackson's opinion unconstitutional, and, as a powerful privileged monopoly, dangerous to society. He himself expressed these ideas freely to Biddle, and at the same time indicated the origin of his dislike of banks:

> *I think it right to be perfectly frank with you. I do not think that the power of Congress extends to charter a Bank ought of the ten mile square. I do not dislike your Bank any more than all banks. But ever since I read the history of the South Sea bubble I have been afraid of banks.*

After this naive and delightfully Jacksonian reason for fearing all banks, after this frank confession of constitutional scruples, no one need henceforth seek for the motives or the origin of Jackson's opposition. He fails to tell Biddle just when he had read the history of the South Sea bubble, but whenever it happened it fixed him against banks. Let it be noted, too, that his dislike was for banks in general and not for the Bank of the United States in particular.

The Charges against the Bank

The subject in connection with the bank which always arouses most interest is its alleged corrupt connection with politics. It may be said at once that there never has been any evidence produced to show that the bank as a national bank ever spent a dollar corruptly. Yet the accusation was repeated so often that historians have been inclined to accept as proved what was only vehemently asserted, and it begot an incurable suspicion which has endured to this day.

It is self-evident that the bank would be affected by political considerations, since from the beginning to the end of its existence it was to a large extent subject to the will and whim of politicians, and it was frequently attacked by them. Had the board of directors been composed exclusively of canonized saints, still the conciliation of politicians and political forces would have been necessary. The only question worthy of discussion is that of the bank's honesty or corruption in this situation.

Biddle in 1829 rejected as totally inadmissible any attempt to create boards on which the political parties were fairly balanced, and declared that political affiliations should not be considered in such selections. He was right in this; but it must not be supposed that the proposition of a political balance was novel, or that Jackson Democrats first suggested it, or that there was any moral obliquity in such an arrangement. When the first government directors were named, President Madison frankly selected them all from his own political party, and the private stockholders, quite certain that the bank must either be a political machine or possess a balance of parties, elected ten Republicans and ten Federalists as their members of the board. Madison and his capable and honest secretary, A. J. Dallas, then struggled successfully to secure the presidency of the bank for a Republican partisan of no particular ability or experience as a banker, and thus the disasters consequent upon the presidency of William Jones are primarily chargeable to James Madison and Alexander James Dallas.

The policy of political balance then inaugurated was religiously pursued all through the administration of William Jones, and certainly through part of that of Langdon Cheves. Writing to Biddle in 1820, John McKim urges him to assist in the election of a Republican director at Baltimore, "as you know that the Republicans are one short of their number, and the necessity of giving us our share of the Directors, as we do hold more than the half of the stock, and it having been Policy to divide the two Partys in the direction, since the Bank was established." When this equal division ceased it is not possible to say, but it may be reasonably presumed that the disintegration of parties under Monroe caused its cessation.

Biddle was opposed to the practice, and fought against it strenuously when it was suggested in the case of the Kentucky branches and the branch in New Hampshire in 1829. He then stated that he considered such an arrangement as largely responsible for the bank's losses in the West in the early years of its career. As to his rumored desire to have the bank anti-Jackson, he repudiated it altogether, and constantly wondered why anyone could suppose that a bank would care which political party was up or which was down. He was never weary of quoting Dean Swift's remark that "money is neither Whig nor Tory," and in asserting that "men lend where they are sure of getting back their money with a profit." This was sound sense, and holding these opinions with deep conviction Biddle was anxious above all to exclude political considerations.

Nevertheless he was not able to carry out his wishes altogether. During Adams's administration members of the party in power were no less ready to complain and to demand assistance from the bank than were the Jackson politicians later. Biddle repulsed them with as little ceremony as he repulsed Ingham, yet he was compelled to consider political affiliations in the appointments to the boards all through his presidency. In January 1824, there was dissatisfaction in Boston with the political complexion of the directorate there, and B. W. Crowninshield was substituted for a Federalist on the parent board in order to give the other party a chance and to assuage "feelings which may hereafter grow into hostility." Again in 1828 he retained the services of C. P. White at New York because it was not expedient to "alienate a member of the Board at such a time—to offend personally a member of that Congress before whom the Bank may probably come for a renewal of its charter," while in November 1832, he was anxious "to conciliate gentlemen who may be useful to the institution."

It will be observed, however, that there was no plan of a political balance in these instances. Another conclusion must also be drawn, that, so far from trying to constitute his boards all of one political party, as the Jackson politicians asserted, Biddle took unusual pains to appoint members of the various parties when he could secure those who were qualified for the positions. After the correspondence with Ingham and the reiterated charges of doing precisely what he wished to avoid, Biddle introduced additional Jackson politicians into the boards. He did this at Baltimore, at New York, at New Orleans, at Portsmouth, at Nashville, at Lexington, and at Utica. He allowed Lewis to name most of the members of the Nashville board, took his advice about the Lexington branch, and ceased his complacency only when he saw reason to suspect that the wily major would soon be naming all the western directorates. In August Lewis wrote saying that he was half ashamed to ask for further favors, but that "Our friends at Louisville, Kentucky, think they are not fairly and equally represented in your Branch at that place," and he forwarded the names of three gentlemen whose appointment would probably "give entire satisfaction to the friends of the administration in that part of the state." This further encroachment upon the province of the bank exhausted the patience of its much-enduring head, and he politely declined to introduce "new members . . . for the purpose of making any political balance." The refusal is creditable to Biddle; it proves that he would not be subservient to the administration even at a most critical moment in the bank's attempts to secure Jackson's assent to a recharter, and that he was fixed in his determination that the bank should not degenerate into a political machine.

It may be argued, however, that while the parent board was free from political chicane and bias, the local boards were not. Such arguments are undoubtedly applicable to the early years of the bank, because in the southern and western states campaigns at times revolved about banking questions and would involve the institution despite itself. Every officer and employee of the Bank of the United States must have been on one side during the struggle between the new and the old court parties in Kentucky, and such occurrences would lead to the conviction that the bank spent money for the purpose of controlling elections which were vital to its interests. It is also certain that a board of directors composed of intelligent businessmen would contain few members of the Jackson Democracy—a condition which would incur suspicion of political favoritism. As the bank's loans would be made mostly to the same class as that from which the directors were selected, a charge of discriminating against Democrats would inevitably arise.

Consequently assertions of corruption at the branches were frequently made. As early as 1825 it was insinuated that the president of the Washington branch, though recognized as incompetent, had retained possession of his office because of his influence with the Monroe administration. In regard to Kentucky frequent charges of unjustifiable political activity were made. Blair asserts of his own knowledge that "bank men" employed bribes to influence the elections, though the phrase "bank men" is scarcely sufficient to include officers of the bank. Like assertions were made in reference to Louisiana. From South Carolina reports came of officials of the branch engaging actively in politics. Hill, of New Hampshire, declared in the Senate that the Portsmouth office "was made a party engine" in 1828, and that "it was the principal instrument" in carrying the state for Adams; while Clayton, of Georgia, asserted that the president of the Norfolk branch had engaged most offensively in politics, publicly declaring that he was "opposed to General Jackson," and becoming involved in fisticuffs as a result.

These are the specific charges of political action which admit of examination. The charge against the president of the Washington office is of no moment. He did indeed exert his supposed influence with the administration to secure his election to the local board, and was severely censured for doing so by the president of the bank. In the New Hampshire case no political acts were adduced, and the only circumstances which gave color to the assertions were that the president there was an old-time Federalist and a friend of Webster. The New Orleans charges were admitted by President Jackson to be baseless; those in regard to South Carolina were of a different character. It was asserted that the president there, who was an active politician, had been seen "superintending . . . the polls at the elections"—which might well be without involving the branch. Unfortunately, this officer insisted on taking an active part in the heated campaign over nullification—opposing that heresy with all his power. Biddle wrote him a letter requesting that he refrain from such action, as it was calculated to injure the bank, and added, "no principle is more fundamental than its total abstinence from politics." Johnson's subsequent activity, however, occasioned complaint on the part of Vice-President Calhoun and Senator Hayne. The charge against the Norfolk officer is of the same character. He was at the polls and opposed to General Jackson, but how this involved the bank it is difficult to see. In regard to the charges against the Kentucky branches, Jackson expressed himself as satisfied that they were without foundation as far as the parent board was concerned. The directors there denied them; while Biddle urged the officers to exercise care in avoiding all cause for such complaints.

The actual status of Biddle's policy never showed better than in 1831, when the charges against the Kentucky offices were renewed. Writing to him in April, the cashier of the Lexington office urges loans to help the anti-Jackson candidate, because funds were needed "to

win for our men." The president of the branch thought they ought to be
furnished, and "so does Mr. Clay. The coming election of Congressmen is all important in its bearing on the Presidential election." To
this Biddle instantly and decisively replied: "I believe it to be a fundamental principle in the administration of the Bank that its officers
should abstain from any connection with what are called politics, to
abstain not in appearance merely, but entirely, candidly and hon-
estly." Thus at the moment that Blair was charging political corruption in Kentucky, Biddle refused assistance which even Henry Clay
thought should be granted. Similarly in 1832, after the veto, Biddle
declared that the bank would take no active part in the campaign,
such action being contrary to its principles. To this resolution he
adhered.

Unquestionably the bank lobbied in its own interests. It did this in
the New York legislature in February and March 1831, to hinder the
adoption of resolutions hostile to it. At the same time it strove to get
through the Pennsylvania legislature a resolution in its favor, C. J.
Ingersoll acting as its champion. Again, during the struggle for recharter, Horace Binney acted as its manager at Washington, while in
1834 the bank used its influence with its friends to elect John Sergeant senator from Pennsylvania. The attempt failed, but prevented
Richard Rush's election. In all these cases, however, there is no reason to suspect the use of corrupt means; while the suspicion that it
used such means to secure recharter in 1832 is absolutely baseless
so far as all the known evidence goes.

What the bank did not do directly, it was frequently charged with
doing indirectly. Its enemies declared, with emphatic repetition, that
it secured the favor of congressmen and politicians by granting them
unusual accommodations on insufficient security and extending to
them favors not granted to other individuals. It must be admitted that
the bank was accustomed to give drafts for the salaries of congressmen, payable at points distant from Washington, without charging
exchange. Biddle said he knew of no such cases, but if they occurred
they were defensible on the ground that congressmen had a right to
their pay wherever "the Treasury chooses to give it to them." This
answer could hardly be considered satisfactory, and the assertion
was frequently made that not only did congressmen receive their pay

wherever they chose to demand it, thus getting the benefit of the exchange, but that in other instances they were accommodated without being charged exchange. Such a practice was certainly open to the objection of being in the nature of granting favors to those from whom favors were to be expected. The same condemnation must fall upon the practice of paying congressmen and government officials before their salaries became due by the passage of the general appropriations act. Adams, a warm champion of the bank, showed that in a single session the amount thus advanced was almost $400,000, "which was equivalent to a loan without interest," and that the amount of interest thus lost to the bank was over $3,000. He was "not without doubts of the propriety of this indulgence."

That congressmen were not to borrow money, or that the bank was not to lend them money, could hardly be argued, since this would be an unwarrantable discrimination against congressmen as congressmen. That the officers of the bank were willing to make loans on easy terms to congressmen is likely, and is illustrated in the case of General Stevens, to whom Biddle granted a loan on his own authority, although he was a stranger, and although the president did not know that the drawers of the notes were of good credit. In June 1829, Biddle justified a loan to Congressman Verplanck, against the objections of Robert Lenox, partly on the ground that it was expedient for the institution to stand well with those who held its future existence in their hands, especially as he believed that "the loan was perfectly safe." In 1831 he permitted John Forsyth to borrow a large sum at a long date on the security of a mortgage, though such loans were against the declared policy of the bank. A similar accommodation was granted to George McDuffie in 1833, for $100,000, the agreement being to loan on mortgage and to renew the note indefinitely. David Crockett's bill was about to be protested, and was renewed by Biddle personally to protect Crockett, and the same favor was accorded Joseph Vance. In 1826 the board released Senator Samuel Smith from his debt consequent upon the Baltimore frauds of 1817–1819. Asbury Dickins, first clerk in the treasury and a valuable friend, was released in 1830, the bank saving about half the debt. Colonel R. M. Johnson and his brother were treated with like kindness in 1824. All these were favors to men who might be politically useful. Moreover, during the years when the bank was attempting to secure a new lease of life, the loans to congressmen were large, and much beyond what had been customary at earlier periods.

It must be remembered, however, that all the loans of the bank were much more extensive than usual at this time, and hence those of congressmen might fairly be expected to be so. Similarly, in settling the debts due when the debtor could not pay, congressmen were not the sole recipients of such favor, but shared it with hundreds of others. Therefore no censure is implied where the favor was not unduly granted, and the evidence of the president's letter books is conclusive that in all the cases named full payment could not be made. Smith's debts had been contracted in 1817–1819 through the criminality of his mercantile partner, and he could not discharge them; Johnson's indebtedness had been incurred at the same time and he was entirely bankrupt; while Dickins's debt had been contracted with the Bank of Columbia, and he was never in a situation to pay it.

On the other hand, in the matter of granting unusual loans to congressmen, the bank seems to have laid itself fairly open to censure. Yet much of this must be mitigated if the loans were safe. Tyler's committee in 1834 reported on this head that of loans made by the Philadelphia office to individuals then in Congress only $400 had been carried to the account of "suspended debt" and one note for $500 protested. These it considered debts which would ultimately be paid. Some cases existed at the branches, but all these loans seem to have been made "upon as good security" as was customary in other cases.

Other charges of indirect bribery were those of paying excessive fees to lawyers and making donations of the bank's money for political effect. Nothing of the kind was discovered. The fees to lawyers were not excessive. No cases of bribes by donations were known by the committee of 1834, and the subject was carefully investigated by the committee of 1832 with results favorable to the bank, the whole amount of donations from 1817 to 1831 aggregating $4,620. The contributions were insignificant and were made for the most part to fire companies, or to turnpikes, with the object of increasing the value of real estate held by the bank or of protecting its property.

The most effective of all the indictments against the bank was that it "subsidized the press." This was a vague phrase, but it was pretty clearly understood by everybody and meant that the bank bribed printers and publishers by granting them accommodations on easy terms, with the expectation of receiving their assistance in return. Of course, editors occasionally needed bank accommodations, yet, as professed molders of public opinion, they were first to take sides either for or against the bank when the subject of recharter came up. In this situation, a loan to an editor favorable to recharter would be called a subsidy, a loan to an editor opposed a bribe. The most prominent editors to secure large loans were Duff Green, of the Washington *Telegraph,* Webb and Noah, of the New York *Courier and Enquirer,* Gales and Seaton, of the *Intelligencer,* Robert Walsh, of the *National Gazette* and the *American Quarterly Review,* Thomas Ritchie, of the Richmond *Enquirer,* Jesper Harding, of the Pennsylvania *Enquirer,* and F. B. Blair, of the *Globe,* though before he established that paper. All were prominent and able editors, some favorable to the bank, some opposed. Suspicion was also aroused by the conversion to the bank's cause of several editors who had been unfriendly. Duff Green ceased to oppose; while Webb and Noah became active supporters instead of bitter opponents.

Numerous cases of attempts to buy up editors were also alleged. Parton intimated that such an attempt was made on Blair. Blair himself makes charges of this character in reference to the New York *Evening Post* and the New York *Standard,* and presents the affidavit of a country editor declaring that "a supporter of the Whig, or Bank candidate" offered him $100 and banking facilities at the Bank of the United States if he would use his influence for the Whig candidate. It is apparent that all this evidence is of the flimsiest, and does not establish in a single instance any connection of the bank with the alleged attempts. In one case "a known friend of the bank" offers a loan, in another "Silas E. Burrows" promises "valuable pecuniary consideration," and in the third it is "a supporter of the Whig" candidate. That there were editors who were not averse to receiving favors scarcely needs to be said. James Gordon Bennett, who always displayed in public the most rancorous antipathy for the bank, nevertheless kept up a friendly correspondence with its president, gave good advice, and on one occasion defined his position thus: "Of course I am opposed to the Bank and must be so—but I suppose you understand that." Three weeks later he hints that he needs money and would like to hear from Biddle. The bank had nothing for him, however.

Biddle's own attitude in relation to "subsidizing" the press has been incidentally left on record by himself, and does honor to his integrity. In 1828 Webster urged upon him the expediency of granting loans to Gales and Seaton in order to sustain their newspaper, which might be useful to the bank. To this Biddle responded warmly that he could not and would not proceed on any such principles:

> *The value of his paper and the advantage of its continuance are considerations entirely foreign to us—and the very circumstance that but for the Bank of the United States any newspaper would be discontinued, or that the Bank had gone out of its way in order to sustain any newspaper either in administration or in opposition would be a subject of reproach and what alone makes reproach uncomfortable of just reproach.*

As this letter was never intended for the public eye, it is the best possible testimony to Biddle's integrity at the time it was written. And yet it was the untoward fate of the man who wrote it, and who in so doing denied accommodations to old and trusted friends at a critical moment in their fortunes and risked offending an intimate and powerful advocate, to be generally regarded as a wholesale briber of editors and publishers.

Of all the loans to editors, those to Webb and Noah, of the New York *Courier and Enquirer,* gained the widest notoriety and created the most intense feeling. This journal had been pronouncedly anti-bank from November 1829 to April 1831. It then changed its attitude and advocated a new charter with modifications, though still professing to support Jackson.

James Gordon Bennett, in his *Memoirs,* declares that the paper was financially embarrassed in 1831, and that Noah, seeing "the breeches pocket of Mr. Biddle open, entered it immediately." It is not necessary to credit Bennett with extraordinary veracity, but he was probably not far wrong. Certain it is that in the spring of 1831 the proprietors of the paper needed more funds, and one of them decided to sell out. At this juncture M. M. Noah, who was desirous of buying up the retiring proprietor's shares, met with Silas E. Burrows, and

Burrows, Webb, and Noah planned to raise the necessary means, and "to change the tone of the *Courier and Enquirer*"—in other words, to bring it out in support of the bank. Burrows was the pivot upon which all the succeeding events turned. He was a vain, loquacious, intruding, scheming merchant, who wished to be regarded as one who bore upon his shoulders the burden of empires. His letters to Biddle are still extant, and are filled with hints of mysterious secrets; chatter of grandiose plans; fulsome laudation at one moment and causeless reproaches at the next; abject petitions for loans to be used in airy ventures; denunciations of the officials of the New York branch; tales of intimacies with presidents and ex-presidents; boasts of imaginary influence over the course of politics; and again with exclamations of fear and violent assertions that he is a persecuted and hunted man. They portray only too clearly an individual possessed of an incurably weak head.

When the trio began operations for securing complete possession of the *Courier and Enquirer,* Webb mentioned to Burrows that he "was prepared to advocate a modified recharter of the bank." Burrows urged him to come out for an "unconditional recharter," and promised Noah that he would raise the funds for the purchase of the half interest in the *Courier and Enquirer* by securing a loan from his father. This proposition was accepted, and Burrows hurried off to Philadelphia to see Biddle, with the object of securing the money there instead of from his father. He told Biddle that he wanted $15,000 for Noah to purchase "a share in a newspaper," and offered the notes of Noah, indorsed by Webb, as security. The exchange committee of the bank authorized the loan at one year and eighteen months. Biddle then furnished Burrows with the money out of his own pocket, without even seeing the notes to secure the sum, and consenting that Burrows should not indorse them thus leaving the responsibility of payment with Noah and Webb. The truth is that Burrows did not then have the notes, for he took the $15,000 to New York, told Noah that he had secured a loan from his father, gave Noah his father's notes instead of the money, took Noah's notes, and then sent them to Biddle, who held them in his own possession for over nine months instead of placing them in the possession of the bank. Here, then, was a large loan made without the receipt of any security at the time on the notes of one partner indorsed by the other—an act in contravention of the rules of the bank; not indorsed by the borrower; and for a long period.

In January 1832, Biddle at last decided to transfer the account to the books, and then the notes, instead of being for one year and for eighteen months, were transformed in to paper to be paid at intervals of six months until October 1836; that is, for from six months to almost five years. In February the investigation of the bank was discussed in Congress, and on the 2d of March Burrows took up the notes, securing a loan at the bank for the purpose, so that the loan made to Webb and Noah was paid by making a new one to Burrows.

The precise relations existing between Biddle and Burrows cannot be determined. In the spring of 1831 Burrows had persuaded Biddle that he was a person of vast though undefined influence in New York politics, and as at that moment the legislature of New York was discussing a resolution denunciatory of the bank, Burrows went to Albany to attempt to prevent the action. It was then that the agreement was made with Webb and Noah. As Burrows could not keep silent, the matter was at once bruited in the public press, whereupon Biddle wrote, asking Burrows to send him a letter saying that he had never "received any authority . . . from anyone connected with the Bank to influence by pecuniary or other means the course of any newspaper in New York or elsewhere." Burrows did not furnish this certificate of good character; but, on the contrary, denominated himself "your agent, confidential agent," and later, in a letter of passionate, childish, and desperate reproach, angrily asserted that he was refused accommodations "whilst the Bank has stifled the press here by rewards of fortunes," and transmitted a bill for services which shows that Biddle had paid him $16,000 and still owed him $1,100. One week later he forwarded another long letter of reproaches, and hinted that he held secrets which would bring a fortune to himself and ruin to the bank; in March 1832, on the other hand, he wrote Biddle: "All discounts made at your bank to me, have been for my accommodation, and individual benefit. Beyond this is unknown to you, and is left for me to explain." He would not appear before the congressional investigating committee, however, and "hopes to God" he will not be called on, and then exclaims: "The moment I knew you had made an entry of these documents, that moment I knew a fortune was at my disposal if I would accept of it, and made without censure by the world, as they would justify me for testifying to all."

It is difficult to assert anything with confidence in the face of such declarations from a man of this character. Burrows may really have thought that Biddle had agreed with him to bribe the New York press; the sums which Biddle had intrusted to his keeping show that he was actually acting for the bank in some capacity; his remarks about the money loaned to him prove that Biddle did not know what he had done with it, and the testimony of Noah and Webb shows that he did not transfer it to them. Biddle's friends evidently regarded Burrows as a bad character, for Bevan writes of him as "a troublesome and unprincipled man," and later as "a very dangerous man, and one in whom no confidence can be placed," at the same time expressing a wish that arrangements "could be speedily made to get W. and N.'s paper out of his possession."

Webb and Noah were accommodated with other loans. In August 1831, they received $20,000, payable 10 percent, every six months. They declared that they could not secure loans from the New York banks because they had supported the bank. On this occasion Noah said that their paper would, if it took part in the agitation for recharter, "go as far in favor of the bank" as it had done in April. In December the partners were back once more, this time for $15,000, claiming that the bank was morally bound to support them, because their course had cut them off from assistance from the New York banks. The loan was granted by the Exchange Committee, though at the time the board was refusing to lend small sums to good customers in Philadelphia. In both cases the notes were drawn by one partner and indorsed by the other.

Nor was this the end. In July 1832, after the veto, Biddle twice brusquely refused further accommodations to Webb, whereupon that gentleman threatened that unless something was done for him the paper would support Jackson. Biddle then consented to see if the loan could not be raised by one of his friends, for which kindness he received the thanks of Webb. Whether anything was done or not is unknown, but Noah retired from the *Courier and Enquirer*. Webb removed the names of Jackson and Van Buren from the head of the editorial columns of the paper and came out in a long article for Clay, Sergeant, and the bank. Let it be added that Webb's notes for

CHEVY CHASE OR **THE BANK RUNNER.** (how Burrows ran on the 1st of Novr. & S. L. followed, and how Burrows distanced him & almost escaped a whipping)

Gallants attend and hear a friend
Rehearse a morrful story;
A tale that's true, tis pity too
Of Burrows' loss of glory.

His Coal Black Mare, in Chatham Square
He rode along so gaily;
But soon his tire, like straw on fire,
Rose when he saw S—L.A—Y.

You fool says S—L, pray why with all
This business do you mix?
If you dont mind full soon you'l find
You'l get some D—d hard Licks!

Ah! Say you so, then off I go.
And Silas did his Steed lace.
S—L followed fast, but lost at last
Both Burrows and the horse race.

He d—d to H—l Cornelius L—
And swore th' offence was rank
That that D—d Post which he saw last
Should go against the Bank.

$18,600 went to protest in February 1833, and that in 1835 he offered to settle for ten cents on the dollar. It does appear as if Biddle had become sadly involved with the *Courier and Enquirer* and could not extricate himself. The loans granted to the editors of this paper would assuredly not have been made to others unless similarly situated.

It is easy to conjecture the arguments which appealed to Biddle in this matter. He had openly announced his belief in the policy of disseminating knowledge of the bank through the press, and of the justice of paying for such publications. In this policy he was supported by men of the most irreproachable character, and it may be added that after the beginning of the campaign of shameless slander and calumny inaugurated by Blair, he was certainly not without justification, and would have been more than an ordinary mortal had he done otherwise than he did. But it was only one step from this legitimate policy to that of making loans as a sort of payment for publications, and perhaps this subtle logic appealed to Biddle. He might regard such loans, even if it could be pointed out that they were not justified by business considerations, as justified by the resolution of the bank to pay for publications. If he had been willing to pay the *Courier and Enquirer* several hundred dollars for the publication of a few columns in a single issue, what possible objection could there be to a loan of $52,000 which would secure every issue of the paper for the bank's cause? As a matter of economy the second method might even be preferable to the first, since there was a chance of securing the repayment of the capital with interest, besides having the support of the paper.

Payments made to printers by the bank for publishing documents, articles, and speeches favorable to recharter were open to the criticism of being political; outside the province of a bank; made out of the money of the stockholders, the largest of whom was the government of the United States itself; and, finally, virtual bribes to the fortunate printers and editors who received the jobs. While the directors felt justified in making these expenditures, yet all these objections were valid, even supposing that the prices paid for the work done were not excessive. Everyone knows that the securing of printing which yields a fair profit is a matter of much moment with publishers, and that those who furnish such business are naturally treated as patrons. In reference to compensation, the Senate committee of 1834 declared that the bank had given no gratuities to printers or publishers, and left it to the Senate to judge whether or not the institution had allowed them "extra compensation." The evidence proves that the rate of payment was moderate.

Another objection to the expenditure was that the president of the bank was permitted to dispose of the funds at his own discretion. Jackson bitterly complained of this in his paper of September 18, 1833, declaring on the authority of the government directors that the sums spent by the bank for printing "during the years 1831 and 1832 were about $80,000." The directors, said Jackson, put "the funds of the bank at the disposition of the president for the purpose of employing the whole press of the country in the service of the bank, to hire writers and newspapers, and to pay out such sums as he pleases to what person and for what services he pleases without the responsibility of rendering any specific account." The criticism was just. The expenditures for extra printing from 1829 to 1834, inclusive, aggregated $65,103.25, and to these were added expenditures by President Biddle, without vouchers, and without designation of the purposes for which they were made. The total of these was $29,605. In whatever light the first of these items may be viewed, the second was totally indefensible. The Senate committee of 1834, though favorable to the bank, condemned the practice and virtually censured the directors for allowing the president to exercise such powers under the resolution of March 11, 1831.

It is to Biddle's credit that he never made any mystery of his policy in regard to paying for publications in the newspapers, and willingly gave his reasons for it. He believed that most of the opposition to the bank was due to ignorance, and that explanatory articles would dispel this ignorance and so put an end to the opposition. Thoroughly convinced that this was true, he continued publishing. He was assuredly mistaken. Ingersoll in 1831 gave it as his opinion that not three members of the Pennsylvania legislature had ever "read or will ever read McDuffie's report, Gallatin's article or the views in the North American and the National Gazette"; while in 1834 Mathew Carey declared that the system of issuing pamphlets dealing with abstruse banking questions at great length was utterly mistaken, that nobody would read them, or, if anybody did, that he would not understand them. This judgment seems sound, as anyone will agree who has read the pamphlets.

The amount of published matter paid for by the bank was very great. It began in April 1830 with Senator Smith's report, and continued for about five years. The bank not only published articles itself, but distributed those of others, and paid newspapers to publish reports. As a consequence, everyone who wrote on banking subjects wanted the bank to pay for his publication. In one case, at least, a pamphlet was published without the privity of the bank, and then recompense was demanded. Newspapers, of course, would not print articles supporting the bank without compensation. A congressman rarely made a friendly speech without expecting its dissemination at the expense of the bank. The most amusing case is that of John Tyler. Tyler was chairman of the Senate investigating committee of 1834, and, voicing the austere public morality characteristic of Virginia Republicanism since the days of Jefferson, criticized the bank for disseminating pamphlets and congressional reports. "Our friend," wrote Webster, "seemed to reserve all his censure for these heads.' Biddle, therefore, felt quite safe in asking Tyler if he wished his report disseminated. The surprise and disgust of the bank's president may easily be guessed when he discovered that Tyler did wish it to the extent of a thousand copies. Whatever credit is due Tyler for his political morality, a sense of humor was evidently not [one of] his prominent characteristics.

That the matter of printing was carried entirely too far will easily be gathered from what has been said, and even the bank's most eager partisans were convinced that this was so. Watmough, who arranged for much of the printing, at last protested. He thought they should cut down the number of congressional speeches published, though he added, with bitter pleasantry, "It is a great assistance to Green, to be sure. He is at best however but a *mauvais sujet,* and scarcely worth what has already been done for him." The printers, in his opinion, were "pretty much all alike—let them handle the money, *au diable,* the rest."

The charge of jobbing in public stocks touched the honor of the president and corporation, and, if proved, established a violation of the law; for the charter declared that the corporation should not "purchase any public debt whatsoever," or sell "more than $2 million thereof in any one year." The specific charge was that the bank jobbed in the 3 percent stock, and that in doing so it had interposed to prevent the payment of the national debt by urging the government's creditors not to present the certificates of the stock when the day of payment came.

The facts were as follows: On the 24th of March 1832, Asbury Dickins, acting secretary of the treasury, informed Biddle that one-half of the 3 percents, amounting to $6.5 million, would be paid off by the government on the 1st of July. The bank would have to furnish the funds from the government deposits held. Unfortunately, the discharge of the debt in this year had been so enormous, and the bank's business so expanded, that it was impossible to raise the sum required by the date specified. Biddle, long before the notice from Dickins, had attempted to reduce the bank's business and so get possession of sufficient specie to meet the government's demands. He had failed in this attempt. He accordingly looked about him for some other means of evading the threatened embarrassment, which would be fatal if it occurred in the midst of the campaign for a renewed charter. Hurrying to Washington, he requested as a temporary relief a postponement of the payment from July 1 to October 1, and offered, on behalf of the bank, to pay the interest on the stock for the three months. His request was granted on this condition. Later the treasury concluded to discharge two-thirds of each certificate in October, and the remainder of the debt on January 1, 1833, thus calling upon the bank for a sum of $13 million within three months' time.

The bank's difficulties under these circumstances are vividly portrayed in the correspondence with the branches, and in a letter of Biddle's to Cadwalader, outlining his plan to secure the means of payment. Biddle thought that local discounts must be diminished wherever possible; that dealings in internal exchange should be materially reduced; that as much money as could be spared should be used to discount paper secured by a deposit of 3 percent stock and to purchase bills of foreign exchange; and that negotiations should be begun with holders of the 3 percents. Cadwalader was doubtful as to the adequacy of this plan, and it was evident that the principal reliance must be in a negotiation with the holders of the stock, in which the bank would secure a loan by paying the interest on the stock in the place of the government, the holders accepting its responsibility and thus relieving the government from all liability. Any other form of loan at this time was hardly feasible, since no one wished to lend.

The board of directors had already authorized the president and the exchange committee to defer "a part of the payments." Proceeding in accordance with this authority, the following plan was adopted: The certificates of foreign holders of the stock were to be surrendered to the bank and by it passed over to the government as evidence of the payment of the debt. The bank itself, however, would not pay the principal, but borrow it from the original holders of the debt, continuing the loan for another year in place of the government and paying the interest during the continuance. The payment of $5 million of the stock was thus to be deferred. To this plan there could not be the least possible objection, either legal or moral, since the government would be discharged of all obligation, the bank simply procuring a new loan to the extent of the $5 million on its own responsibility. The operation would be the same as if it had paid the debt outright and then immediately borrowed it back from the original holders on its own account.

On the day that the directors authorized the postponement of the stock, Biddle opened negotiations with T. W. Ludlow, of New York, but soon perceived that there was little chance of getting the transaction settled in time to be of service. He therefore dispatched General Cadwalader to England to make arrangements with the Barings to defer the payment of $5 million of the stock. This mission succeeded. The Barings agreed to invite the foreign holders of the 3 percents to retain their stock until October 1833, while the Bank of the United States was to continue the payment of the interest quarterly and to pay the principal at the date named. Since this would probably not suffice to defer $5 million as much of the stock as possible was to be bought up by the Barings for the bank, at the best terms, not over $91 on $100. The certificates were to remain with the Barings, or with the holders of them.

It will be noticed that this arrangement differed considerably from the first plan of the bank, inasmuch as the Barings were authorized to buy stock for the bank, and also to withhold the certificates, which would leave the debt still unpaid. The bank would be culpable in both particulars for it was prohibited by its charter from purchasing any public debt, and the arrangement for deferring the delivery of the certificates was an unjustifiable interference with the government's plan to discharge the debt. Cadwalader's agreement was, therefore, both morally wrong and illegal. But this would not necessarily involve the bank, for the vital question was: Had he authority to make such an agreement? In answer to this question Cadwalader distinctly averred that he alone was responsible, his instructions not having contemplated the purchase of the stock. In support of his admission are the declarations of the directors that no such agreement was contemplated, and Biddle's disavowal of that part of it which was patently illegal on the ground that the institution was forbidden by its charter "to purchase any public debt whatsoever." Unless there was an infinite amount of shabby lying, and that, too, under oath, the corporation was not guilty. The presumption that everybody lied will hardly be considered tenable.

The disavowal of Cadwalader's contract gave rise to new complications. Biddle insisted that the certificates of the stock must be sent to the United States in order that he might turn them over to the secretary of the treasury. The Barings had already purchased $1,428,-974.54 and got $2,376,481.45 postponed. They now concluded to buy the latter also if the owners would not consent to the bank's revised terms, which were to the effect that new certificates should be given for the old ones surrendered, the bank to continue paying the interest. Many of the foreign holders agreed to these terms, and the Barings secured their certificates and forwarded them to the United States.

The affair made a great noise, and kept the bank's advocates busy explaining for many months. Biddle was particularly sensitive about the charge of violating the charter. That the bank should encourage the holders of the debt not to present the certificates for payment, he apparently considered of little importance and of no concern to anyone but the bank. Writing on the subject he revealed the depth and the keenness of his feeling:

> *With regard to the return of the certificates the Government cannot oblige any body to present his certificate—the Government stops the interest—but cannot compel a stockholder to take his principal. . . . But supposing that the certificates are delayed for a few months, what harm does that do to any body? The interest has stopped—the money remains*

in the Treasury; so that instead of depriving the Government of the use of its funds, directly the reverse is true, for the Government retains the funds and pays no interest.

But that the bank, the agent of the government, should urge the holders to delay presentation of the certificates, when its business was to procure them for the government at once, was another proposition, and one not to be justified by such arguments. Moreover, the assertions that "the money remains in the Treasury," "the Government retains the funds," were not strictly true, unless the bank and the treasury were identical, for the bank retained the funds and the government had no further use of them.

Suspicious souls will consequently continue to believe that Biddle's explanations were not veracious, but in morals as in law it is well to give the accused the benefit of the doubt. The evidence of the bank's integrity was sufficient for J. Q. Adams, Gulian C. Verplanck, Albert Gallatin, and Thomas Cooper, and may well be accepted. What is certain is that after Biddle's disavowal the bank returned to its legal position, if it had ever deliberately left it, and the postponement of the 3 percents did not take place.

The most serious charges from the point of view of proper and safe business were those which imputed usurpation of the authority and power of the board of directors, by the president and the exchange committee, and the use of such power to loan funds to favored individuals on unusual terms.

The charge of loaning large sums of money to favorites was made in the case of T. Biddle & Co. The bank replied by asserting that the firm acted as its brokers, which is undoubted, and that the loans were made to them to loan for the bank. This is likely. Professor Sumner's assertion that precisely such loans led later to the ruin of the bank is not apropos, because the later loans were made deliberately at a moment when it was intended to close up the bank's business, and were of an entirely different nature.

The president of a bank, if he is a real and active executive, a man of energy, of autocratic temper, of tact and skill, will always secure power over his board, provided that he wishes to do so. In the case of the Bank of the United States this was rendered easier by the position of the president. Under the by-laws he was *ex officio* a member of every committee. This power in committee was increased by his right under the rules of 1833 to name them all with one exception. In addition it must be recollected that his tenure of office was continuous, while that of the directors was intermittent. Again, most of the voting for directors was done by proxy, and out of 4,533 proxies in 1832, Biddle in person held 1,436, and was joint holder in the case of 1,684 others. While he thus held a controlling number of the votes of distant stockholders, those resident in Philadelphia rarely attended elections, and consequently the holders of proxies had power to elect the directors if they chose.

Nicholas Biddle was a man of intense energy, autocratic in temper, and possessing supreme confidence in his own judgment. It was inevitable that he should rule and not merely reign, and the proofs that he did rule are observable everywhere. He appointed the committees of the bank after 1828, though the rules giving him this power were not adopted until 1833; he does not want the bank's books examined by the government directors, and he gives orders that the books must not be examined by them, though only the board could rightfully do this; he desires new directors at the central board and writes, "General Cadwalader and myself have thought it was for the interest of the Bank to make the change," though it would be difficult to find in the charter any clause giving General Cadwalader and Nicholas Biddle authority to appoint new directors.

Though such power might not in itself be objectionable, it was certainly liable to abuse, and under Biddle something like abuse can be detected. The most serious charge was that R. M. Whitney, who asserted in 1832 that the president of the bank (1) made discounts on his own authority; (2) that in doing so he favored his relatives, T. Biddle & Co.; (3) that he made such loans without charging interest; (4) that a custom had obtained of permitting brokers to receive money from the teller's drawer as temporary loans, leaving stock certificates as security; (5) that these transactions were not entered on the books of the bank, and consequently never came to the knowledge of the directors. To substantiate his charges, Whitney told a very circumstantial story to the effect that the cashier and assistant cashier had reported to him specific transactions of this character in May 1824; that he with them went to the first teller's drawer and found security for two temporary loans of large sums; that they then went to the discount clerk's desk and found two notes for large sums which had been discounted by the president alone, and not entered on the books. He said that he instructed the officers "to enter on the books the money that had been loaned from the Teller's Drawer," and that this was done under the head of "bills receivable"; that he then went at once to President Biddle and "desired that nothing of a similar nature should occur while" he remained a director. The president "colored up a good deal" and said that there should not. Whitney had taken a memorandum of the sums at the time and produced it in corroboration of his assertions. He gave exact dates for the transactions.

Unfortunately for him, his evidence broke down at every one of the essential points most needing corroboration. In regard to the charge that the president made discounts on his own authority, ex-Cashier Wilson, who was said to have given the information and was summoned to support Whitney, swore positively that the notes referred to had been discounted by the board and not by the president. Both the officers who, Whitney asserted, had communicated to him the facts about the loan swore that they had no recollection of such an interview. The first teller and the discount clerk declared that they had no knowledge of the alleged visit to their desks. The officers also swore that no single director had authority to order entries made on the books, and in case such an order was given no clerk would obey it. Mr. Andrews furnished evidence in the books to show that the sum of $45,000 was actually entered on the day the loan was made, and consequently could not have been ordered entered by Whitney. In regard to the charge of favoritism to the Biddles, the evidence adduced was conclusive that the president had not been guilty. That interest had been paid on all accommodations granted to the firm was irrefutably established by the testimony, by the books of the bank, and by those of the firm of T. Biddle & Co. Finally, to Whitney's complete discomfiture, it was proved that President Biddle was in Washington when the particular loans referred to were made in Philadelphia, and so could not have made them, nor could he have been interviewed then by Whitney in regard to the loans. The entire case was so overwhelmingly against Whitney that he was compelled to admit that the two loans were not made by the president; that the interview with him so confidently alleged did not take place at the time stated; that interest had been paid on the loans; and that he was not sure that he had directed the entries to be made. The committee, though hostile to the bank, passed a majority resolution declaring that in their opinion the charges were "without foundation."

Yet before the very committee which heard these charges and admitted their disproof, it was proved beyond question that the president of the bank had on his own responsibility bought bills of exchange; that he had granted interest to T. Biddle & Co. on loans by them to the bank, without the consent of anyone and against the protests of the cashier; that on March 23, 1832, he had discounted a note for $3,500 for General Stevens, a congressman and a stranger to him, without consulting either the exchange committee or the board, and this in spite of the fact that the board met the same day. In May 1831, Biddle also granted a loan to the War Department, though he had "had no opportunity of consulting the Board of Directors on the subject."

These cases are, however, the only ones which a thorough search has revealed. Nor would it be rational to expect that many cases existed, since Biddle was so autocratic that his will would be pretty certain to obtain at the board. This was particularly likely because the directors rarely attended a session of the board in any number. On one occasion McIlvaine writes Biddle that no quorum could be secured, and on another he says, "we had the unusually large Board of eight this morning." With a directorate so little devoted to the irksome duties of their positions, it was inevitable that power should fall into the hands of a few, and it is not surprising to find an acquaintance appealing to Biddle for a loan on the ground that "you always get your way with the Board."

Even if Biddle had not controlled the board, still he might easily control the committee of exchange, which was small and appointed by himself, and over which he presided. The essential charge was that this committee supplanted the board completely. That the committee itself had no reason for existing could not be urged, since the purchase and discounting of bills of exchange might frequently need to be made between discount days, and the board met only twice a week. Horace Binney consequently upheld the exchange committee as indispensable "to the due management of the parent bank." The question still remains: Did it act as the agent or the master of the board?

The exchange department was created early in the history of the bank, and a committee to manage the department naturally followed. As exchange operations were at first very limited, the committee was of little weight; but with the stupendous growth of such dealings under Biddle's system it became very important. It was now appointed quarterly by the president, though down to 1828 it had been selected by rotation, so that all members might sit upon it. In the early days, too, the functions of the committee consisted in the management of only exchange operations, while in 1832 an officer of the bank could say that "the principal object of having the Exchange Committee" was to discount notes on days that the board of directors did not sit. At this time the committee purchased "bills both foreign and domestic, and, in the absence of the Board," discounted "domestic bills on any part of the United States." It also discounted promissory notes. In brief, it might "be said, in some measure, to represent the board . . . to act for the board" even in the ordinary business of the bank. In acting, however, it was authorized by votes of the directorate, sometimes to perform specific duties, as in the case of the 3 percents, sometimes to operate generally, as by the resolutions of the 9th of July 1830, which authorized the committee "to loan on the collateral security of approved public stock, large sums of money, at a rate of discount not lower than five percent." The government directors in 1833 objected to the making of discounts by the committee, moving to restrict it to exchange purchases; but, nevertheless, the board as a whole approved.

Such authority and such powers might not be objectionable, provided that the board kept itself informed of the transactions entered into by the committee and checked them when necessary. But the discounts were not generally "laid before the directors for their approval or rejection," but were "acted upon definitely by the committee," the directors not members of the exchange committee meanwhile knowing no "more of the nature of the operations than other persons." Such discounts were, however, entered upon the books and submitted to the board after being made, with the exception of loans on "bills receivable," which never came before it at all.

In 1831, moreover, the loans on "bills receivable," that is, loans secured by stock, began to increase notably. This was ominous, when it is recollected that Biddle early in his administration had condemned such loans as bad banking. But in all this the committee acted under the board's authority.

A committee of five, including the president and cashier—a committee "expressly invested with an authority which, from its very nature, exempted" it "from many of the ordinary rules of discounting," which discounted promissory notes four days out of every week and controlled the enormous exchange operations of the bank, was likely to absorb power, likely to abuse its authority. There can, indeed, be no doubt that this was the result. After the downfall of the bank, certain of the directors accused Biddle of having destroyed the institution, the specific charges being that a resolution of March 6, 1835, gave the complete control of the bank into the hands of the president and the exchange committee, that this committee exercised its authority to loan money on the pledge of the stock of incorporated companies, no matter what the companies were like or what their operations were, and that these loans ruined the bank. Biddle's accusers, however, omitted the extremely important qualification that such powers had been primarily granted to the committee five years earlier, and Biddle answered their charge that the committee dealt in regular discounts by proving that this had long been the custom, and had been authorized by the board, as is apparent enough from what has already been said. This, however, was only to push back the charges to a date five years earlier. The directors had no answer, because Biddle's rejoinder proved that they were equally guilty, having been members of the board at the time, and having voted for the obnoxious resolutions, besides declaring as members of examining committees that the business was sound. They had partly forestalled this answer, however, by declaring that the committee on the state of the bank never really investigated its affairs, but accepted statements made by the president, while many of the transactions were concealed under the item of "bills receivable." The conclusion is irresistible that abuses did exist, and were participated in by both accused and accusers. Biddle could not controvert the charge; the directors could not carry it to its logical conclusion because it inculpated them.

That abuses existed after 1830 must be admitted, and this is the principal point. But admitting this—admitting that the president and the exchange committee controlled the business of the bank, in regard to dealings in foreign and domestic exchange, to loans on stock, and to discounting between discount days, while the president even made discounts absolutely on his own authority—admitting all this, yet it does not follow that they were to be held responsible for the losses accruing. The board gave this authority in many cases, and, where it did not, it might have checked the practice, for the dealings of the exchange committee were placed sooner or later before the entire board, and the transactions might be known at any time. All the business of the bank was to be investigated by a committee appointed by the directors four times a year, and if this committee was efficient, all errors and all transactions should have been known to it, and through it to the board. If, therefore, bad business was done, the board, and not the president or the exchange committee, was responsible. The censure must lie here, and it must be heavy, for of all the charges examined this is the only one thoroughly substantiated, and the only one of great and perilous import.

. . . Up to the period of the Bank War, the connection between the bank and the government was an immense benefit to both, but particularly to the government. But having stated this conclusion, there is a corollary which is just as inevitable. With the growth of the Union, with the increase of national wealth and of population, the bank would have been progressively useful. From this point of view, it becomes obvious that Jackson and his supporters committed an offense against the nation when they destroyed the bank. The magnitude and enormity of that offense can only be faintly realized, but one is certainly justified in saying that few greater enormities are chargeable to politicians than the destruction of the Bank of the United States. It was the overthrow of a machine capable of incalculable service to this country—a service which can be rendered by no bank not similarly organized. Would it not be better for the nation if it could command that service today? Why should it be almost unanimously admitted that a bank of this type is of paramount importance to the finances and commerce of England, France, Germany, Austria, Russia, and yet denied that a similar bank would be of equal value to the United States? No answer to this question can be found in our political organization, none in the nature of American institutions, none in the history of our country, none in the nature of men as citizens of a republic, none in such a bank's political power; for the bank possessed no political power. In truth, there is no answer.

If, finally, it is necessary to acknowledge, in the words of Daniel Webster, that this form of a bank for the United States is an "obsolete idea," it ought, at least, to be so much the easier to understand and to admit the services which such an institution once performed at so great a profit to the people; it ought to be easy to give the due meed of praise, and no more than the due measure of blame. When this is done, it will have to be acknowledged that the old bank, in its services to the government, was far superior to any other banking system known in this country.

Bray Hammond

JACKSON, BIDDLE, AND THE BANK OF THE UNITED STATES

Bray Hammond served for some twenty years with the United States Federal Reserve Board. During that time he wrote an outstanding study entitled Banks and Politics in America from the Revolution to the Civil War. *In this major contribution to United States banking history he stressed the role of central banking, an emphasis which reflects his long association with the Federal Reserve System. In 1958, the year following the publication of this book, Hammond was awarded the Pulitzer Prize in history.*

More than forty years have passed since Catterall's monograph on the second Bank of the United States was published, and, though that account has never been superseded, it antedates all recent literature on central banking and therefore presents inadequately the public purposes of the bank. Furthermore, it includes nothing about the bank's Pennsylvania successor, which failed, and thus omits the denouement of Biddle's conflict with Jackson. The inevitable effect of

From the *Journal of Economic History* 7 (May 1947): 1–23, by permission of the New York University Press.

the failure, in the rough justice of history, was to make Jackson seem right and Biddle wrong; and this impression, especially in the absence of attention to the purpose and functions of the bank, seems in recent years to have been strengthened. I think it needs correction.

The Bank of the United States—the B.U.S. as Biddle and others often called it—was a national institution of complex beginnings, for its establishment in 1816 derived from the extreme fiscal needs of the federal government, the disorder of an unregulated currency, and the promotional ambitions of businessmen.[1] The bank had an immense amount of private business—as all central banks then had and as many still have—yet it was even more definitely a government bank than was the Bank of England, the Bank of France, or any other similar institution at the time. The federal government owned one fifth of its capital and was its largest single stockholder, whereas the capital of other central banks was wholly private. Government ownership of central-bank stock has become common only in very recent years.[2] Five of the bank's twenty-five directors, under the terms of its charter, were appointed by the President of the United States, and no one of these five might be a director of any other bank. Two of its three successive presidents—William Jones and Nicholas Biddle—were chosen from among these government directors. The charter made the bank depository of the government and accountable to Congress and the Secretary of the Treasury.

On this depository relation hinged control over the extension of credit by banks in general, which is the essential function of a central bank. The government's receipts arose principally from taxes paid by importers to customs collectors;[3] these tax payments were in bank notes, the use of checks not then being the rule; the bank notes were

[1] On the organization of the bank, besides R. C. H. Catterall, *Second Bank of the U. S.* (Chicago: The University of Chicago Press, 1903), see Raymond Walters, Jr., "Origin of the Second Bank of the U. S.," *The Journal of Political Economy* 53 (1945): 115.
[2] The Bank of England and the Bank of France came under government ownership in 1945. The modern term "central bank" was not used till nearly a century after Biddle's death. Hamilton used the term "public bank," and the nineteenth-century equivalent was "bank of issue."
[3] E. R. Taus, *Central Banking Functions of the U. S. Treasury, 1789–1941* (New York: Columbia University Press, 1943), Appendixes III and IV; Davis R. Dewey, *Financial History of the U. S.* (New York: Longmans, Green and Company, 1931), p. 168; John Spencer Bassett, *The Life of Andrew Jackson* (New York: The Macmillan Company, 1931), p. 586.

mostly those of private banks, which were numerous and provided the bulk of the money in circulation; the B.U.S. received these notes on deposit from the customs collectors and, becoming thereby creditor of the private banks that issued them, presented them to the latter for payment. Banks that extended credit properly and maintained adequate gold and silver reserves were able to pay their obligations promptly on demand. Those that overextended themselves were not. The pressure of the central bank upon the private banks was constant, and its effect was to restrict their lending and their issue of notes. In this fashion, it curbed the tendency of the banks to lend too much and so depreciate their circulation.[4] Its regulatory powers were dependent on the private banks' falling currently into debt to it. The regulatory powers now in effect under the Federal Reserve Act depend upon the opposite relation—that is, upon the private banks' maintaining balances with the Federal Reserve Banks. The private banks were then debtors to the central bank; they are now creditors. The regulatory powers of the United States Bank were simpler, more direct, and perhaps more effective than those of the Federal Reserve Banks, though they would not be so under present-day conditions.

It was notorious that large and influential numbers of the private banks and official state banks resented this regulation of their lending power. All but the more conservative found it intolerable to be let and hindered by the dunning of the B.U.S. and forced to reduce their debts instead of enlarging their loans. Many of them had the effrontery to insist as a matter of right that they be allowed to pay the central bank if and when they pleased.[5] The effort of various states, especially Maryland and Ohio, to levy prohibitory taxes on the United States Bank's branches reflects this desire of the private banks to escape regulation quite as much as it reflects the states' jealousy of their "invaded" sovereignty; the efforts were economic as well as political.[6]

---

[4] I use the term "private banks" in preference to the common term "state banks" because it brings out the essential differences between the central bank and the units of the banking system regulated by it. I therefore include as private those "state banks" proper owned in whole or part by state governments; for functionally these "state banks" proper differed little if any from the private banks.

[5] R. C. H. Catterall, *Second Bank, p. 85.*

[6] *McCulloch* v. *Maryland* (1819), 4 Wheaton, p. 315; *Osborn* v. *Bank of the United States* (1824), 9 Wheaton, p. 737. The arguments in these cases were constitutional, not economic.

In 1831, Gallatin commended the bank for its conduct during the twenties; it had "effectually checked excessive issues" by the state banks; "that very purpose" for which it had been established had been fulfilled. On the regulatory operation of the bank, "which requires particular attention and vigilance and must be carried on with great firmness and due forbearance, depends almost exclusively the stability of the currency. . . ." The country's "reliance for a sound currency and, therefore, for a just performance of contracts rests on that institution."[7] In 1833 he wrote to Horsley Palmer, of the Bank of England, that "the Bank of the United States must not be considered as affording a complete remedy," for the ills of overexpansion, "but as the best and most practicable which can be applied"; and its action "had been irreproachable" in maintaining a proper reserve position "as late as November 1830."[8] Though Gallatin did not say so, this was in effect praise of Nicholas Biddle's administration of the bank.

The powerful expansion of the economy in the nineteenth century made it necessary for the regulatory action of the bank to be mostly one of restraint, but there was occasion also for it to afford ease as holder of the ultimate reserves and lender of last resort. One of the first things it did was to end the general suspension that the country had been enduring for more than two years; and a crucial factor in the willingness and ability of the private banks to resume payment of their obligations was the pledge of the United States Bank that it would support them.[9] This Vera Smith writes, was "a very early declaration of the view that it is the duty of the central bank to act as lender of last resort."[10]

The regulatory functions of the bank were not always well performed. Its first president, William Jones, was a politician who extended credit recklessly, rendered the bank impotent to keep the private banks in line, and nearly bankrupted it—all in a matter of three years. Langdon Cheves put the bank back in a sound condition by stern procedures that were unavoidably unpopular. When Nicholas

---

[7] Albert Gallatin, *Writings,* ed. Henry Adams (Philadelphia: J. B. Lippincott and Company, 1879), III: 334, 336, 390;6 II: 426.

[8] Ibid., II: 461. See also *Niles' Weekly Register* 35 (1828–1829): 37.

[9] R. C. H. Catterall, *Second Bank,* pp. 24–26; American State Papers, *Finance* (Washington: Gales and Seaton, 1858), IV: 768–769.

[10] Vera C. Smith, *Rationale of Central Banking* (London: P. S. King and Son, 1936), p. 40.

Biddle succeeded Cheves in 1823, the bank was strong in every respect but good will. Biddle repressed the desires of the stockholders for larger dividends, keeping the rate down and accumulating reserves. The art of central banking was not so clearly recognized then as it has since become, but Biddle advanced it, and with better luck he might well be memorable for having developed means of mitigating the tendency to disastrous, periodic crises characteristic of the nineteenth century in the United States.[11]

But Biddle, with all his superior talents, was not very discreet. He had an airy way of speaking that shocked his more credulous enemies and did him irreparable harm; and, when he described the functions of the bank, he contrived to give a livelier impression of its power than of its usefulness. Once when asked by a Senate committee if the B.U.S. ever oppressed the state banks, he said, "never": although nearly all of them might have been destroyed, many had been saved and still more had been relieved. This was ineffable in a man of Biddle's exceptional abilities. It put a normal situation in a sinister and uncouth light. A wanton abuse of regulatory powers is always possible, and abstention from it is not to be boasted of—any more than a decent man would boast of not choosing to be a burglar. By talking so, Biddle made his opponents feel sure he had let the cat out of the bag. For Thomas Hart Benton he had proved entirely too much—that he had a dangerous power "over the business and fortunes of nearly all the people."[12] Jackson referred in his veto to Biddle's remark, and Roger Taney was still shuddering at the disclosure many years later. He believed then and he believed still, he wrote, that there was a scheme to close every state bank in the Union. He believed "that the matter had been thought of, and that the manner in which it could be done was well understood."[13] That people believed such things, Biddle had his own jauntiness, naïveté, and political ineptitude to thank.

[11] Statements on Biddle's central-bank policy will be found in Reginald C. McGrane, *Correspondence of Nicholas Biddle* (Boston: Houghton Mifflin Company, 1919), pp. 34–36, 51, 56–58. Catterall discusses the subject admirably in his chapter v, with the limitation that central banking was no better understood in his day than in Biddle's—if as well. See also J. S. Bassett, *Andrew Jackson*, pp. 585–586.
[12] T. H. Benton, *Thirty Years' View* (New York: D. Appleton and Company, 1897), I: 159.
[13] C. B. Swisher, *Life of Taney* (New York: The Macmillan Company, 1935), pp. 166–169.

When Jackson became President in 1829, the B.U.S. had survived what then seemed its most crucial difficulties. The Supreme Court had affirmed and reaffirmed its constitutionality and ended the attempts of unfriendly states to interfere with it. The Treasury had long recognized its efficient services as official depository. The currency was in excellent condition. Yet in his first annual message, Jackson told Congress that "both the constitutionality and the expediency of the law creating the bank were well questioned by a large portion of our fellow-citizens, and it must be admitted by all that it has failed in the great end of establishing a uniform and sound currency."

There is nothing remarkable about Jackson's doubts of the bank's constitutionality, for he did not defer his own judgment to John Marshall's nor, in general, had the Supreme Court's opinions attained their later prestige.[14] His statement that the bank had failed in establishing a good currency is more difficult to understand, for it was plainly untrue in the usual sense of the words. But he was evidently using the words in the special sense of locofoco hard-money doctrine, according to which the only good money was gold and silver; the Constitution authorized Congress to coin it and regulate its value; the states were forbidden to issue paper and the federal government was not empowered to do so. Jackson, wrote C. J. Ingersoll, "considers all the state banks unconstitutional and impolitic and thinks that there should be no currency but coin. . . ."[15] There were practical considerations no less important than the legal. It was evident to the anti-bank people that banking was a means by which a relatively small number of persons enjoyed the privilege of creating money to be lent, for the money obtained by borrowers at banks was in the form of the banks' own notes. The fruits of the abuse were obvious: notes were over-issued, their redemption was evaded, they lost their value, and the innocent husbandman and mechanic who were paid in them were cheated and pauperized. "It is absurd," wrote Taney, "to

---

[14] Even Gallatin in 1831 took pains to defend the bank's constitutionality without a reference to the court's decisions, of which he remarked in a footnote he had not known. Gallatin, *Writings*, III: 327. He was in Europe when *McCulloch* v. *Maryland* was decided, but not *Osborn* v. *Bank of the United States*. It is notable that he would discuss constitutionality without learning till he was through that the Supreme Court had said something on the subject.
[15] R. C. McGrane, *Correspondence of Biddle*, 172. For Benton's ideas, see his *Thirty Years' View*, I: 436.

talk about a sound and stable paper currency."[16] There was no such thing. So, in Jackson's opinion, if the United States Bank was not establishing a metallic currency, it was not establishing a constitutional or sound and uniform one. His words might seem wild to the contaminated, like Gallatin and Biddle, but they were plain gospel truth to his sturdy antibank, hard-money agrarians.[17]

Hard money was a cardinal tenet of the left wing of the Democratic party. It belonged with an idealism in which America was still a land of refuge and freedom rather than a place to make money. Its aim was to clip the wings of commerce and finance by restricting the credit that paper money enabled them to obtain. There would then be no vast debt, no inflation, no demoralizing price changes; there would be no fluctuant or disappearing values, no swollen fortunes, and no grinding poverty. The precious metals would impose an automatic and uncompromising limit on the volatile tendencies of trade. "When there was a gold and silver circulation," said an agrarian in the Iowa constitutional convention of 1844, "there were no fluctuations; everything moved on smoothly and harmoniously."[18] The Jacksonians were even more devoted to the discipline of gold than the monetary conservatives of the present century.

There was also a pro-bank, "paper-money wing," which harbored the Democratic party's less spiritual virtues.[19] Its strength lay with free enterprise, that is, with the new generation of businessmen, promoters, and speculators, who found the old Hamiltonian order of the Federalists too stodgy and confining. These were "Democrats by trade," as distinguished from "Democrats in principle"; one of the latter wrote sarcastically in the *Democratic Review* in 1838, "Being a good Democrat, that is to say, a Democrat *by trade* (Heaven forfend that any son of mine should be a Democrat *in principle*)—being a good Democrat by trade, he got a snug slice of the public depo-

[16] J. S. Bassett, *Correspondence of Andrew Jackson* V (Washington, D.C.: Carnegie Institution, 1931): 491; Benton, *Thirty Years' View,* I: 436.
[17] The principal argument against the bank's constitutionality was not this, of course, but that Congress had no power to charter a bank outside the District of Columbia.
[18] Benjamin F. Shambaugh, *Fragments of the Debates of the Iowa Constitutional Conventions of 1844 and 1846* (Iowa City: State Historical Society of Iowa, 1900), pp. 69, 70, 71.
[19] Col. Benton on Banks and Currency, *Hunt's Merchants' Magazine* 38 (January 1858): 560–561.

sites."[20] Fifty years before, business had fostered the erection of a strong federal government and inclined toward monopoly; in the early nineteenth century it began to appreciate the advantages offered by laissez faire and to feel that it had more to gain and less to fear from the states than from the federal government. This led it to take on the coloration and vocabulary of Jacksonian democracy and to exalt the rugged individualism of the entrepreneur and speculator along with that of the pioneer.

The private banks and their friends had helped to kill the first Bank of the United States twenty years before, but the strength they could muster against the second was much greater. Herein lies the principal difference between the situation of the old bank when Jefferson became President in 1801 and the situation of the second when Jackson became President in 1829. Both men disapproved of the national bank and yet were inhibited by its being accepted in their own party and performing well its evidently important functions. There were also the differences that Jefferson was more amenable to reason than Jackson, that he had in Gallatin a better adviser than any Jackson had, and that the bank was under a more passive management in his day than in Jackson's. But of most importance was the greater pressure the private banks were able to exert in Jackson's time than in Jefferson's. Between 1801 and 1829 their number had greatly increased, as had the volume of their business and the demand for credit. The records indicate that in 1801 there were 31 banks, in 1829 there were 329, and in 1837 there were 788—an increase of 140 percent during Jackson's administration alone.[21] These banks were associated to a marked extent with the Democratic party, especially in New York. Their opposition to federal regulation was therefore far greater in 1829 than in 1801, and it did more for Jackson's victory over the national bank than did the zeal of his hard-money locofocos. De Tocqueville wrote that "the slightest observation" enabled one to see the advantages of the B.U.S. to the country and mentioned as most striking the uniform value of the currency it

[20] *The United States Magazine and Democratic Review* 3 (December 1838): 368. Alexander Hamilton's son, James A. Hamilton, a friend of Jackson and a speculator in New York real estate, seems to have been a Democrat by trade.
[21] United States Comptroller of the Currency, *Annual Report,* 1916, pp. 913–914.

furnished. But the private banks, he said, submitted with impatience to "this salutary control" exercised by the B.U.S. They bought over newspapers. "They roused the local passions and the blind democratic instinct of the country to aid their cause. . . ."[22] Without them, it is doubtful if the Jacksonians could have destroyed the B.U.S.

The Jacksonian effort to realize the hard-money ideals was admirable, viewed as Quixotism. For however much good one may find in these ideals, nothing could have been more unsuited than they were to the American setting. In an austere land or among a contemplative and self-denying people they might have survived but not in one so amply endowed as the United States and so much dominated by an energetic and acquisitive European stock. Nowhere on earth was the spirit of enterprise to be more fierce, the urge for exploitation more restless, or the demand for credit more importunate. The rise of these reprobated forces spurred the agrarians, and as business itself grew they came to seek nothing less than complete prohibition of banking.[23] Yet they chose to destroy first the institution which was curbing the ills they disapproved, and to that end they leagued with the perpetrators of those ills.[24] Jackson made himself, as de Tocqueville observed, the instrument of the private banks.[25] He took the government's funds out of the central bank, where they were less liable to speculative use and put them in the private banks, where they were fuel to the fire.[26] He pressed the retirement of the public debt, and he acquiesced in distribution of the federal surplus.[27] These things fomented the very evils he deplored and made the

[22] Alexis de Tocqueville, *Democracy in America,* ed. Phillips Bradley (New York: Albert A. Knopf and Company, 1945), I: 409.

[23] In a number of western states and territories they achieved prohibition: in Arkansas, Illinois, Iowa, Wisconsin, California, and Oregon—though in the last two the impetus was more than agrarian.

[24] T. H. Benton, *Thirty Years' View,* I: 158.

[25] Alexis de Tocqueville, *Democracy in America,* I: 409.

[26] Taney made himself ridiculous: he told the pet banks the government funds would enable them to lend more, he gave them checks on the B.U.S. to protect them from the monster, and then he helplessly asked them not to use the checks.—R. C. H. Catterall, *Second Bank,* pp. 302–305. United States Secretary of the Treasury, *Annual Reports* 3 (1833): 369; 23d Congress, 1st Session, *Senate Document No. 16,* 321 ff.

[27] Retirement of the public debt was inflationary in that it spread a feeling of elate satisfaction and closed a field for conservative investment. Gallatin had thought the retirement would be a good thing but later found to his dismay that it was "a signal for an astonishing increase in the indebtedness of the community at large."—Henry Adams, *Life of Albert Gallatin* (Philadelphia: J. B. Lippincott and Company, 1879), p. 656.

Jacksonian inflation one of the worst in American history. They quite outweighed the Maysville veto, which checked federal expenditures on internal improvements, and the specie circular, which crudely and belatedly paralyzed bank credit.

As a result, Jackson's presidency escaped by only two months from ending like Hoover's in 1933. Far from reaching the happy point where the private banks could be extirpated and the hands of the exploiters and speculators could be tied, Jackson succeeded only in leaving the house swept and garnished for them; and the last state of the economy was worse than the first. He professed to be the deliverer of his people from the oppressions of the mammoth—but instead he delivered the private banks from federal control and his people to speculation. No more striking example could be found of a leader fostering the very evil he was angrily wishing out of the way.[28]

But this was the inevitable result of the agrarian effort to ride two horses bound in opposite directions: one being monetary policy and the other states' rights. Monetary policy must be national, as the Constitution doubly provides. The agrarians wanted the policy to be national, but they eschewed the practicable way of making it that, and, instead of strengthening the national authority over the monetary system, they destroyed it. Where they were unencumbered by this fatal aversion to centralized power, they accomplished considerable. In Indiana they set up an official State Bank, with branches, which from 1834 to 1853 was the only source of bank credit permitted and yet was ample for all but the most aggressive money-makers, who finally ended its monopoly. In Missouri, they established the Bank of Missouri, with branches, a state monopoly which lasted from 1837 to 1857, when it too succumbed to free enterprise. And in Iowa, another monopoly, the Bank of Iowa, with branches, was in operation from 1858 till 1865, when free banking penetrated the state under authority of the National Bank Act. These instances indicate that if the hard-money agrarians had had a conception of national government less

---

[28] See a contemporary English observer, "Causes and Consequences of the Crisis in the American Trade," *Edinburgh Review* 65 (July 1837): 227–228. The impetus given new banks by the prospect of closing the B.U.S. was observed everywhere. Benton exclaimed that he had not joined in putting it down in order "to put up a wilderness of local banks."—24th Congress, 2d Session, January 1837, *Register of Debates,* p. 610. See also Jabez Hammond, *History of Political Parties in New York* (Cooperstown: H. and E. Phinney, 1846), II: 434, 489.

incompatible with their social purposes, they might have tempered rather than worsened the rampant excesses of nineteenth-century expansion that so offended them.[29]

But as it was, they helped an acquisitive democracy take over the conservative system of bank credit introduced by Hamilton and by the merchants of Philadelphia and New York and limber it up to suit the popular wish to get rich quick. Wringing their hands, they let bank credit become the convenient key to wealth—the means of making capital accessible in abundance to millions of go-getting Americans who otherwise could not have exploited their natural resources with such whirlwind energy. The excesses of that energy have forced the Jacksonian hard-money heroics to be slowly undone: the federal government's authority over money, the Treasury's close operating contact with the banking system, and the central-bank controls over credit have been haltingly restored. Credit itself, in the surviving American tradition, is not the virus the agrarians held it to be but the lifeblood of business and agriculture, and the Jacksonian hard-money philosophy has been completely forgotten, especially by Jackson's own political posterity.

Jackson had not committed himself against the bank during the early part of his first term but worried both those who wanted him to support recharter and those who wanted him to prevent it. In November 1829 he was friendly to Biddle and assured him that he had no more against the B.U.S. than against "all banks." The next month he slurred the bank in his message to Congress. In 1831 when the cabinet was changed, two important portfolios went to friends of Biddle: Livingston became Secretary of State and McLane Secretary of the Treasury. Both wanted the bank continued and hoped to influence Jackson. Biddle deferred to their hopes, but the tension was evidently too severe for him. The bank's enemies were growing more provocative, and in the summer of 1831 his brother, a director of the bank's St. Louis branch, was killed in a duel, more than usually shocking, which arose from the controversy over recharter.[30] What-

[29] See Hugh McCulloch, *Men and Measures of Half a Century* (New York: Charles Scribner's Sons, 1889); John Ray Cable, *The Bank of the State of Missouri* (New York: Columbia University Press, 1923); Howard H. Preston, *History of Banking in Iowa* (Iowa City: State Historical Society of Iowa, 1922).
[30] *St. Louis Beacon*, September 1, 1831, September 22, 1831; *Niles' Weekly Register*,

ever the reasons, he let impatience get the upper hand and decided that the bank, without further temporizing, should ask Congress that the charter be renewed.[31]

Jackson was offended by this direct action, and notwithstanding improvements in the new charter and concessions to his views, he vetoed the bill of renewal. The economic reasoning of the veto message was, in Catterall's language, "beneath contempt," and the most appealing allegations in it were "demonstrably and grossly false."[32] Biddle was deluded enough to have 30,000 copies printed and distributed in the bank's own interest. One may regard this as evidence of contempt for Jackson or of a faith in the democracy as sincere as Jackson's own; but it is also evidence of the limitations on Biddle's political sense. In the election that fall the bank was the leading issue, and hopes for recharter went to nothing with Jackson's overwhelming majority. Jackson's purpose now was to stop using the bank as government depository. How firmly accepted it was in Washington as the peculiar agency of the government is indicated by the resistance he encountered. He had to get rid of two Treasury heads successively before he found a third who would execute his wishes, the law giving only the Secretary of the Treasury the power to remove the government's deposits from the bank; and he had also to disregard a House resolution declaring that the government deposits were safe as they were.

With loss of the deposits, the bank lost the means of regulating the private banks' extension of credit. Biddle had made enough mistakes already, but he now made the fatal one of failing to resign and let the bank be liquidated; there is a limit beyond which the head of a central bank cannot decently go against the head of the government, even when he is right and the head of the government is wrong. Moreover, although a central bank is a very useful institution, it never possesses the kind of virtues that count in conflict against an intensely popular leader. By resigning, Biddle would have stultified Jackson and justified himself, as it turned out; for when the panic came in 1837, Jackson would have got the blame, with considerable justice. Furthermore,

September 17, 1831, p. 37. The duel was fought with pistols at five feet, Major Biddle being nearsighted, and each man killed the other.
[31] R. C. H. Catterall, *Second Bank,* pp. 214 ff.
[32] Ibid., p. 239.

Biddle would have spared himself a tragic end. The bank was in a better condition than it came to be later, and conditions were much more favorable for liquidation, in spite of the recession of 1833–1834. Incidentally, this recession was produced, it was averred, by a vindictive curtailment of the bank's loans. There certainly was resentment mixed into the bank's policy, but on the other hand, the bank could not go out of existence, as its enemies desired, without curtailing its credit, and curtailment is always unpopular, scarcely less in a period of general expansion than in one of depression.

Instead of going out of existence the bank became a private corporation under Pennsylvania charter in February 1836, a fortnight before its federal charter expired.[33] A little more than a year later the panic of 1837 broke. It began May 10 and involved all the banks in the country, about 800 in number, with an aggregate circulation of $150 million and deposits of $125 million. It precipitated three distinct monetary programs—one of hard money by the anti-bank administration in Washington, one of easy money by Biddle in Philadelphia, and one of convertibility by the banks of Wall Street under the sage but incongruous leadership of the venerable Jeffersonian, Albert Gallatin.

The administration, with Van Buren now President, took the opportunity to urge an independent Treasury system, with complete "divorce of bank and state." Its course was that urged by Jackson, who wrote, July 9, 1837:

> *Now is the time to separate the Government from all banks, receive and disburse the revenue in nothing but gold and silver coin, and the circulation of our coin through all public disbursements will regulate the currency forever hereafter. Keep the Government free from all embarrassments, whilst it leaves the commercial community to trade upon its own capital, and the banks to accommodate it with such exchange and credit as best suits their own interests—both being money making concerns, devoid of patriotism, looking alone to their own interests—regardless of all others. It has been, and ever will be a curse to the Government to have any en-*

---

[33] The authorized capital of the bank under Pennsylvania charter was $35 million, as it had been under national charter. It appears, however, that the shares ($7 million par) held by the government under the national charter were not reissued to new owners and that the actual paid-in capital of the Pennsylvania corporation was only $28 million.—John J. Knox, *History of Banking* (New York: Bradford, Rhodes, and Company, 1903), pp. 78–79.

> *tanglement or interest with either, more than a general superintending care of all.*[34]

Wall Street paid little attention to this program but set about preparations to resume specie payments as soon as possible, getting its own house in order and urging the banks elsewhere to send delegates to a convention "for the purpose," in Gallatin's words, "of agreeing on a uniform course of measures and on the time when the resumption should take place."[35]

Nicholas Biddle took a course opposed to that of both Wall Street and the administration. He demanded that the Treasury scheme be abandoned and the specie circular repealed. He contended that Jackson's policies were responsible for the financial distress and that the basic condition of recovery was their repudiation by Congress. Till these things were done, the banks should not resume redemption of their notes. Wall Street's program he denounced as premature and sacrificial. He advocated instead an active and flexible policy that should be remedial for the prostrate economy—that should check the credit contraction and the fall of prices. His own objects during the past eighteen months, he wrote James Gordon Bennett, October 1838, had been "to sustain the national character abroad by paying our debts and at the same time to protect the securities and the staples of the country from the ruinous depreciation to which they were inevitably sinking."[36] It was evident to him, he wrote John Quincy Adams in December, "that if resort was had to rigid curtailments, the ability to pay would be proportionally diminished; . . . the only true system was to keep the country as much at ease as consisted with its safety, so as to enable the debtors to collect their resources for the discharge of their debts."[37] Lenity for the banks would mean lenity for their debtors, foreclosures and bankruptcies would be avoided, and values protected from collapse. Suspension, he had already said, was "wholly conventional between the banks and the community" and

[34] J. S. Bassett, *Correspondence of Jackson*, V: 495, 498, 500, 504 ff.; Condy Raguet, *Financial Register*, II (Philadelphia: Adam Waldie, 1838): 58.
[35] Albert Gallatin, *Writings*, III: 398.
[36] Presidents' Letter Book, No. 1, 542, Biddle MSS, Library of Congress.
[37] 29th Congress, 1st Session, *House Document No. 226*, p. 405.

arose from "their mutual conviction that it is for their mutual benefit."[38]

The situation was one in which the more conservative settled back
to let deflation, as it came to be called a century later, run its bitter
course; and the hard-money agrarians sardonically joined them in
hoping for the worst. But both the agrarians and Wall Street testified
to the popularity of Biddle's ideas. Governor Ford of Illinois observed,
with the sarcasm of a hard-money Democrat, that although the banks
owed more than they could pay and although the people owed each
other and the banks more than they could pay, "yet if the whole
people could be persuaded to believe the incredible falsehood that
all were able to pay, this was 'confidence.' "[39] In Wall Street it was
said that suspension made lawbreakers of every one. "Instead of the
permanent and uniform standard of value provided by the Constitution, and by which all contracts were intended to be regulated, we
have at once fifty different and fluctuating standards, agreeing only in
one respect, that of impairing the sanctity of contracts."[40] The be-
lievers in Biddle were themselves eloquent in the new faith. Following
the later debacle of the B.U.S., the Philadelphia *Gazette* said:

> *The immediate effect of the suspension will be an ease in the money
> market, a cessation of those cares and disquietudes with which the busi-
> ness men of our community have been annoyed. . . . The great error . . .
> to which all subsequent errors are in a measure to be traced was in the
> premature resumption in August 1838. . . . The banks are just as good,
> and better and more solid, under a season of suspension as under its
> opposite.*[41]

Meanwhile, the New York banks had succeeded in resuming payment of their obligations, May 10, 1838, the anniversary of the suspension. This was a real hard-money achievement, due largely to
Gallatin and the Bank of England, in which the professedly hard-
money administration had little if any part. Instead it had to violate
with its eyes open the professions that Jackson had violated without

---

[38] Condy Raguet, *Financial Register,* I: 342–346.
[39] Thomas Ford, *History of Illinois* (Chicago: S. C. Griggs and Company; New York:
Ivison and Phinney, 1854), p. 227.
[40] Report of delegates to the Bank Convention, New York, November 1837; Condy
Raguet, *Financial Register,* I: 229.
[41] *Philadelphia Gazette,* October 10, 1839.

knowing what he was doing. While still trying to distribute a federal "surplus" which had turned into a deficit, it had to resort to issues of Treasury notes, which its hard-money zealots believed unconstitutional. It had to go still further and tolerate what Biddle had demanded: the specie circular was repealed in May 1838, the subtreasury bill was defeated in June, and in July the Treasury had to accept—to its substantial relief—a credit of four to five million dollars on the books of the Bank of the United States in anticipated payment of amounts due the government in liquidation of its shares.[42] This last transaction made the bank a depository of the government some five years after Jackson had ordered that its predecessor, a better institution, cease to be used as depository.

By the fall of 1838, banks everywhere were back on a specie basis, and, although this was mainly due to the efforts of Wall Street and Albert Gallatin, it was Biddle who had the prestige. He was riding on the crest. "All that it was designed to do has been done," he wrote John Quincy Adams in December 1838; and he was about to retire.[43] Two months later, February 1839, he was Van Buren's guest of honor at the White House. "This dinner went off very well," according to James A. Hamilton, "Biddle evidently feeling as the conqueror. He was facetious and in intimate converse with the President."[44] A month later Biddle retired from the bank, its affairs being, he said, in a state of great prosperity and in able hands.[45] The same day the directors were unanimous in describing him as one who had "performed so much and so faithfully" and was leaving the bank prosperous in all its relations . . . and secure in the respect and esteem of all who are connected with it in foreign or domestic intercourse."[46]

---

[42] These represented payment of $7.9 million to the government for its stock in the bank. This sum included a premium of about $1 million, besides which the government had received dividends of over $7 million during the twenty years of the bank's existence. The net gain to the government from its original investment of $7 million, which it paid for in bonds, is estimated by Knox at $6 million and by Catterall at $8 million.—John J. Knox, *History of Banking*, p. 79; R. C. H. Catterall, *Second Bank*, p. 474. In the settlement for the government stock, agreed upon in 1837 (Catterall, *Second Bank*, pp. 373–375), the administration had held out for a premium in a way which indicated it had no doubt of the bank's solvency.

[43] 29th Congress, 1st Session, *House Document No. 226*, p. 408.

[44] R. C. McGrane, *Correspondence of Biddle*, p. 337; *Reminiscences of James A. Hamilton* (New York: Charles Scribner's Sons, 1869), p. 312.

[45] *Niles' Weekly Register* 54 (April 6, 1839): 84.

[46] 29th Congress, 1st Session, *House Document No. 226*, p. 486.

Six months later, in the fall of 1839, the bank suspended payment of its obligations. It resumed and then suspended again. In 1841, after two years of dismayed inquiry and recrimination, it was assigned to trustees for liquidation.

The stockholders were stunned, and then they turned on Biddle. In the summer of 1840 he was told that he owed the bank an "over-advance" of about $320,000 on an old account. This he denied. Nevertheless, "though he did not recognize the claim" and although "neither law or equity made it necessary to pay," he did so—mostly in Texas bonds which were accepted at more than market value. The stockholders next turned to litigation and thereafter seem to have kept Biddle continuously in the courts. In January 1842, he and former associates in the bank were arrested on charges of criminal conspiracy and put on $10,000 bail each. The charge was that they had conspired "to cheat and defraud the bank by obtaining therefrom large advances upon shipments of cotton to Europe," and "by the unlawful receipt and expenditure of large sums of money, the application of which is not specified upon the books."[47] The court of General Sessions was occupied two weeks with habeas corpus hearings, twenty witnesses being examined and "all the books and papers of the bank brought into court, where they underwent a most searching investigation." Biddle's attorney let his case stand on the evidence of the prosecutors. "As soon as the testimony for the prosecution was finished, the counsel for Mr. Biddle offered to leave the matter to the court without argument."[48] The court found evidence lacking that the acts charged involved fraud; for they were known to the directors and approved by them. Of any fraudulent coalition it found nothing to justify even a reasonable suspicion.[49] Two judges concurred in this decision; one dissented.

A few weeks later another suit was instituted. The stockholders filed a bill of equity in which they asked that Biddle and one of his former associates be required to account for $400,000 of the bank's

---

[47] 29th Congress, 1st Session, *House Document No. 226,* 419 ff., 475 ff.; also opinion of Judge Barton, *Philadelphia Inquirer,* May 10, 1842.

[48] *Philadelphia Public Ledger,* April 11, 1842.

[49] *Philadelphia Public Ledger,* April 30, 1842. The court had much to say of "the singularly loose method" by which the directors had conducted the business of the corporation.

funds. The bill was dismissed December 1844, the court holding that information which might incriminate the defendants could not be required of them.[50] But Biddle was no longer living. He had died ten months before, February 27, 1844, aged fifty-eight.

The failure of the B.U.S. leaves two questions one would like to have answered: What was the actual condition of the bank? How responsible was Biddle for it? The Jacksonians had easy answers, of course, and jeered triumphantly; matters had proved to be even worse than they had said, Biddle had known the bank was rotten, and having enriched himself he had striven to leap clear in time but had been caught. The Democratic press was hot with invective and ribald ridicule of the great Regulator, the old Nick, the prestidigitatorial wizard who had crowned a career of astounding performances by consummately destroying everything he had done, and himself with it.[51]

To say with Biddle's political enemies that the bank was "rotten" is putting it both vigorously and vaguely. No one can be precise in such a matter, for in a long and complicated liquidation involving suits and technical decisions respecting the admissibility of claims, the completeness of the settlement must be subject to interpretation. But, according to a trustee quoted by Knox, the creditors were paid in full, principal and interest, though the bank's capital was entirely absorbed, and the stockholders got nothing.[52] This would mean a shrinkage of about one fourth of the value of the bank's assets, roughly speaking. The 7,000 bank failures in the United States in the ten years, 1921–1930, entailed estimated losses of about one third of the total deposit liabilities.[53] The comparison is crude, but I think it warrants the opinion that the condition of the B.U.S. was rotten only in a hyperbolical sense. Moreover, it is to be borne in mind that values usually diminish in liquidation, that the portfolio to be liquidated was the country's largest, and that the process, which ran to 1856, had to be undertaken in a period when buyers were not eager

[50] *Bank of the United States* v. *Biddle,* Parsons' Select Cases in Equity (Philadelphia, 1888), II: 33 ff.
[51] *Democratic Review* 3 (December 1838): 372–373.
[52] John J. Knox, *History of Banking,* p. 79.
[53] Federal Deposit Insurance Corporation, *Annual Report* (Washington, 1940), p. 66.

nor prices buoyant. The stockholders in 1841 insisted to the legislature that the bank could pay its creditors and requested lenity so that losses might be minimized.[54] These things make me think that the bank in 1839 may have been in a situation little if any worse than that which Jones had got its predecessor into twenty years before and from which Cheves rescued it.

As for the second question—Biddle's responsibility—it seems to me clear that policies put into effect by him led to the bank's failure but that he had no realization or suspicion of what was developing. The policies included prodigal loans on stocks, especially to officers and directors of the bank, heavy investments in corporate stocks and speculative bonds, and purchases of cotton and other agricultural commodities for export. The cotton transactions were undertaken in the emergency of 1837 as a means of sustaining domestic commodity prices and providing European exchange. They succeeded initially, but once begun they were hard to stop, and they produced loss, litigation, and recrimination that was probably more damaging to Biddle himself than to the bank. The loan and investment policy was begun as early as 1835 when it looked as if the bank would have to liquidate: the active assets were converted into loans on stocks in preparation for a long period of liquidation. But when the Pennsylvania charter was obtained, the policy was not abandoned. Instead it was adapted to the vaster prospects of manifest destiny and empire building. Loans were made with a lax grandiosity. "It seems to have been sufficient," according to a stockholders' committee report later, "to obtain money on loan, to pledge the stock of 'an incorporated company,' however remote its operations or uncertain its prospects." Partly from choice and partly from the extortionate requirements of its charter—which Biddle should never have accepted—the bank also became the owner of such stocks outright; in 1840 it had shares in more than twenty other banks, some of which it wholly controlled, and great holdings in railways, toll bridges, turnpikes, and canals, besides speculative bonds issued to finance "public improvements."[55]

---

[54] 29th Congress, 1st Session, *House Document No. 226,* p. 533.

[55] Laws of Pennsylvania 1835–1836, p. 43; 29th Congress, 1st Session, *House Document No. 226,* p. 532. See report of the stockholders' committee, April 3, 1841, 29th Congress, 1st Session, *House Document No. 226,* esp. pp. 414–416, 425 ff. This report confirms, it seems to me, the opinion of Judge Barton a year later. I do not go into

These investments immobilized the bank's funds so that it was without active means to repay the government for its stock, to honor its $20 million of circulating notes, which soon began to be rapidly presented for redemption, and to meet its charter obligations, which in five years made it divert more than a third of its capital "to purposes of the state." To meet these requirements, the bank was driven into the market as borrower, both at home and abroad. These borrowings were begun by Biddle, and his successors turned to them more and more. Hence the bank came to be progressively incurring new obligations harder to meet than the old. The pressure mounted swiftly, so that a situation of apparent comfort in the spring of 1839 had passed into one of agony in the fall. These were the six months between Biddle's retirement and the bank's suspension. The bank had for years been growing more and more illiquid, but the condition had remained concealed by confidence. Once the illiquidity was suspected, however, the bank's creditors woke up with a start, and its obligations became instantly menacing. The suddenness of the change depended not on existence of the condition but on recognition of it.

According to one view, Biddle cannot be blamed for the bank's failure—it happened six months after he had retired. Well, granted that Biddle was gone, the bank was in the hands of successors who besides being heirs to his policies had been trained in his school. And this school, according to the evidence of stockholders' reports and court records, was one of extreme administrative inefficiency. The directors, dazzled by Biddle, knew nothing and approved everything. There were special procedures for special transactions, items being carried in the teller's drawer till it was expedient to post them. Accounts of the old bank were continued on the books of the new as if the corporate continuity was unbroken; and the notes of the old were kept in circulation by the new—a practice which particularly outraged Gallatin. It was in this atmosphere that Biddle's successors learned to manage the bank, and if they came to grief it cannot be

the cotton transactions, which Judge Barton discusses at length, because to discuss them adequately takes too much space. They show Biddle's audacity, ingenuity, and casuistry, but it is not clear that they cost the bank much, except indirectly by deterioration of management. The loan policy, though less irregular, did the bank more direct damage.

said that it was merely because they had not his ability. He would have come to grief himself.[56]

That Biddle must bear responsibility for the bank's condition is one thing; but that he had a guilty consciousness of its condition is quite another. Although the tradition of his dishonesty is held both by the Jacksonian partisans and by some scholars, I think it rests on a trite and stiffly moralistic view of the facts. If he realized how seriously wrong things were, it was an instance of objective analysis and cold self-appraisal unique in his career. I cannot believe him capable of it. He was eminently of a sanguine disposition, as is emphasized in the characterization of him by Catterall, who has given him more attention than any other historian. Caution and modesty were probably never among his more conspicuous virtues, and Jackson's attack did not enhance them. In the years 1836 to 1839, when he was laying down a new course for the bank, he was at the height of his career, it then seemed, and flushed with victory. He had blundered when he forced the issue of recharter in 1832, and Jackson had whipped him in the elections that year, in the veto, and in the removal of the deposits in 1833. But by 1838 he seemed to have retrieved his blunder and defeat. He had found sanctuary for the bank in the Pennsylvania jurisdiction, where Jackson could only gnash his teeth at it. He could point scornfully at the situation compounded of the panic of 1837, the specie circular, and distribution of the federal surplus. By 1839 he was the honored guest of Van Buren in the White House, and he could boast that the bank was again a government depository, that the independent Treasury scheme was rejected, and that the specie circular was repealed. He had triumphed over the Jacksonians on the points he cared most about. He even claimed credit for resumption, patronized Wall Street, and acted as the impresario of national monetary policy. It was in the fatuous mood of wishful thinking and expansive imagination stimulated by these illusive developments that he administered the bank after the failure of Jackson's attempt to annihilate him. If Biddle, at the height of his success in the winter of 1838–1839, examined his achievements objectively and concluded that all he had done mounted up to either a colossal fraud or

---

[56] For some account of the bank's methods, see Sister M. Grace Madeleine, *Monetary and Banking Theories of Jacksonian Democracy* (Philadelphia: The Dolphin Press, 1943), chaps. iv and v. The author seems to believe Biddle morally culpable.

FIGURE 5. Set to between Old Hickory (Jackson) and Bully Nick (Biddle), which Jackson won by vetoing recharter and withdrawing United States deposits. (Courtesy of the Print Department, Boston Public Library)

a colossal mistake, he must have been a very remarkable character indeed. Yet that is what the tradition of his moral guilt requires one to believe. I find more credible the less dramatic possibility that, being a man of very sanguine susceptibilities, he was simply carried away by success and self-confidence, by the grand scale of his activities, and by the daily exercise of more power, as he put it, than the President of the United States possessed. I believe he had lost the faculty of recognizing his own mistakes. The series of letters he wrote in 1841—prolix, specious, declamatory compositions in which he unconvincingly insisted that the bank had been in sound condition when he left it—seem to me the pathetic efforts of a man confounded by other things than guilt: by surprise, incredulousness, grief, anxiety, and shock.[57] His friends were at no less a loss; the most they could say in his favor was to protest at those who had been his sycophants while hoping to prosper but who turned against him with a "malicious prosecution" when their common fortunes collapsed.[58]

The hostility of Jackson to the Bank of the United States was in the first instance a matter of principle, the bank belonging to a monetary system and to a theory of federal powers which he disapproved; but later he and his followers could allege also that the bank was rotten and Biddle dishonest. That allegation was, in fact, emphasized more than the original principle. But if the bank was not rotten and Biddle was not dishonest, then what may be called the moral grounds for Jackson's action disappear leaving no defense except in charity to his good intentions. All he did was destroy a wisely developed monetary system. The administration of that system by the B.U.S. was admirable but might have been strengthened and improved had not Jackson's views been so radical and his temper so intransigent. In particular, had his demoralizing attack never been made Biddle would not have been stimulated to undertake his later grandiose and tragic course. But the blame must be shared by Biddle. The fury and the folly of these two ruined an excellent monetary system—as good as any the country has ever possessed—and left a reckless, booming anarchy.

When the career of Nicholas Biddle is given the study its importance deserves, it may appear that the earlier part of it, when he was a central banker, was something less than brilliant and that the later part, when he was an empire builder, was something worse than overweening. But, as it is, the evidence indicates an inventive, facile, dynamic person—vain and not too painfully honest under pressure—who encountered a bigoted interference with his extremely able management of an institution purposing to restrain the inflationary abuse

57 29th Congress, 1st Session, *House Document No. 226*, pp. 475–516.
58 *Philadelphia Public Ledger*, April 1, 1842.

of bank credit; who naïvely trusted the rightness of his position, condemned his adversary, defied him, and, after a smart defeat which he refused to acknowledge, achieved an illusory victory; who then, with overblown confidence in his own judgment, in the economic future of the country, and in the alchemic powers of bank credit, committed himself to empire building; who did things the ingenious if not the right way; and who reckoned on a faster and less fluctuant growth than the country actually had. In all this he went with the times. When an opposition that was locofoco on one side and laissez faire on the other overcame him, he joined the latter and likelier of the two. Having been stripped of the Hamiltonian garments of central control, he gladly put on the gayer ones of free enterprise. Yet Biddle was attracted more by the statesmanship of enterprise than by enterprise itself. As a central banker, his policy had been governed properly by public interest rather than profit.[59] As empire builder also, he led the bank into affairs of national scope and purpose.[60] He upheld the nation's foreign financial obligations. He intervened with both parties on behalf of Texas, whose government he had financed.[61] He resisted Jackson's monetary measures with a determination more patriotic than discreet. His retirement from the bank at the age of fifty-three must have been greatly influenced, and very reasonably, by political ambitions. Only a few weeks before announcing that he would retire, he had been advised by Thomas Cooper that his candidacy for President of the United States was not immediately practicable because of the "prevailing ignorance and prejudice about banks"—the general suspension being still a recent matter—and that "some years hence" prospects might be better.[62] The bank's difficulties from 1839 on blanked out these prospects wholly. They did more. Biddle had rebounded from the earlier frustration that ended his career as central banker; from the disaster to his later career he had no power to turn. John Quincy Adams had dinner with him *en famille,* November 22, 1840, and talked long with him. "Biddle," he wrote, "broods with

[59] See his critisim of "mere men of business" as administrators of the B.U.S.—R. C. McGrane, *Correspondence of Biddle,* p. 27.
[60] It will be recalled that, in his earlier literary days, he prepared a popular edition of the Lewis and Clark journals.
[61] R. C. McGrane, *Correspondence of Biddle,* pp. 325, 333, 335; C. H. Van Tyne, *Letters of Daniel Webster* (New York: McClure, Phillips and Company, 1902), p. 213.
[62] R. C. McGrane, *Correspondence of Biddle,* p. 333. See also earlier correspondence with Thomas Cooper regarding the presidency, pp. 272, 277–282, 293, 296, 323.

smiling face and stifled groans over the wreck of splendid blasted expectations and ruined hopes. A fair mind, a brilliant genius, a generous temper, an honest heart, waylaid and led astray by prosperity, suffering the penalty of scarcely voluntary error—'tis piteous to behold."[63] He died a little more than three years later, in reduced circumstances if not insolvent.

Besides the Jacksonian view of Biddle and the view that I have opposed to it, there is another I have already mentioned. Its distinction is its calm silence about the unhappy events, whether discreditable or tragic, of Biddle's last years. In R. C. McGrane's *Panic of 1837,* the bank's failure is alluded to, and Biddle's connection with it is dismissed in a footnote: "It should be noted that Biddle was now out of office, and can not be held responsible for what the bank did at this period." In the published correspondence of Nicholas Biddle, edited by Mr. McGrane, there is nothing that deals with the things that made Biddle's last years so miserably unlike those of his prime—the bank's failure, the loss of money and esteem, the prosecution of suits against him. And similarly in the article on Biddle in the *Dictionary of American Biography,* no mention is made of his last years being clouded by any trouble whatsoever. Such reticence and piety contrast genteelly with the bitterness he actually suffered and with the judgment that he belonged in jail.[64]

Two things combined to give Biddle's fall a supererogatory blackness. One was the sheer drama of the event. The largest corporation in the country—one of the largest in the world—had fallen suddenly from its splendid success into sprawling collapse at the very feet of the genius who had only recently with grand gestures relinquished its management. It was a denouement that stimulated the imagination to make worse what was already bad enough. The other aggravation of the story came from political motives. Biddle and the bank had never been warmed to by the Whigs, and Biddle's own ties were less with

[63] John Quincy Adams, *Memoirs,* ed. C. F. Adams (Philadelphia: J. B. Lippincott and Company, 1876), X: 361.
[64] Reginald C. McGrane, *The Panic of 1837; Some Financial Problems of the Jacksonian Era* (Chicago: The University of Chicago Press, 1924), p. 205; R. C. McGrane, *Correspondence of Biddle.* The Jacksonian opinion of Biddle is reflected in Arthur M. Schlesinger, Jr.'s, *Age of Jackson* (Boston: Little, Brown and Company, 1945), which I have not referred to in this essay because I reviewed it in the May 1946 issue of this Journal.

them than with the Democrats, but the latter naturally sought to make the bank seem Whig.[65] They had great success; the debacle helped to disintegrate the Whigs and strengthened the Jacksonians immeasurably. As a result, partisan views have dominated subsequent judgments and given Biddle the incidental and thankless role of darkened background to the glories of Andrew Jackson; and his achievements in credit policy, especially in the earlier and more admirable phase when he was a pioneer central banker, have been forgotten. Nowhere has he been studied adequately in his own right as a man of significant accomplishments, shortcomings, and misfortunes. Yet, in intellectual capacity, force of character, public spirit, and lasting influence, he was comparable with any of the contemporaries of his prime.

The withering that overtook Biddle's fame did not extend to his philosophy and example, which turned out to be triumphant, though with no acknowledgment to him. The monetary views of Gallatin and of Jackson are both obsolete, but Biddle's have a sort of pragmatic orthodoxy. He sought to make monetary policy flexible and compensatory rather than rigid. His easy-money doctrine had its source in a vision of national development to which abundant credit was essential. The majority of his countrymen have agreed with him. They have dismissed the man, but they have followed his ideas, especially his worse ones. They have shared his bullishness and his energy. They have not liked Jackson's primitive ideals of a simple, agrarian society, except in their nostalgic moods. They have not understood Gallatin's noble aversion for the fierce spirit of enterprise. They have exploited the country's resources with abandon, they have plunged into all the debt they could, they have realized a fantastic growth, and they have slighted its cost. Gallatin personified the country's intelligence and Jackson its folklore, but Biddle personified its behavior. They closed

[65] It is not clear which party Biddle supposed might make him president. The second Bank of the United States was both nurtured and destroyed within the Democratic party. Its creators and friends included Madison, Monroe, Gallatin, and Crawford; its three presidents, Jones, Cheves, and Biddle, were party members. Its greatest enemies were likewise pillars of the party—Jackson himself, Benton, and Taney. Jackson's cabinet was divided. The Whigs championed the bank less for its own sake than because Jackson's course left them no choice, and they abandoned it with relief as soon as they could. They were not interested in having bank credit restricted.

their careers in high honor—he closed his in opprobrium and be-
wilderment.

Arthur M. Schlesinger, Jr.

THE BANK WAR

*Teacher, historian, and ardent political activist, Arthur Schlesinger, Jr. kindled
a revival of interest in the Jacksonian period of American history by the
publication in 1945 of his Pulitzer Prize-winning book,* The Age of Jackson.
*Few important interpretations of the history of the United States have been
more widely read by historians as well as the general public—few have
generated more enthusiasm or provoked more controversy.*

Beginnings of the Bank War

In 1836 the charter of the Second Bank of the United States was to
expire. This institution was not in the later sense a national bank. It
was a banking corporation, located in Philadelphia, privately controlled, but possessing unique and profitable relations with the government. To its capital of thirty-five million dollars, the government
had subscribed one fifth. It served as repository of the public funds,
which it could use for its own banking purposes without payment of
interest. It could issue bank notes up to the physical ability of the
president and cashier to sign them; after 1827 it evaded this limitation
by the invention of "branch drafts," which looked and circulated
like notes but were actually bills of exchange. The Bank was not to
be taxed by the states and no similar institution was to be chartered
by Congress. In return for these privileges the Bank paid a bonus of
one and a half million dollars, transferred public funds and made
public payments without charge, and allowed the government to
appoint five out of the twenty-five directors. The Secretary of the

Treasury could remove the government deposits provided he laid the reasons before Congress.

Even advocates of the Bank conceded that this charter bestowed too much power. That staunch conservative Hezekiah Niles, writing in the heat of the fight for renewal, declared he "would not have the present bank re-chartered, with its present power . . . for the reason that the bank has more power than we would grant to any set of men, unless responsible to the people" (though he ultimately supported the Bank). Nathan Appleton, who had tried vainly to modify the charter in 1832, wrote carefully but emphatically in 1841: "A great central power, independent of the general or state governments, is an anomaly in our system. Such a power over the currency is the most tremendous which can be established. Without the assurance that it will be managed by men, free from the common imperfections of human nature, we are safer without it."

There could be no question about the reality of the Bank's power. It enjoyed a virtual monopoly of the currency and practically complete control over credit and the price level. Biddle's own testimony disclosed its extent:—

> Q.3. *Has the bank at any time oppressed any of the State banks?*
> A. *Never. There are very few banks which might not have been destroyed by an exertion of the powers of the bank. None have ever been injured.*

To radical Democrats like Taney, Biddle's tone implied that he thought himself entitled to credit for his forbearance. "It is this power concentrated in the hands of a few individuals," Taney declared, "—exercised in secret and unseen although constantly felt—irresponsible and above the control of the people or the Government for the 20 years of its charter, that is sufficient to awaken any man in the country if the danger is brought distinctly to his view."

There could be no question either about the Bank's pretensions to complete independence of popular control. Biddle brooked no opposition from within, and the government representatives sat through the directors' meetings baffled and indignant. "I never saw such a Board of *directors*," raged Henry D. Gilpin, "—it is a misuse of terms of *directed*. . . . We know absolutely nothing. There is no

consultation, no exchanges of sentiments, no production of correspondence, but merely a rapid, superficial, general statement, or a
reference to a Committee which will probably never report." He
added, "We are perfect cyphers."

Biddle not only suppressed all internal dissent but insisted flatly
that the Bank was not accountable to the government or the people.
In 1824 the president of the Washington branch had written Biddle,
"As . . . there are other interests to be attended to [besides those
of the Bank], especially that of the Government, I have deemed it
proper to see and consult with the President." Biddle hotly replied,

*If . . . you think that there are other interests to be attended to besides
those with which you are charged by the administration of the bank, we
deem it right to correct what is a total misapprehension. . . . The moment
this appointment [of the five government directors] takes place the Executive has completely fulfilled its functions. The entire responsibility is
thenceforward in the directors, and no officer of the Government, from
the President downwards, has the least right, the least authority, the least
pretence, for interference in the concerns of the bank. . . . This invocation
of the Government, therefore . . . is totally inconsistent with the temper
and spirit which belong to the officers of the bank, who should regard
only the rights of the bank and the instructions of those who govern it,
and who should be at all times prepared to execute the orders of the
board, in direct opposition, if need be, to the personal interests and wishes
of the President and every officer of the Government.*

In Biddle's eyes the Bank was thus an independent corporation, on
a level with the state, and not responsible to it except as the narrow-
est interpretation of the charter compelled. Biddle tried to strengthen
this position by flourishing a theory that the Bank was beyond political
good or evil, but Alexander Hamilton had written with far more
candor that "such a bank is not a mere matter of private property,
but a political machine of the greatest importance to the State." The
Second Bank of the United States was, in fact, as Hamilton had intended such a bank should be, the keystone in the alliance between
the government and the business community.

Though conservative Jeffersonians, led by Madison and Gallatin,
had come to accept Hamilton's Bank as necessary, John Taylor's
dialectics and Randolph's invective kept anti-Bank feeling alive, and
men in the old radical tradition remained profoundly convinced of

the evil of paper money. Jackson's hard-money views prompted his opposition to the Tennessee relief system in 1820. "Every one that knows me," as he told Polk in 1833, "does know, that I have been always opposed to the U. States Bank, nay all Banks."[1] Benton, from talks with Macon and Randolph and his observations of the collapse of the paper system in 1819, similarly concluded that the only safeguard against future disaster lay in restricting the system; and that, to this end, the government should deal only in gold and silver, thus withdrawing support from the issues of privately owned banks. Van Buren, Cambreleng, Taney and Polk more or less shared these views.

The ordinary follower of Jackson in the West also regarded the Bank with strong latent antagonism, but for very different reasons. Its policy in 1819 of recalling specie and checking the note issue of state banks had gained it few friends in any class, and, in Kentucky especially, the Relief War kept resentments alive. But this anti-Bank feeling owed little to reasoned distrust of paper money or to a Jeffersonian desire for specie. As a debtor section the West naturally preferred cheap money; and Kentucky, for example, which most vociferously opposed the United States Bank, also resorted most ardently to wildcat banking of its own. The crux of the Kentucky fight against the Bank was not the paper system, but outside control: the Bank's sin lay not in circulating paper money itself, but in restraining its circulation by Kentucky banks. Almost nowhere, apart from doctrinaires like Jackson and Benton, did westerners object to state banks under local control.

Indeed, during the eighteen-twenties, even the Philadelphia Bank to a considerable degree overcame the western prejudices against it.[2] In Tennessee, for example, until 1829 "both [Governor William] Carroll and the legislature favored federal as well as state banks,

---

[1] Jackson to Polk, December 23, 1833. Jackson told Nicholas Biddle late in 1829, "I do not dislike your Bank any more than all banks." Cf. C. J. Ingersoll to Biddle, February 2, 1832: "General Jackson's antipathy is not to the Bank of the United States in particular, but to all banks whatever. He considers all the State Banks unconstitutional and impolitic and thinks that there should be no Currency but coin." All serious students of the Bank War agree that Jackson's hostility to the Bank was of long standing and based on principle, not the result of a burst of temper over the conduct of a branch at Portsmouth, New Hampshire, or elsewhere.

[2] This was less true in Missouri, where there was considerable hard-money sentiment which the most careful student of the question ascribes in large part to Benton's personal influence.

nor does anything in the history of the state indicate that there was any general feeling against such institutions before Jackson became President."[3] Caleb Atwater, a lusty Jackson man from Ohio and something of a professional westerner, expressed a widespread feeling when he wrote in 1831, "Refuse to recharter the bank, and Pittsburgh, Cincinnati, Louisville, St. Louis, Nashville, and New Orleans, will be crushed at one blow." Even Frank Blair's first large-scale blast against the Bank in the *Argus of Western America* after Jackson's election did not come until December 23, 1829, many months after eastern groups had begun to agitate the question. This editorial —actually prefaced by an anti-Bank quote from a Van Buren paper in New York—appealed to the Kentucky fear of eastern control; and all through 1830 the *Argus* continued to focus on the power and privileges of the Bank and the consequent peril to the Commonwealth Bank of Kentucky, never on the general implications of the paper system.

Some writers have talked of frontier life as if it bred traits of "individualism" and equality which made westerners mystically opposed to banks. Actually, like all other groups in the population, westerners favored banks when they thought they could profit by them and fought them when they thought others were profiting at their expense. The western enthusiasm for an assault on the Bank came, not from an intuitive democratic *Weltschmerz* born in the American forest, nor from a Jeffersonian dislike of banks, but from a farmer-debtor desire to throw off restraints on the local issue of paper money.

Similar objections to control from Philadelphia ranged many easterners against the Bank. State institutions hoped, by falling heir to the government deposits, to enlarge their banking capital, at no expense to themselves. Special grievances multiplied the motives. The state banks of New York, for example, envied the United States Bank because its loan operations were not restricted by Van Buren's safety-

[3] T. P. Abernethy, "Andrew Jackson and the Rise of Southwestern Democracy," *American Historical Review,* 33:70. Cf. St. George L. Sioussat, "Some Phases of Tennessee Politics in the Jackson Period," ibid., 14:69: "though originally predisposed to hostility against the Bank of the United States, Tennessee, or rather the dominant western portion of the state, was yet quite willing to accept the benefits of a branch of the great bank, as long as times were good and credit was easy, and only gradually listened to and joined in the attack on that institution, which was begun in the year of Jackson's inauguration."

fund system. New York City had long resented the choice of Philadelphia as the nation's financial capital. Thus in a fight against the Bank Jackson could expect the backing of a decent minority of the local banking interests.

But there was still another and more reliable source of support. In March 1829, after the grim depression winter, a group of Philadelphia workingmen, under the very shadow of the Bank, called a meeting "opposed to the chartering of any more new banks." The hard times were blamed upon the "too great extension of paper credit," and the gathering concluded by appointing a committee, "without confining ourselves to the working classes," to draw up a report on the banking system. The committee, which was dominated by intellectuals, included two leading economists, William M. Gouge, editor of the *Philadelphia Gazette,* and Condy Raguet, editor of the *Free Trade Advocate,* as well as William Duane, the famous old Jeffersonian journalist, his son William J. Duane, a lawyer, Roberts Vaux, the philanthropist, Reuben M. Whitney, a disgruntled businessman and former director of the Bank, and William English and James Ronaldson, two trade-union leaders. A week later the committee pronounced its verdict on the paper system:—

> *That banks are useful as offices of deposit and transfer, we readily admit; but we cannot see that the benefits they confer in this way are so great as to compensate for the evils they produce, in . . . laying the foundation of* artificial *inequality of wealth, and, thereby, of* artificial *inequality of power. . . . If the present system of banking and paper money be extended and perpetuated, the great body of the working people must give over all hopes of ever acquiring any property.*

This view was spreading rapidly through the middle and northern states of the East in the late eighteen-twenties. The working class was no more affected by an instinctive antipathy toward banking than the backwoodsmen beyond the Alleghenies; but they never enjoyed the western opportunity of having banks under their own control. Their opposition, instead of remaining fitful and capricious, began slowly to harden into formal anti-banking principle. Their bitter collective experience with paper money brought them to the same doctrines which Jackson and Benton gained from the Jeffersonian inheritance.

The war against the Bank thus enlisted the enthusiastic support

of two basically antagonistic groups: on the one hand, debtor interests of the West and local banking interests of the East; on the other,
eastern workingmen and champions of the radical Jeffersonian tradition. The essential incompatibility between cheap money and hard
could be somewhat concealed in the clamor of the crusade. Yet that
incompatibility remained, and it came to represent increasingly a
difference between the western and eastern wings of the party, as
the state banking group gradually abandoned the Jackson ranks. It
was, indeed, a new form of the distinction between western and
eastern readings of "equality." The West, in its quest for political
democracy and home rule, did not object to paper money under local
control, while the submerged classes of the East, seeking economic
democracy, fought the whole banking swindle, as it seemed to them,
root and branch.

The administration took care not to offend its cheap-money ad-
herents by openly avowing hard-money ideas. Yet, the drift was un-
mistakable, and it rendered ineffective some of Jackson's western
followers for which the battle was being pressed on lines they could
not understand. Richard M. Johnson, for example, a staunch relief
man and ancient foe of the Bank, served on the House committee
which investigated the Bank in 1832; but he could take no real part
in a hearing dominated by Cambreleng's hard-money views, and,
though he signed Cambreleng's report, he confessed later that he had
not asked a question or looked at a Bank book. In general, the western politicians, torn between the hard-money leanings of the White
House and the cheap-money preferences of the folks back home,
tended to pursue an erratic course.

Only the intellectuals, who did not have to think about reelection,
effected a quick adjustment. Amos Kendall, who had been originally
a hard-money man, perhaps from his eastern upbringing, found no
difficulty in reverting to his earlier opinions. Frank Blair also rapidly
shifted his ground after coming to Washington. These were not basic
reversals of position. Their allegiance, after all, had been primarily
to a social class, not to a set of financial theories. The experience
of the Kentucky relief system taught that salvation was not to be
bought so cheaply: however much inflation might temporarily benefit
a frontier state with a large debtor element, it was at best a risky
expedient, imposed by political necessity; it never could serve as the

basis of a national economic policy. Kendall and Blair, liberated from their local obligations, naturally turned to hard-money ideas as affording the only permanent solutions for the financial problems in favor of the non-business classes.

Thomas Hart Benton had long awaited the opportunity to fight for this solution. In the eighteen-twenties, when he fumed about the paper system, Nathaniel Macon would remark that it was useless to attempt reform unless the administration was with you. Now, at last, the administration seemed to be with him. Jackson's first message had expressed grave doubts about the constitutionality and expediency of the Bank. In 1830 the President continued to make ominous allusions to the subject of recharter. But the administration position was still not clear. Jackson's views were widely regarded as the expressions of private prejudice, not of party policy. Few people interpreted the Maysville veto as opening a campaign which might end by involving the Bank.[4] Even now, the Bank was confidently conducting backstairs negotiations with Secretary McLane to work out a formula for recharter, and it had inspired an effective press campaign to counteract Jackson's pronouncements. Benton, watching impatiently, concluded that someone (who else but Benton?) would have to set forth the hard-money case.

He tried several times to get the floor in the Senate, but the friends of the Bank succeeded always in silencing him by parliamentary technicalities. Finally, on February 2, 1831, he outmaneuvered the opposition and launched his comprehensive indictment:—

First: Mr. President, I object to the renewal of the charter . . . because I look upon the bank as an institution too great and powerful to be tolerated in a Government of free and equal laws. . . .

Secondly, I object . . . because its tendencies are dangerous and perni-

---

[4] Nicholas Biddle's statement in 1830 that opposition to recharter was "not . . . a cabinet measure, nor a party measure, but a personal measure" was accurate. Biddle to Samuel Smith, January 2, 1830. Few anticipated the emergence of the Bank as the crucial issue. Webster wrote to Clay on May 29, 1830, "The great ground of difference will be Tariff and Internal Improvements." Cf. Hezekiah Niles's comment on a letter by A. L. Dabney of Virginia: "His remark that it is the tariff and internal improvement policy that now divides the parties in the United States, is certainly true." *Niles' Register,* August 14, 1830. As late as 1831, Tocqueville was told repeatedly, among others by Biddle, that no real issues divided the parties. Tocqueville, who was a surprisingly poor political reporter, later incorporated this theory in his famous work.

*cious to the Government and the people. . . . It tends to aggravate the
inequality of fortunes; to make the rich richer, and the poor poorer; to
multiply nabobs and paupers. . . .*

*Thirdly, I object . . . on account of the exclusive privileges, and anti-
republican monopoly, which it gives to the stockholders.*

And his own policy? "Gold and silver is the best currency for a
republic," he thundered; "it suits the men of middle property and
the working people best; and if I was going to establish a working
man's party, it should be on the basis of hard money; a hard-money
party against a paper party." The words reverberated through the
hall—"a hard-money party against a paper party"—as Mr. Webster
of Massachusetts hastily rose to call for a vote which defeated Benton's resolution against recharter.

But the words also reverberated through the country. The *Globe*
speedily reprinted the speech, the party press took it up, and pamphlets carried it through the land, to be read excitedly by oil lamp
and candlelight, talked over heatedly in taverns and around fireplaces,
on steamboats and stagecoaches, along the crooked ways of Boston
and the busy streets of New York and on isolated farms in New
Hampshire, Missouri, Iowa, Michigan, Arkansas. Nathaniel Macon
read it with deep pleasure in North Carolina. "You deserve the thanks
of every man, who lives by the sweat of his face," he told Benton,
adding with sturdy candor, ". . . I observe some bad grammar,—you
must pardon my freedom."

Nicholas Biddle, in his fine offices on Chestnut Street, was dis-
turbed by much more than Benton's grammar. This able, suave and
cosmopolitan Philadelphian was only thirty-seven when he became
president of the Bank in 1823. He had been known mainly as a
literary man—an early training which instilled a weakness for writing
public letters that would often prove embarrassing. One English
traveler pronounced him "the most perfect specimen of an American
gentleman that I had yet seen" and commended his "exemption from
national characteristics."

As head of the Bank, he inclined to pursue an active policy; but
up to 1830 all his ventures had succeeded, he had taken no unnecessary risks (except perhaps for the "branch draft" device), and
his judgment was universally respected. Yet, for all his ability, he

suffered from a fatal self-confidence, a disposition to underrate his opponents and a lack of political imagination. He sought now to make a deal with the administration, while working on public opinion by newspaper articles, loans to editors and personal contacts. But his ultimate reliance was on two of the nation's giants, Henry Clay and Daniel Webster.

Henry Clay was the most beloved politician of the day. He was tall and a little stooped, with a sandy complexion, gray, twinkling eyes, and a sardonic and somewhat sensual mouth, cut straight across the face. In conversation he was swift and sparkling, full of anecdote and swearing freely. Reclining lazily on a sofa, surrounded by friends, snuffbox in hand, he would talk on for hours with a long, drawling intonation and significant taps on the snuffbox as he cracked his jokes. John Quincy Adams called him only half-educated, but added, "His school has been the world, and in that he is a proficient. His morals, public and private, are loose, but he has all the virtues indispensable to a popular man."

Brilliant, reckless, fascinating, indolent, Clay was irresistibly attractive. Exhilarated by his sense of personal power, he loved to dominate his human environment everywhere, in Congress and at party councils, at dinner and in conversation; but he was not meanly ambitious. If he possessed few settled principles and small analytical curiosity, he had broad and exciting visions, which took the place of ideas.

It was these rapt visions which made him so thrilling an orator. His rich and musical voice could make drama out of a motion for adjournment, and Clay took care that it ordinarily had much more to occupy itself with. His brilliance of gesture—the sharp nods of the head, the stamp of the foot, the pointed finger, the open palm, the tight-clenched fist—made the emotion visible as well as audible. He carried all, not by logic, not by knowledge, but by storm, by charm and courage and fire. His rhetoric was often tasteless and inflated, his matter often inconsequential. "The time is fast approaching," someone remarked in 1843, "when the wonder will be as great, how his speeches could have been so thrilling, as it now is, how Mr. Burke's could have been so dull." Yet he transfixed the American imagination as few public figures ever have. The country may not have trusted him, but it loved him.

Daniel Webster lacked precisely that talent for stirring the popular imagination. He was an awe-inspiring figure, solid as granite, with strong shoulders and an iron frame. His dark, craggy head was unforgettable; strangers always recognized the jet-black hair, the jutting brow, the large smoldering eyes, and the "mastiff-mouth," as Carlyle saw it, "accurately closed." Yet, he inclined to be taciturn in public, except when he worked up, with the aid of brandy, a heavy geniality for social purposes. He loved his comfort too much: liquor and rest, duck-shooting at Marshfield and adulation in Boston. His intellectual ability was great, but he used it only under the spur of crisis. In his great speeches inspiration would take charge of his deep booming voice, and he would shake the world. Then he was, as Emerson remembered him, "the great cannon loaded to the lips." But when inspiration lagged he became simply pompous.

The nation never gave its heart to Webster. The merchants of Boston did, along with a share of their purses, and also the speculators of Wall Street and rich men everywhere. But the plain man did not much respond to him, except for a few Yankee farmers in New Hampshire, who liked to hobnob with statesmen. "He gives the idea of great power," said one English observer, "but does not inspire 'abandon.' " The people, who trusted Jackson and loved Clay, could neither trust nor love Webster. He never won the people simply because he never gave himself to them. He had, as Francis Lieber said, "no instinct for the massive movements."

Clay fought for Biddle and his Bank because it fitted in with his superb vision of America, but Webster fought for it in great part because it was a dependable source of private revenue. "I believe my retainer has not been renewed or *refreshed* as usual," he wrote at one point when the Bank had its back to the wall. "If it be wished that my relation to the Bank should be continued, it may be well to send me the usual retainers." How could Daniel Webster expect the American people to follow him through hell and high water when he would not lead unless someone made up a purse for him?[5]

---

[5] Stephen Vincent Benét's recent skillful attempt to make Webster a hero of myth would have surprised many of Webster's contemporaries. The real Webster lacked the generosity and warm humanity of Mr. Benét's hero, and would have opposed many of the things which Mr. Benét himself has stood for today. In fact, the least plausible part of Mr. Bénét's charming tale is not that a New Hampshire man should sell his soul to the devil, or that Benedict Arnold and Simon Girty should be on

In the House, Biddle could count on aid almost as formidable. John Quincy Adams, the ex-President, had come out of retirement to defend the American System in this moment of its peril. Adams, as Emerson noted, was no gentleman of the old school, "but a bruiser . . . an old roué who cannot live on slops but must have sulphuric acid in his tea!" He loved the rough-and-tumble of debate and neither asked quarter nor gave any. Sometimes he would lash himself into a rage, his body swaying with anger, his voice breaking, and the top of his head, usually white as alabaster, flushing a passionate red. Old age made him majestic and terrifying, with that bald and noble head, the cracked voice, the heavy figure clad in a faded frock coat. "Alone, unspoken to, unconsulted, never consulting with others, he sits apart, wrapped in his reveries," reported a Washington correspondent in 1837, ". . . looks enfeebled, but yet he is never tired; worn out, but ever ready for combat; melancholy, but let a witty thing fall from any member, and that old man's face is wreathed in smiles."

Adam's protégé, Edward Everett, the great rhetorician, could also be relied on to embellish Biddle's case with splendid exordiums and perorations; and George McDuffie, an experienced politician from South Carolina, was entrusted with the actual charge of the bill in the House. To strengthen the Bank forces, Biddle induced Horace Binney, the noted Philadelphia lawyer, to run for Congress. Binney had served as Bank lobbyist in Washington in the spring of 1832, and the next year took his seat as legislator.

In Clay, Webster, Adams, Everett, McDuffie and Binney, Biddle had a team whose personal following, abilities and oratory promised to overwhelm the best efforts of the administration. As the skirmishes began, he might be pardoned if he failed to regard Jackson, Benton and the Kitchen Cabinet as constituting a serious threat.

In the spring of 1830 a House committee, directed by George McDuffie, had brought in a report clearing the Bank of the charges made by Jackson in his first message to Congress. Jackson returned to the subject in more detail in his second message, and Benton's speech in 1831 thrust the question vigorously to the fore.

tap for jury service, but that Daniel Webster should be found arguing against the sanctity of contract.

Biddle would have much preferred to keep the Bank out of politics altogether. His one interest was in renewing the charter. This he would do with Jackson's help, if possible; with Clay's, if necessary. Thus, during 1830 and 1831 he carefully explored the chances of winning over the President. The active cooperation of McLane and Livingston and the evident division in Jackson's party raised Biddle's hopes. The President, in the meantime, while saying quietly that his views had not changed, allowed McLane to recommend recharter in his Treasury report and barely mentioned the Bank question in his message of 1831.

But for all his amiability Jackson remained unyielding, while the Van Buren group seemed irrevocably hostile. Henry Clay, fearful lest so good an issue slip through his fingers, kept pressing Biddle to let him make recharter a party question. Biddle hesitated, considered, stalled, watched the National Republican convention nominate Clay, with John Sergeant, a lawyer for the Bank, as running mate, read the party address denouncing Jackson's views on the Bank—and on January 9, 1832, petitions for recharter were presented in each House of Congress.

Benton, certain that the Bank could carry Congress, realized that the administration's only hope lay in postponement. Accordingly he had a good many obstructionist amendments prepared for the Senate, and in the House he set in motion plans for an investigating committee. Late in February, A. S. Clayton of Georgia moved the appointment of such a committee, defending the proposal from unexpectedly hot attacks by reading from hasty notes provided by Benton, twisting the paper around his finger so that no one would recognize the handwriting.

The Bank forces could hardly refuse this request without raising strange suspicions. Yet, they first resisted it, then tried to keep it in their own hands, then tried to restrict its scope—overruling McDuffie who understood perfectly the futility of these tactics—with the result that by the time the committee was appointed the Bank had lost considerable prestige through the country. McDuffie, John Quincy Adams and J. G. Watmough, Biddle's vestpocket representative, served on the committee as friends of the Bank, with Cambreleng, Clayton, Richard M. Johnson and Francis Thomas of Maryland as opponents. After six weeks in Philadelphia, examining records and questioning witnesses, it issued three reports: a majority report against the Bank, and two minority dissents, one by Adams.[6]

In May the fight began in earnest. Biddle had already sent an advance guard of crack lobbyists, but, with the crucial struggle about to start, he took personal command. By now he was growing drunk with power. When Nathan Appleton, Massachusetts mill owner and member of the House, proposed the charter be modified, Biddle scorned the suggestion, and Clay interceded with Appleton, begging him to vote for the measure as it stood. "Should Jackson veto it," exclaimed Clay with an oath, "I shall veto him!"

On June 11 the bill passed the Senate, 28–20, and on July 3 it passed the House, 107–85. When Biddle made a smiling appearance on the floor after the passage, members crowded round to shake his hand. A riotous party in his lodgings celebrated the victory late into the night.

Veto

Jessie Benton knew she must keep still and not fidget or squirm, even when General Jackson twisted his fingers too tightly in her curls. The old man, who loved children, liked to have Benton bring his enchanting daughter to the White House. Jessie, clinging to her father's hand, trying to match his strides, would climb breathlessly up the long stairs to the upper room where, with sunshine flooding in through tall south windows, they would find the General in his

---

[6] The operations of this committee confound naive theories of economic determinism. All the opponents of the Bank were in debt to it (Clayton, $400; Johnson, $650; Thomas, $650; Cambreleng, $400), while the friends of the Bank owed it much less (McDuffie, $500; Watmough, $300; Adams, nothing). Though the Jacksonians made a good deal of the Bank's loans to Congressmen, there was not much correlation between the size of the loans and the intensity of the devotion to the Bank.

This statement does not apply at all, however, to loans to newspaper editors; and Taney's analysis of one Congressman's change of opinion after a large loan was certainly true for a small number of individual cases. "Now I do not mean to say," wrote Taney, "that he was directly bribed to give this vote. From the character he sustained and from what I knew of him I think he would have resented any thing that he regarded as an attempt to corrupt him. But he wanted the money—and felt grateful for the favor: and perhaps he thought that an institution which was so useful to him, and had behaved with so much kindness, could not be injurious or dangerous to the public, and that it would be as well to continue it. Men under the influence of interest or passion . . . do not always acknowledge even to themselves the motives upon which they really act. They sometimes persuade themselves that they are acting, on a motive consistent with their own self-respect, and sense of right, and shut their eyes to the one which in fact governs their conduct."

big rocking chair close to the roaring wood fire. The child instinctively responded to the lonely old man's desire for "a bright unconscious affectionate little life near him," and would sit by his side while his hand rested on her head. Sometimes, in the heat of discussion, his long bony fingers took a grip that made Jessie look at her father but give no other sign. Soon Benton would contrive to send her off to play with the children of Andrew Jackson Donelson, the President's private secretary. Then the talk would resume. In the latter days of 1831 the discussions grew particularly long and tense.

Jackson's grim calm during that year cloaked no basic wavering of purpose. With characteristic political tact he presented an irresolute and amenable face to the world in order to hold the party together. Benton and Kendall were in his confidence, but very few others. His apparent moderation deceived not only Biddle but many of the Bank's enemies. James A. Hamilton considered making a hurried trip to London to discuss Jackson's vacillations with Van Buren; and William Dunlap, the artist, voiced the misgivings of many liberals in his remark to Fenimore Cooper that Jackson had "proved weaker than could have been anticipated; yet those who hold under him will hold to him and strive to hold him up."

In particular, Jackson's cabinet misinterpreted his pose. McLane, Livingston and Taney were all convinced that compromise was possible, greatly to the relief of the two and the despair of the third. Taney was coming to believe that he stood alone in the cabinet and almost in the country in opposing recharter. In the meantime, the Bank's alacrity in opening new offices and making long-term loans, though its charter was soon to expire, seemed "conclusive evidence of its determination to fasten itself by means of its money so firmly on the country that it will be impossible . . . to shake it off without producing the most severe and extensive public suffering.—And this very attempt," he cried, "calls for prompt resistance—for future resistance will be in vain if the charter is renewed."

But who would lead the resistance? He watched the debates drag on and the votes pile up through the spring of 1832 with mounting apprehension. In the late spring, having to attend the Maryland Court of Appeals, he decided to prepare a memorandum setting forth his conviction that recharter should be vetoed. He finished it the night before his departure and notified the President that the opinion would be delivered as soon as the bill was passed.

On July 3 Jackson received the bill. Hearing the news, Martin Van Buren, just back from England, went straight on to Washington, arriving at midnight. The General, still awake, stretched on a sick-bed, pale and haggard and propped up by pillows, grasped his friend's hand. Passing his other hand through his snow-white hair, he said firmly but without passion, "The bank, Mr. Van Buren, is trying to kill me, *but I will kill it!*"

A day or two later, Taney, busy in Annapolis, received word to hurry back to Washington. He found the President out of bed and eager for action. He had read Taney's memorandum with emphatic agreement and then had heard the arguments of the rest of the cabinet. While disapproving the bill, they wanted him to place his rejection on grounds which would allow the question to be reopened in the future. Jackson, unwilling to compromise, then turned to Amos Kendall for a first draft of the veto message. Andrew J. Donelson was now revising Kendall's draft in the room across the hall. Would Taney help? The lean, determined face of the Attorney General expressed no reservations.

It took three days to finish the document. The first day Taney and Donelson worked alone, except for Jackson and Ralph Earl, an artist who lived at the White House and used this room as a studio, painting away, oblivious of the tense consultations, the hasty scribbles, the words crossed out, the phrases laboriously worked over, the notes torn up and discarded. On the second day Levi Woodbury, having decided to change his stand, made an unabashed appearance and assisted till the job was done. Jackson meanwhile passed in and out of the room, listening to the different parts, weighing the various suggestions and directing what should be inserted or altered.

The message, dated July 10, burst like a thunderclap over the nation. Its core was a ringing statement of Jackson's belief in the essential rights of the common man. "It is to be regretted, that the rich and powerful too often bend the acts of government to their selfish purposes," Jackson declared.

> *Distinctions in society will always exist under every just government. Equality of talents, of education, or of wealth can not be produced by*

*human institutions. In the full enjoyment of the gifts of Heaven and the
fruits of superior industry, economy, and virtue, every man is equally entitled to protection by law; but when the laws undertake to add to these
natural and just advantages artificial distinctions . . . to make the rich
richer and the potent more powerful, the humble members of society—
the farmers, mechanics, and laborers—who have neither the time nor the
means of securing like favors to themselves, have a right to complain of
the injustice of their Government.*

But the case against the Bank could not rest simply on generalities.
Jackson's real opposition, of course, and that of Benton, Taney and
Kendall, arose from their hard-money views. Yet, a great part of their
backing came from cheap-money men. Thus powerful hard-money
arguments—the economic argument that the paper system caused
periodic depressions, and the social argument that it built up an
aristocracy—were unavailable because they were as fatal to the
debtor and state banking positions as to the Bank itself.

The veto message was brilliantly successful in meeting this di-
lemma. It diverted attention from the basic contradiction by its passages of resounding and demagogic language; it played down the
strictly economic analysis; and it particularly sought to lull western
fears by dwelling on the hardships worked by the long arm of the
Bank in the Mississippi Valley. Its main emphasis fell, first, on the
case against the Bank as unconstitutional, and then on the political
argument that the Bank represented too great a centralization of
power under private control. The stress on the "great evils to our
country and its institutions [which] might flow from such a concentration of power in the hands of a few men irresponsible to the people"
sounded good to the state banks and to the West, both of which had
chafed long enough at the ascendancy of Chestnut Street. The message thus thrust to the foreground the issues on which all enemies
of the Bank could unite, while the special aims of the hard-money
school remained safely under cover.[7]

The distinction between "the humble members of society" and

---

[7] The Bank controversy elicited a few examples of what would be a natural modern
argument: that the Bank was clothed with the public interest. Henry D. Gilpin, a
former government director of the Bank and Attorney General under Van Buren,
suggested somewhat this argument in 1836: "I am not sure that Dallas has put the
argument [against the bank] in its strongest form—that such an institution is essentially *public*, affecting the general value of property and exercising powers too broad

"the rich and powerful" drew quick reactions from both classes. The common man through the land responded enthusiastically to his leader's appeal. "The veto works well everywhere," Jackson could report from the Hermitage in August; "it has put down the Bank instead of prostrating me."

But men who believed that the political power of the business community should increase with its wealth were deeply alarmed. When Jackson said, "It is not conceivable how the present stockholders can have any claim to the special favor of the Government," did he mean that the common man had the same rights as the rich and wellborn to control of the state? The Bank of the United States, according to the plan of Hamilton, would serve as the indispensable make-weight for property against the sway of numbers. Did not the veto message attack the very premises of Federalism, rejecting its axioms, destroying its keystone and rallying the groups in society bent on its annihilation?

No wonder Nicholas Biddle roared to Henry Clay, "It has all the fury of a chained panther, biting the bars of his cage. It is really a manifesto of anarchy, such as Marat or Robespierre might have issued to the mob of the Faubourg St. Antoine." Or, as Alexander H. Everett wrote in Boston's conservative daily, the *Advertiser*, "For the first time, perhaps, in the history of civilized communities, the Chief Magistrate of a great nation . . . is found appealing to the worst passions of the uninformed part of the people, and endeavoring to stir up the poor against the rich." Webster, rising gravely in the Senate, summed up the indictment:

> *It manifestly seeks to influence the poor against the rich. It wantonly attacks whole classes of the people, for the purpose of turning against them the prejudices and resentments of other classes. It is a State paper which finds no topic too exciting for its use, no passion too inflammable for its address and its solicitation.*

For Webster, as for Jackson, it was becoming a battle between antagonistic philosophies of government: one declaring, like Webster

to be regarded as private acts—and that whether public or private the chief legislative body have a right to rescind a franchise, as they have to take private property, when the public welfare requires it." Gilpin to Van Buren, September 14, 1836.

at the Massachusetts convention, that property should control the state; the other denying that property had a superior claim to governmental privileges and benefits.

The veto struck consternation through some parts of the Democratic party. The summer and fall of 1832 saw a hasty recasting of party lines. In Boston, the ex-Federalist silk-stocking Democrats scurried back to their natural political allegiances, even at the cost of associating once again with John Quincy Adams. In New York, conservative politicians like G. V. Verplanck and businessmen like Moses H. Grinnell abandoned the radicals. Almost every city had its meeting of "original Jackson men" to disown the administration and renounce its works.

Two-thirds of the press, largely perhaps because of advertising pressure, supported the Bank.[8] Even such a theoretically unpolitical family magazine as the *Saturday Evening Post* had opinions which led the *Washington Globe* to denounce it, in terms which would appeal to later generations, for conveying "its stealthy political influence into the bosom of such *families* as avoided the contests of politics." Biddle also hired such august journals as Robert Walsh's *American Quarterly Review* to print pro-Bank articles.

A part of the business community stuck by Jackson. Some merchants opposed the concentration of power in the Bank. Some distrusted Biddle. Some hoped the Bank would be replaced by a Democratic Bank of the United States in which they might hold stock. Some were investors or officers in state banks with an eye on the government deposits. But they made up a small part of the whole. "Since landing in America," noted young Tocqueville, "I have prac-

---

[8] Two-thirds was the estimate of W. M. Holland in 1835; Van Buren's own estimate was three-fourths. As for the cause, as a discerning English traveler pointed out, "Relying chiefly, if not entirely, on their advertisements for support, and these being furnished by persons engaged in the mercantile and trading operations, they can hardly dare offend those on whom they are so dependent. . . . Hence they are almost all Whigs." The report of the Philadelphia workingmen's committee of 1829, largely the work of two editors, W. M. Gouge and Condy Raguet, charged: "Even now it is impossible to obtain entrance into many papers for free disquisitions of the [banking] system. The conductor of a public journal who ventures on so bold a step, risks his means of subsistence." Biddle's newspaper loans were notorious. The most celebrated example was the reversal of the policy of the *New York Courier and Enquirer,* formerly a strong Jackson paper, on receiving loans which aggregated to nearly $53,000 and were very risky business ventures.

tically acquired proof that all the enlightened classes are opposed to General Jackson."[9]

As the day of election drew near, the universal debate went on with increasing acrimony, from the shacks of Maine fishermen to the parlors of Philadelphia and the plantations of Alabama. An epidemic of cholera swept through the North in the first months of summer. "If it could only carry off Jackson and a few other of our politicians by trade," wrote Henry C. Carey, Philadelphia publisher and economist, "I would submit to all the inconveniences of it for a month or two." The din of politics, filling the cabin of a ship bound for America, wearied a charming British actress: "Oh, hang General Jackson!" cried Fanny Kemble.

August gave way to September, September to October, and the clamor grew increasingly furious. Jackson men paraded the streets in the glare of torches, singing campaign songs, carrying hickory poles, gathering around huge bonfires blazing high into the night. Late in October, Horace Binney solemnly told a Philadelphia audience that "the preservation of the Constitution itself" depended on the defeat of Jackson, congratulating them that the right of a free election could still be exercised with safety. "How long it will continue so, or how long the enjoyment of it will be of any value to you, are questions upon which the short remainder of the present year will probably furnish materials for a decisive judgment." Fanny Kemble, resting in Philadelphia after her successes in Washington (where she had dazzled Chief Justice Marshall and Justice Story as well as Frank Blair of the *Globe*), was assured by her friends that Henry Clay, "the leader of the aristocratic party," was already certain of election.

But the people had not spoken. Soon their time came: "The news from the voting States," Rufus Choate wrote to Edward Everett, "blows over us like a great cold storm." The results rolled in: Jackson, 219, Clay, 49, John Floyd, 11, William Wirt, 7.[10] The bitterness

---

[9] For Tocqueville the "enlightened classes" were the merchants and lawyers.

[10] A later President's [Franklin D. Roosevelt] judgment on Jackson's opposition has bearing on both their experiences. "An overwhelming proportion of the material power of the Nation was against him. The great media for the dissemination of information and the molding of public opinion fought him. Haughty and sterile intellectualism opposed him. Musty reaction disapproved him. Hollow and outworn traditionalism shook a trembling finger at him. It seemed sometimes that all were against him—all but the people of the United States."

with which conservatism faced the future flared up briefly in a post-election editorial in Joseph T. Buckingham's *Boston Courier*. "Yet there is one comfort left: God has promised that the days of the wicked shall be short; the wicked is old and feeble, and he may die before he can be elected. It is the duty of every good Christian to pray to our Maker to have pity on us."[11]

Jackson's reelection and the popular acclaim following the nullification crisis only reinforced the administration's resolve to press the offensive against the American "Nobility System." The first necessity was to destroy its "head," the Bank. But the charter still had well over three years to run. The Bank was still backed by the National Republican party, most of the press and many leading citizens. And the custody of the government deposits, the radicals feared, provided the Bank with campaign funds for recharter. Generous loans, subsidies and retainers, strategically distributed, might substantially change public opinion before 1836. Moreover, the government deposits, by enabling the Bank to take most of the specie out of circulation in exchange for its bank notes, might place Biddle in a position, just before the election of 1836, to create a financial panic and insure the success of Bank candidates and the recharter of the Bank.

The solution lay in withdrawing the deposits. This would cripple the Bank's attempt to convulse the money market and probably provoke it into an all-out fight against the only man who could whip it, thus foreclosing the issue once and for all. Jackson seems to have decided on this course shortly after his reelection. It was his own plan, "conceived by him," as Benton later wrote, "carried out by him, defended by him, and its fate dependent upon him." Taney,

[11] It continues in similar vein, declaring that the works of Paine "do not furnish Atheists with a single argument against the existence of a benign Providence, half so strong as the continuance of the misrule of Andrew Jackson. . . . We are constrained to acknowledge that the experiment of an absolutely liberal government has failed. . . . Heaven be praised that Massachusetts and Connecticut have escaped the moral and political contagion! As for the rest, they have proved themselves slaves, born to be commanded—they have put the whip into the hands of one who has shown every inclination to be absolute master, and it is some consolation to think that he will probably ere long lay it upon their backs till they howl again. . . . Who doubts that if all who are unable to read or write had been excluded from the polls, Andrew Jackson could not have been elected?"

Kendall and Blair actively supported him while Barry added his crumbling influence. Benton, vastly pleased, for some reason played little part in working out the details. Woodbury remained inscrutable, with McLane, Livingston and Cass all hostile.

McLane and Biddle, indeed, went quickly to work to forestall the President. A special Treasury investigator reported early in 1833 that the Bank was sound, and in March the House upheld a majority report of the Ways and Means Committee declaring the funds perfectly safe in the Bank's custody. These incidents only confirmed the radicals' conviction of the extent of Biddle's power.

The campaign for removal slowed down in May and June, during the President's trip to New York and New England. No overt act had yet destroyed his almost universal popularity, and the tour proved a long triumphal procession, marked by the thunder of cannon, the cheering of crowds, pompous reception committees and interminable banquets. General Jackson, though tormented by a throbbing pain in his side and the bleeding of his lungs, remained resolute and erect through it all.[12]. . . At Concord he finally collapsed and was hurried back to Washington.

In the meantime the transfer of Livingston to the French ministry and of McLane to the State Department had created a vacancy in the Treasury for which McLane proposed William J. Duane, the Philadelphia lawyer who had signed the anti-Bank report of the workingmen's meeting in March 1829. Jackson approved, and Duane took office on June 1. This appointment raised fresh difficulties. Though Duane could hardly have been much surprised on learning Jackson's sentiments about removal, he played an equivocal part, neither accepting nor opposing the President's views, but stalling and obstructing. Kendall and Reuben M. Whitney, another veteran of the workingmen's meeting in 1829, were working out the details of a system of deposit in selected state banks, and Duane finally agreed to resign if, after Kendall's report, he still found himself unable to take the desired action.

July, as usual, was unbearable in Washington. Jackson, sick and weary, prepared to go to Ripraps in Virginia for a rest. Where, in

[12] A description of the tour is here omitted.—Ed.

this moment of loneliness, stood the Vice-President? Van Buren at first had opposed immediate removal. The imminence of 1836, and his role as heir-apparent, had probably intensified his natural caution. Sometime in the spring, during a heated discussion with Van Buren, Amos Kendall, rising from his seat in excitement, warned that a Bank victory in 1836 was certain unless it were stripped of the power it gained from managing the public money: "I can live under a corrupt despotism, as well as any other man, by keeping out of its way, which I shall certainly do." Impressed by Kendall's vehemence, Van Buren changed his attitude, though he never allowed himself to become identified with the measure. His own private council, the Albany Regency, was divided, Silas Wright favoring delay, while A. C. Flagg and John A. Dix supported the President. During August and September Van Buren traveled around New York, first to Saratoga, then, with Washington Irving, taking a four-week tour of the Dutch settlements on Long Island and the North River, always one step ahead of the Washington mail. For once he was living up to his reputation.[13]

Frank Blair accompanied Jackson to the seaside, where the two households spent a pleasant month, the invigorating salt air restoring Jackson's appetite and improving his health. Letters bombarded the President, pleading with him not to disturb the deposits. What seemed an organized campaign only strengthened his purpose: "Mr. Blair, Providence may change me but it is not in the power of man to do it. In spare moments, he shaped his notes into a militant and uncompromising document. Returned to the White House late in August, he resolved to end the matter before Congress convened.

On September 10 he presented Kendall's report on the state banks to the cabinet. Taney and Woodbury backed the proposal to discontinue placing funds with the Bank on October 1, while McLane, Cass and Duane vigorously opposed it. Duane's assent as Secretary of the Treasury was necessary for the action. By September 14 Jackson, having tortuously overcome his scruples against discharging persons who disagreed with him, suggested to Duane that he resign; perhaps he might be named Minister to Russia. Duane refused.

---

[13] Wright added as another argument against removal the fear that "such men and mausers as Jas. A. Hamilton and Jesse Hoyt" might try to benefit in stock speculation by prior knowledge of removal.

The next day Jackson handed Taney for revision the fiery paper he had dictated at Ripraps. On the eighteenth he read this paper to the cabinet. Two days later the *Globe* announced the plan to cease deposits in the Bank after October 1. Duane continued in frightened obstinacy, agreeing to the removal of neither the deposits nor himself. "He is either the weakest mortal, or the most strange composition I have ever met with," Jackson wrote in exasperation. The next five days exhausted even the President's patience. He dismissed Duane and appointed Taney to the place.[14]

He now faced the threatened resignations of McLane and Cass. A friend of the Secretary of War told Blair that Cass would remain if a paragraph in the President's statement would exempt him from responsibility. Jackson, amused at the suggestion that Cass might be held responsible, said, "I am very willing to let the public know that I take the whole responsibility," and conceded the point. The amended message went off to the *Globe* for publication, and the next morning Blair took Taney the proofs. Taney, black cigar in mouth and feet on table, listened as Andrew J. Donelson read the message aloud. "How under heaven did that get in?" exclaimed Taney on hearing the inserted passage. When Blair explained, Taney observed, "This has saved Cass and McLane; but for it they would have gone out and have been ruined—as it is, they will remain and do us much mischief."

The radical Jacksonians exulted at the removal. "This is the crowning glory of A. J.'s life and the most important service he has ever rendered his country," cried Nicholas P. Trist, the intelligent young Virginian who served as the President's secretary. "Independently of its misdeeds, the mere *power*,—the bare existence of such a power—is a thing irreconcilable with the nature and spirit of our institutions." Benton pronounced it "the most masterly movement in politics which the age had witnessed." The *Boston Post* put it in the same class as Christ's expelling the money-changers from the Temple. The sturdy and rebellious William Cobbett, in England, called it "one

---

[14] Duane published in 1838 a plaintive defense of his odd behavior, called *Narrative and Correspondence Concerning the Removal of the Deposites* and correctly described by the *New York Evening Post*, May 14, 1839, as a work of "feeble bitterness."

of the greatest acts of his whole wonderful life." Jovial Charles
Gordon Greene, editor of the *Boston Post*, even composed an epitaph for the Bank: "*Biddled, Diddled, and Undone.*"

But Biddle was not yet convinced that it was the Bank which
needed the epitaph.

Counterattack

The new storm of denunciation made the attack on the veto seem a
model of good temper. Biddle, convinced by midsummer that the deposits were doomed, began in August to fight back. Employing to
the full his power over the state banks, he commenced to present
their notes for redemption, reduce discounts and call in loans. While
claiming to be simply winding up business in preparation for the
expiration of the charter, he was in fact embarked on the campaign
the radicals above all had feared: the deliberate creation of a panic
in order to blackmail the government into rechartering the Bank.
"Nothing but the evidence of suffering abroad will produce any effect
in Congress," he wrote privately to a friend. ". . . if . . . the Bank
permits itself to be frightened or coaxed into any relaxation of its
present measures, the relief will itself be cited as evidence that the
measures of the Govt. are not injurious or oppressive, and the Bank
will inevitably be prostrated." "My own course is decided," he informed another, "—all the other Banks and all the merchants may
break, but the Bank of the United States shall not break."

The strategy was at first brilliantly successful. The business community, already incensed by Jackson's measures, was easily persuaded that deflation was the inevitable consequence of removal. The
contraction of loans by the Bank tightened credit all along the line.
Businesses failed, men were thrown out of work, money was unob-
tainable. Memorials, petitions, letters, delegations and protests of
every kind deluged Congress.

The friends of the administration now needed all their skill. Thomas
Hart Benton still swaggered through the Capitol, a host in himself,
and still rose to make his crushing speeches, pausing only to apply
a double glass to his eye as he read the tedious, yet essential, sta-
tistics. But his footwork was slow, and the brunt of the defense in

Senate debates fell rather on the shoulders of John Forsythe of Georgia, a good southern politician, talented, facile and endowed with strong political loyalties which served him in place of principles. No one excelled Forsythe in the guerrilla aspects of debate, in reconnoitering and skirmishing, in leading the assault and covering the retreat.

In Isaac Hill of New Hampshire, Andrew Jackson had another firm defender. . . . The special representative of Van Buren was Silas Wright, the Senator from New York. . . .[15]

Roger B. Taney set forth the issue in the report he rendered to the House early in the session. "It is a fixed principle of our political institutions," he declared, "to guard against the unnecessary accumulation of power over persons and property in any hands. And no hands are less worthy to be trusted with it than those of a moneyed corporation." What would be the future of American democracy if the course of the government was to be regulated by fear of the Bank? "They may now demand the possession of the public money, or the renewal of the charter; and if these objects are yielded to them from apprehensions of their power, or from the suffering which rapid curtailments on their part are inflicting on the community, what may they not next require? Will submission render such a corporation more forbearing in its course?"

This was indeed the question: if Mr. Biddle's panic could coerce the Congress into restoring the deposits, would not the Bank, strengthened by the deposits, in the same manner coerce the Congress into recharter; and as its power grew, would not its demands become more exigent, until democracy was dead? "For, rely upon it," as Taney warned again in a speech in Maryland the next summer, "if the deposits are restored, the Bank is surely rechartered. And if, after all its enormities, it obtains an extension of its charter for a single year, the contest is over, and we may quietly resign ourselves to the chains with which it is prepared to bind us."

The Bank forces were now reinforced by the support, under complex and tenuous conditions, of John C. Calhoun. The philosopher from South Carolina proved helpful in lifting the issue to more ele-

[15] Descriptions of Hill and Wright are here omitted.—Ed.

vated planes of discussion. He sharply denied that the struggle was over the question of Bank or no Bank. If it were, "if it involved the existence of the banking system, . . . I would hesitate, long hesitate, before I would be found under the banner of the system." What then was it all about? "I answer, it is a struggle between the executive and legislative departments of the Government; a struggle, not in relation to the existence of the bank, but which, Congress or the President, should have the power to create a bank, and the consequent control over the currency of the country. This is the real question."

While this was hardly the real question, it was certainly a far nobler question than the discredited plea for recharter. It fitted neatly into the ancient picture of Jackson as a backwoods Caesar, bent on establishing a military dictatorship; and it supplied an issue on which the friends of the Bank and the friends of nullification could unite in an anti-Jackson front. Clay sounded the new keynote before a hushed Senate and packed galleries on the day after Christmas. "We are in the midst of a revolution," he declared, "hitherto bloodless, but rapidly tending towards a total change of the pure republican character of the Government, and to the concentration of all power in the hands of one man." The currency had been undermined, the recharter vetoed against the will of the Congress, the system of internal improvements crushed, the tariff imperiled, and now liberty and the Constitution were themselves in danger. "If Congress do not apply an instantaneous and effective remedy, the fatal collapse will soon come on, and we shall die—ignobly die—base, mean, and abject slaves; the scorn and contempt of mankind; unpitied, unwept, unmourned!"

Webster took up the attack, arguing the imminence of despotism with massive logic; Silas Wright replied, and Webster slashed back at Wright. (The two men disliked each other. Webster thought Wright "the most over-rated man" he had ever met, while Wright, regarding Webster as the Bank's henchman, had only contempt for his views "as far as he is competent to entertain views today which will govern his action tomorrow.") For a moment in his rejoinder, Webster glanced from the fictitious issue to the real one. "Sir," he exclaimed, holding a newspaper clipping in his hand and turning his great, stern, dark face on Wright, "I see . . . plain declarations that the present controversy is but a strife between one part of the community and another. I hear it boasted as the unfailing security, the solid ground,

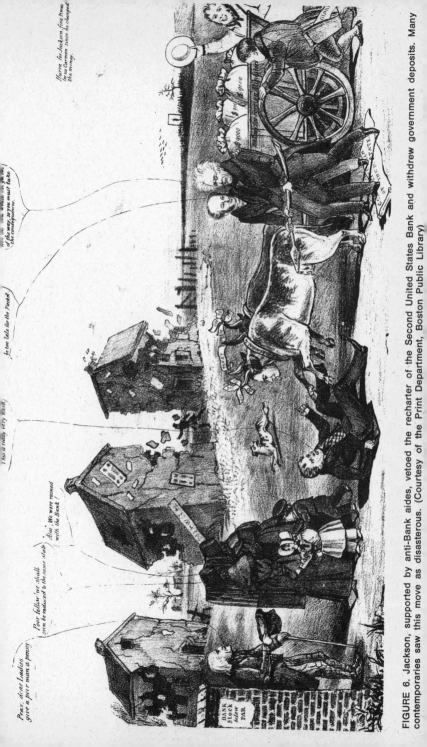

FIGURE 6. Jackson, supported by anti-Bank aides, vetoed the recharter of the Second United States Bank and withdrew government deposits. Many contemporaries saw this move as disasterous. (Courtesy of the Print Department, Boston Public Library)

never to be shaken, on which recent measures rest, that the poor naturally hate the rich." The great voice throbbed with indignation. Whoever was wicked enough thus to attack the Bank, "by arraying one class against another . . . deserves to be marked especially as the poor man's curse!"

But the Bank forces took care most of the time to avoid such issues, and the debates turned more and more on constitutionality. On February 5 a resolution passed declaring Taney's reasons for removal unsatisfactory, and on March 28 came another charging Jackson with having acted in derogation of the Constitution. When Jackson replied by a long protest, the Senate refused to enter it in its records, and the session came to a bitter end.

Events moved more favorably in the House. The quiet, remorseless leadership of James K. Polk kept the discussion to the point. "The Bank of the United States has set itself up as a great irresponsible rival power of the Government," he declared; and if it won this fight, no man thereafter could expect "to arrive at the first station in this great republic, without first making terms with the despot." He assailed the attempt to divert the debate into quibbles about constitutionality. "The present is, in substance and in fact, the question of recharter or no recharter. The question is, in fact, whether we shall have the republic without the bank, or the bank without the republic."

Horace Binney replied in a three-day attack on the removal; but it was in terms of argument rather than invective, and Jackson, amiably inviting him to dinner, showed him, as Binney wrote back to an amazed Philadelphia, "a succession of the most obliging civilities, of the most marked and striking kind, from the beginning to the end of a really excellent dinner in every possible sense." Cambreleng responded to Binney, and Samuel Beardsley, a rather conservative New York Democrat, added, in words which seemed to unveil the secret purposes of Jackson and Amos Kendall, that, if the credit and commerce of the country depended upon the Bank, "I, for one, say perish credit; perish commerce; . . . give us a broken, a deranged, and a worthless currency, rather than the ignoble and corrupting tyranny of an irresponsible corporation."

Perish credit; perish commerce: these chilling words struck terror in the hearts of the more apprehensive conservatives. Was not this the whole drift of the administration policy? First, the Maysville veto, then the Bank veto, then the removal of the deposits—who knew what would follow? "How far this Catilinarian conspiracy has been carried, who but the miscreants concerned in the plot can now discolse to the nation?" snarled fiery Tristram Burges, of Rhode Island. "Have they already parcelled out our cities and villages, and appointed some Lentulus to superintend their conflagration?" But Polk steered straight to his objectives, through all these furious gales, carrying through the House forthright resolutions against recharter, against restoration of the deposits, and in favor of a new deposit system employing state banks.

The President meanwhile remained unshaken by all the uproar. James Fenimore Cooper began to believe that "hickory will prove to be stronger than gold," and he need never have doubted. One day it was reported in Washington that a Baltimore mob was threatening to camp on Capitol Hill till the deposits were restored. A group of quaking administration Congressmen beseeched Jackson to say what was to be done. "Gentlemen," the old General reassured them with grim humor, "I shall be glad to see this federal mob on Capitol Hill. I will fix their heads on the iron palisades around the square to assist your deliberation. The leaders I will hang as high as Haman to deter forever all attempts to control the legislation of the Congress by intimidation and design."

Delegations of businessmen, from New York, Baltimore and Philadelphia, also beset the President. Jackson, disliking to argue with people who were either fools enough to believe Nicholas Biddle or knaves enough to work for him, would make his unshakable determination clear by launching into fearful tirades against the Bank. A deputation from New York found him writing at his desk, smoking fiercely away at his long pipe. He excused himself, finished the paper and rose. "Now gentlemen, what is your pleasure with me?" James G. King, son of Rufus King, had hardly spoken a few sentences of a prepared address asking for relief when Jackson interrupted angrily: "Go to Nicholas Biddle. We have no money here, gentlemen. Biddle has all the money. He has millions of specie in his vaults, at this moment, lying idle, and yet you come to *me* to save you from breaking." And so on, with mounting vehemence, until the visitors departed. The man who had introduced them was overtaken by a messenger on the White House stairs and asked to return to the President's office.

He found Jackson chuckling over the interview: "Didn't I manage them well?"

A Philadelphia delegation barely announced its mission when Jackson broke in with an excited speech. *"Andrew Jackson* never would restore the deposites to the bank—*Andrew Jackson* would never recharter that monster of corruption. . . . sooner than live in a country where such a power prevailed, he would seek an asylum in the wilds of Arabia." (Biddle, on hearing this, observed that he might "as well send at once and engage lodgings.") A Baltimore deputation, waiting on Taney, declared that, unless the government changed its policy, a large part of the business community would fail, and understood Taney to reply, "If *all* did fail, the policy of the government would not be changed." Jackson provided little more sympathy. "The failures that are now taking place," he told them, "are amongst the stock-jobbers, brokers, and gamblers, and would to God, they were all swept from the land!" *Go to Nicholas Biddle* was Jackson's refrain, until he felt that his interviews had been so deliberately misquoted that he would receive no more committees.

"The Nation Stands on the Very Brink of a Horrible Precipice," exclaimed Hezekiah Niles, in March, on behalf of the business community. A month later he announced with alarm that it is later than you think: *"Things cannot remain and stand still. . . .* Wives, children and property—liberty and peace—are the things which are under consideration. . . . A worse or better state must soon happen." Fanny Kemble turned a moment from her army of admirers to note that everything threatened "change and disintegration." While playing "The Inconstant" in Philadelphia, she toasted *"Here's the deposites back again"* in one scene, and the audience roared its approval. Late in the summer another English lady, sharp-eyed, spinsterish and deaf, arrived in America. The first person Harriet Martineau met was quick to inform her that the nation was on the verge of a military despotism.

The "natural aristocracy" was everywhere shocked into fantasies of collapse. Chancellor Kent departed from judicial calm to proclaim comprehensively: "I look upon Jackson as a detestable, ignorant, reckless, vain & malignant tyrant." Justice Story was sufficiently under the influence of Clay's rhetoric to observe, "Though we live under the form of a republic we are in fact under the absolute rule of a single man." He felt himself called back as in a dream to the last days of the Roman republic, when the mob shouted for Caesar, and liberty expired with the dark and prophetic words of Cicero. "It has been remarked with much justice and truth," a Missouri businessman wrote Frank Blair, "that the merchants through the United States, as a class, are opposed to our present Administration."

On the very day that Story was delivering himself of his classical vision, Edward Everett told an English banker, "The present contest is nothing less than a war of Numbers against Property." He reported the rise of the mob with horror. "In Philadelphia, after the powerful expression of sentiment proceeding from the merchants and men of business, [Congressman] Southerland cooly observed that this was only the view of Chestnut Street and Market Street; that he went to the lanes and alleys, where they held a different language." Appalling —and only one man, Daniel Webster, could save the nation, though this, of course, required certain preliminaries! Everett was candid: "If our friends in Boston mean that their houses, their lands, their stocks shall really be their own much longer, they must make the effort; they must make it at once. It is but $1000 each for one hundred gentlemen."

But Biddle could not hope to fool the business community indefinitely. More and more merchants were coming to believe that he was carrying the money pressure farther than necessary, and few would agree that it was worth breaking "all the other Banks and all the merchants" to restore Nicholas Biddle to power. Late in February, Governor George Wolf of Pennsylvania, hitherto a leading Bank Democrat, came out against the Bank. Clay probably sensed the reaction in March when Van Buren offered to bet him a suit of clothes on the elections in Virginia and New York City. The Senator responded gallantly that if the people did support the administration, he would fear self-government had failed; but it is noticeable that he did not take up the Vice-President's wager.

In the same month, the leading merchants of Boston gathered at Faneuil Hall to appoint a committee to go to Washington with another petition. When Nathan Appleton, the chairman, reached New York, he discovered his old suspicion of Biddle's motives confirmed by James G. King and Albert Gallatin. King, as chairman of a New York committee, had already threatened the Bank with exposure if it did not change its policy. (*Go to Nicholas Biddle,* the old General had said; James G. King was quick to get the point.) Though Biddle had ignored earlier attempts at persuasion, this threat spoke in another tone, and he hurried to New York for personal consultations. Appleton and others of the Boston committee backed up King and Gallatin, informing Biddle that he knew very well the contraction was not necessary for the safety of the Bank, and that his whole object was to extort a charter from the government. Biddle could not talk himself out of the hole, and he knew that repudiation by Gallatin, an honored champion of the Bank, would be fatal. "Hence the Bank had to do something," as he explained to Watmough, the Bank lackey, "for the evil of such an announcement would have been enormous." So during April the pressure relaxed, but in May it resumed with greater violence than before, though even Webster now counseled prudence.

On returning to Boston, Appleton found that, though the politicians proposed to support Biddle at any cost, the business community had lost all patience. When the contraction continued into June, he wrote a long letter to the directors of the Boston branch for transmission to Biddle. Signed by many of the solidest and most conservative merchants—such men as George Bond, Henry Lee, Warren Dutton, Amos Lawrence, G. W. Lyman, W. P. Eustis—and also approved by Abbott Lawrence and William Appleton, it abundantly documented the Jacksonian indictment from a quarter whose every predilection was on the side of Nicholas Biddle.

> *It is well understood that the Bank is pursuing a regular system of contraction apparently at the rate of about a million of Dollars per month,— the effects of which have been a renewal, since the first of May, of the pressure on the money market, and which threatens to Paralize business for the future, indefinitely, so long as it shall be continued. At the same time the Statement of the Bank for the month of June shows a degree of strength wholly unprecedented in the history of the Bank, and its ability, with perfect safety to itself, not merely to relieve the pressure, but to make discounts far beyond the present actual wants of the community.*
>
> *No satisfactory reason has been assigned for this course. It has sometimes been put forward, that it is necessary for the Bank, preparatory to wind up its concerns on the expiration of its charter—but however good a reason that may be for reducing the amount of pure accommodation loans, it cannot be considered any reason for refusing to employ its funds in discounting business paper in the commercial cities, or on the pledge of its own on other stocks.—It is not supposed that this ground of the*

necessity of this course preparatory to winding up its concerns, has been taken by the Bank, since if it were sound it would go far to justify the government, in the removal of the deposites. . . .

Under these circumstances it is not perhaps surprising that public opinion, even amongst the most intelligent of our commercial men of the Whig Party, should attribute to the Bank the design, unnecessarily if not wantonly to continue the pressure for the purpose of operating upon the fall elections. And it is quite apparent, that the general diffusion of this opinion, must operate most unfavorably upon the Bank, and in some measure upon the party which supports it.—It may even create a necessity for the Whigs in self-defense to separate themselves entirely from that institution.—In this state of things the subscribers are of opinion, that the interest of the Bank, of the country and of the party, requires a change of measures, and that no time should be lost in adopting it, as the only mode of averting a most dangerous crisis.

Biddle responded evasively and desperately, apparently even denying that there was any systematic curtailment of discounts. In a second letter Appleton blasted Biddle's claims with a grim array of evidence, mostly taken from the Bank's own statements, concluding with the harsh but essential question: "what is the policy of the Bank? why is it pursuing a course of policy so utterly irreconcilable with the ordinary principles of Banking?"[16]

Biddle acknowledged the answer himself on September 16 when he gave the lie direct to the case for curtailment by suddenly entering on a policy of expansion. After reducing its loans by well over eighteen million dollars from August 1, 1833, to November 1, 1834, under the plea of winding up its affairs, the Bank in the next five months *increased* its loans by almost fourteen and a half million. On June 1, 1835, the loans were almost what they were when Biddle's campaign began in August 1833, and the note circulation was actually greater than ever before. The panic was over, and the Bank had not recovered the deposits.

Somewhere along the way, Biddle had lost his grip on reality. Ambition, vanity and love of power had crossed the thin line to megalo-

---

[16] Appleton's opinion of Biddle did not improve with time. "The case of the U. States Bank," he wrote in 1853, ". . . was the result of Mr. Biddle's wanton abuse of the power intrusted to him. He pursued a course of unnecessary contraction under the pretence that it was necessary to the winding up of the Bank, until after the rising of Congress, when finding that he could not coerce them into renewal of the charter he most wantonly and recklessly increased his discounts." Appleton to Samuel Hooper, February 21, 1853.

mania. So little had he understood the American people that he ordered the circulation of thirty thousand copies of the Bank veto as a campaign document for Henry Clay. He completely misconceived the grounds of the Jacksonian attack; and, when the President stated them, Biddle brushed the explanation aside as mere demagogy. As late as the summer of 1833, he still believed that Jackson's secret purpose was to found a new national bank of his own.

Senator Theodore Frelinghuysen of New Jersey, his friend and defender, found the exact image for such a man. "There," Frelinghuysen observed with satisfaction, speaking on the effects of the panic, "sits Mr. Biddle, in the presidency of the Bank, as calm as a summer's morning, with his directors around him, receiving his salary, with everything moving on harmoniously: and has this stroke reached him? No, sir. The blow has fallen on the friends of the President [Jackson] and the country." What a touching picture of innocent virtue! (Roger B. Taney muttered ungraciously, "Nero is said to have fiddled while Rome was burning, but I have not learned from history that even his courtiers praised him for doing so.")

Biddle continued to console himself by fantasy. "My theory in regard to the present condition of the country is in a few words this," he wrote in 1835. "For the last few years the Executive power of the Govt. has been wielded by a mere gang of banditti. I know these people perfectly—keep the police on them constantly—and in my deliberate judgment, there is not on the the face of the earth a more profligate crew." He warned the alumni of Princeton of the insolent ambitions of "some frontier Cataline." "It cannot be," he concluded with a flash of bravado, "that our free nation can long endure the vulgar dominion of ignorance and profligacy. You will live to see the laws re-established—these banditti will be scourged back to their caverns—the penitentiary will reclaim its fugitives in office, and the only remembrance which history will preserve of them, is the energy with which you resisted and defeated them."

Hard Money

The determination which enabled Jackson to resist the hysteria of panic came basically from the possession of an alternative policy of his own. Madison had surrendered to a corresponding, though less intense, pressure in 1816 because he had no constructive program to offer. But, for Jackson, the emotions and ideas which underlay the hard-money case against the Bank were crystallizing into a coherent and concrete set of measures, designed to capture the government for "the humble members of society," as Hamilton's system had captured it for "the rich and powerful."

The Jeffersonian tradition provided the main inspiration for this program. The Virginia condemnation of paper money, pronounced by Jefferson, formulated profoundly by Taylor, kept pure and uncompromising by Macon and Randolph, had passed on as a vital ideological legacy to Jackson, Benton, Van Buren, Polk, Cambreleng. Yet it was handed down as a series of keen but despairing criticisms delivered in the shadow of an invincible industrialism. The creative statesmen of the Jackson administration now proposed to transform it into a positive governmental policy.

The Bank War played an indispensable role in the precipitation of hard-money ideas. It dramatized currency questions in a way which captured the imagination of the people and excited their desire for further action on the financial front. It enlisted the enthusiasm of intellectuals, stimulating them to further analysis, widening the range and competence of economic theory. It tightened class lines, and the new bitterness of feeling sharpened the intellectual weapons.

Above all, the Bank War triumphantly established Jackson in the confidence of the people. Their faith in him had survived ordeals and won vindication: thereafter, when faced by a choice between Jackson and a cherished policy, most of them would choose Jackson. The effect of this mandate was particularly to sell the West on an intricate economic program, which many westerners did not understand and which ran counter to their preconceptions.

The uncertainty about the West had postponed the avowal of the hard-money system.[17] The veto message, written by three men of known hard-money convictions, Jackson, Taney and Kendall, sup-

---

[17] Orestes A. Brownson later declared that he had been urged in 1831 by "men high in the confidence of the party . . . to support the administration of that day, on the ground that it was opposed to all corporate banking, whether state or national." This was, of course, long before any such purpose was avowed as party policy.

pressed mention of the doctrine, as if by main force. But the election of 1832 increased Jackson's confidence. He could have lost the entire West and still have broken even with Clay, but he carried the whole West except for Kentucky.[18] He now felt certain of vigorous national support, and also of probable western support, even for his economic ideas. Not all the West would follow, of course, and even three leaders from his own state turned against him on the currency question: his old friend Hugh Lawson White, young and able John Bell, and the picturesque if somewhat phony frontiersman, Davy Crockett. Others of his western supporters, like Robert J. Walker of Mississippi, were careful to disclaim any hard-money leanings.[19] But, on the whole, the magic of Jackson's name was fairly certain to win western approval for almost anything.

He thus was emboldened to come out publicly for the hard-money policy, expressing himself first in his interview with the Philadelphia delegation a few days before his second inaugural. His objective, he said, was gradually to reduce the circulation of paper, by forbidding deposit banks to issue small notes and by refusing such notes in payment for taxes, until all notes under twenty dollars would be eliminated and "thus a metallic currency be ensured for all the common purposes of life, while the use of bank notes would be confined to those engaged in commerce."

Soon after, he reorganized his cabinet, turning it for the first time into an effective unit. McLane and Duane, both evidently hostile to a radical economic policy, were replaced by John Forsythe in the State Department and Roger B. Taney in the Treasury. William T. Barry, whose incompetence as Postmaster General finally drove

---

[18] The "West" here includes Alabama, Mississippi, Louisiana, Kentucky, Tennessee, Ohio, Indiana, Illinois and Missouri. Jackson had only to carry one western state to get a majority of the electoral votes.

[19] "God save us from the wild, visionary, ruinous, and impractical schemes of the senator of Missouri," Walker cried in 1837. ". . . Sir, in resistance to the power of the Bank of the United States, in opposition to the re-establishment of any similar institution, the Senator from Missouri would find Mr. W. with him; but he could not enlist as a recruit in this new crusade against the banks of his own and every other State in the Union. . . . [It] was not, he believed, anticipated by any one of his constituents." Note Walker's emphasis on "resistance to the power of the Bank" as his main motive in fighting it. In 1840, when Walker, now a strong hard-money man, undertook to explain the origins of the hard-money policy, he correctly declared: "The workingmen of the city of New York, next, perhaps to the patriot Jackson and the Senator from Missouri, may be justly considered the original Loco Focos and hard money men of the Union."

even Jackson to despair, was succeeded by Amos Kendall. Benjamin F. Butler of New York, Van Buren's former law partner, followed Taney as Attorney General, and, after Taney's eventual rejection by the Senate, Levi Woodbury was promoted to the Treasury. In this circle of staunch hard-money men Lewis Cass could only relapse into mournful silence. The administration was now streamlined for action.

The hard-money system owed many of its maxims and dogmas to the Jeffersonians, and much of its vitality to the northern workingmen who backed it so warmly; but the man to whom, after Jackson, Benton and Taney, it perhaps owed most for its emergence as a constructive policy was William M. Gouge, the Philadelphia editor and economist. Gouge put the hard-money doctrines in the clearest form, furnished the most cogent indictment of the paper system, stated the general problems in a way (unlike the Jeffersonian) relevant to a society where finance capitalism was well entrenched, and proved unfailingly resourceful in working out the practical measures to realize his policy. Thirty-seven years old in 1833, he had been from 1823 to 1831 editor and part proprietor of the *Philadelphia Gazette.* For the next two years, he busied himself with a treatise on the banking system, published in Philadelphia in February 1833, under the title *A Short History of Paper Money and Banking in the United States.*[20]

The work consisted of an analysis of the social consequences of the paper system, followed by a detailed account of the history of paper money in America. The first section set forth the broad theoretical case, while the second provided the crushing documentation. Facts were Gouge's most powerful weapons; and in a plain, circumstantial way, occasionally flavored by irony, constantly buttressed by names, dates and citations, he supplied a crisp and comprehensive statement of the hard-money position.

The book became an instant success. Probably no work in economics had ever circulated so widely in the United States. The first edition was nearly exhausted by the fall of 1834, and, in 1835, it was reprinted in cheap stereotyped form to sell for twenty-

[20] Gouge's own copy, with interleaved notes, is in the Harvard College Library.

five cents. By 1837 it had gone into a third edition. It was serialized in the *New York Evening Post* in 1834, and later in the *Washington Globe* and many other papers. William Cobbett published an English edition, and an abridged version was translated into French and printed at Brussels. All the radicals of the day read it voraciously— William Leggett, Theophilus Fisk, Orestes A. Brownson, William Cullen Bryant—and paid cordial tribute to the author. It delighted Frank Blair, was passed from hand to hand in the inner circle of the government; and early in 1835 Gouge was called down to Washington to take a job under Levi Woodbury in the Treasury Department. There his terse and hard-hitting memoranda were to exert for many years an important influence on financial policy.

The book's success was deserved. Its historical sections went unchallenged, even by the most ardent defenders of the system; and Gouge's keenness of analysis, as well as his accuracy, has won the approval of our ablest historians of banking. When it was first published Condy Raguet called it "decidedly the best work on Banking that we have ever met with." Modern students have treated it with similar respect. As William Graham Sumner, no friend of Jacksonian democracy, put it, Gouge "studied this system [of paper money] in its operation more thoroughly and with more intelligence than anybody else." A popular jingle expressed contemporary appreciation:—

> *Of modern books, the best I know—*
> *The author all the world is thanking—*
> *One written more for use than show,*
> *Is quaintly titled, "Gouge on Banking."*

> *But still improvements might be made,*
> *Whilst books on books the world is scrouging,*
> *Let Biddle try to help the trade,*
> *And write one titled, "Banks on Gouging."*[21]

The hard-money policy was conceived by Gouge and its other

---

[21] The leading modern historian of early banking theories [Miller] remarks: "Gouge was one of the most thorough students of our early banking and also one of its keenest and most influential critics."

champions as a total alternative to the Hamiltonian system. Its central point was the exclusion of banks from control over the currency. It was not, as its opponents persisted in describing it, a demand for the annihilation of the banking system and the establishment of an exclusively metallic currency. It proposed merely to limit bank paper to commercial transactions, and to confine banks to the functions of deposit and discount, slowly withdrawing from them the privilege of note issue.

The main purposes were three. One was essentially economic: to prevent periodic depressions; another essentially political: to prevent the rise within the state of independent powers, not responsible to the people and able to defy the government; and the third essentially social: to prevent the rule of a moneyed aristocracy systematically exploiting the "humble members of society."

The economic argument was brought to public attention largely by Benton and Gouge, and it drew somewhat on the reports of the English bullionists. The political was, of course, central in the American tradition; it was perhaps the particular contribution of the frontier to this controversy, and had been thrust forward during the Kentucky Relief War. The social argument represented the Jeffersonian legacy and was indebted considerably in its details to John Taylor of Caroline. As political expediency dictated, one could be stressed at certain times and others concealed. The Bank veto, for example, confined itself mainly to the second argument, with some suggestions of the third. But, after the election of 1832 had demonstrated the national confidence in Jackson, the administration began to urge all three. Gouge's book stated them conveniently, and Jackson's Farewell Address provided an excellent brief summary.

The economic argument turned ultimately on varying attitudes toward the concrete economy as an environment for living, rather than on disagreement over abstract principles. Alexander Hamilton in his eagerness to make out a case for paper money had once argued that note issue constituted "an absolute increase of capital," but this obviously untenable view was pretty well abandoned by 1830. Even the most fervent admirers of paper money acknowledged the value of increasing the proportion of specie in the circulating medium. Nicholas Biddle himself in some moods was a hard-money man.[22] Daniel Webster loudly and constantly proclaimed the evils of overissue, except when he had to vote on a measure intended to prevent it.

Yet men like Biddle and Webster plainly preferred in last analysis a speculative economy, with quick expansion, huge gains and huge risks. During the investigation of the Bank by the Clayton Committee, when Cambreleng asked whether the existing banking system did not encourage speculation, Biddle replied: "Until the nature of man is changed, men will become speculators and bankrupts—under any system—and I do not perceive that our own is specially calculated to create them." Cambreleng became more specific. Would not the system be more healthy if note issue were forbidden? Biddle hedged: "I fear I do not comprehend all this. . . . That banks do occasional mischief there can be no doubt; but until some valuable improvement is found which supplies unmixed good, this is no objection to them. And constituted as they now are, the banks of the United States may be considered safe instruments of commerce."

Biddle and men like him were willing to take the chance of depression in exchange for the thrills and opportunities of boom. But others confronted a speculative situation with much less confidence. Men of small and fairly fixed income—farmers, laborers, mechanics, petty shopkeepers, many of the southern planters—felt themselves the victims of baffling and malevolent economic forces which they could not profit by or control.

On the most obvious level, the working classes believed that they were regularly cheated by paper money. A good portion of the small notes they received in wages were depreciated, worthless or counterfeit. Unscrupulous employers even bought up depreciated notes and palmed them off on their workingmen at face value. And, in the larger economic picture, all the stable-income classes had to stand by helpless and impotent during the unpredictable rise and fall of prices or ebb and flow of credit. Their reaction to a

[22] In 1832 Biddle recommended the following reforms: "First, to widen the basis of the metallic circulation, by abolishing the use of small notes. . . . And second, to annex to the non-payment of specie by the banks, so heavy a penalty . . . as would deprive the banks of all temptation to incur the risk of insolvency."

gambling economy was not delight at the opening up of chances for gain, but an intense feeling of insecurity. Jackson expressed their pent-up exasperation in his exclamation to the Baltimore committee on stock-jobbers, brokers and gamblers—"would to God, they were all swept from the land!"

The administration proposed to rescue the working classes from this treacherous economic order. "It is time," declared Taney, "that the just claims of this portion of society should be regarded in our legislation in relation to the currency. So far we have been providing facilities for those employed in extensive commerce, and have left the mechanic and the laborer to all the hazards of an insecure and unstable circulating medium." Jackson pronounced it "the duty of every government, so to regulate its currency as to protect this numerous class, as far as practicable, from the impositions of avarice and fraud."

Prompted by these aims, the Jacksonians began to sketch out fairly coherent theories of self-generating business cycles. Condy Raguet was perhaps the first to adumbrate the general theory, and Gouge set forth the classic description in his *Paper Money*.

In its simplest outline the theory was this: Banks incline to over-issue their notes. Prices then rise, and a speculative fever begins to spread. Excited by the appearance of prosperity that accompanies boom, people spend freely. The general expansion of credit leads to overtrading and inflation. Every new business operation on credit creates more promissory notes, and these increase the demand for discounts, till finally the currency depreciates so greatly that specie is required for export in order to pay foreign debts. With specie at a premium, contraction sets in. Banks call in their loans, timid people start runs on banks, contraction turns to panic, and panic to collapse. "One man is unable to pay his debts," wrote Gouge. "His creditor depended on him for the means of paying a third person to whom he is himself indebted. The circle extends through society. Multitudes become bankrupt, and a few successful speculators get possession of the earnings and savings of many of their frugal and industrious neighbors."

The more careful analysts pointed out the complex interdependence of bank credit and general business activity, but political pamphleteers skipped the subtleties and blamed depressions on the paper-money system alone. Bank paper, they argued, stimulated the original boom psychology by beguiling businessmen into overtrading at times of rising prices. It linked the whole system so intimately that the failure of one merchant might prevent a dozen others from meeting their obligations. And most particularly, the expansion or contraction of paper in circulation bore only a perverse and futile relation to actual business needs. In the words of George Bancroft, it "expands when rising prices require a check to enterprise, and contracts when falling prices make credit most desirable." Or, as Theophilus Fisk put it with more venom, "The moment a spirit of speculation can be excited, the banks increase the flame by pouring oil upon it; the instant a reaction takes place, they add to the distress a thousand fold."

If by modern standards highly inadequate, this currency theory of depression yet represented a considerable advance over no theory at all. Very little was then said of general overproduction as a cause of depression. Some men, like Robert Rantoul, Jr., laid special stress on the glutting of markets as a factor in crisis; but many would agree with Gouge's note on such arguments, that "if the real wants of the community, and not their ability to pay, be considered, it will not, perhaps, be found that any one useful trade or profession has too many members," and accept his emphasis on the problem of "ability to pay." In 1843 Orestes A. Brownson in a brilliant passage placed the blame squarely on "our vicious method of distributing the products of labor." "More can be produced, in any given year," he wrote, "with the present productive power, than can be sold in any given five years." The fault lies in distribution.

> We create a surplus—that is a surplus, not when we consider the wants of the people, but when we consider the state of the markets—and then must slacken our hand till the surplus is worked off. During this time, while we are working off the surplus, while the mills run short time, or stop altogether, the workmen must want employment. The evil is inherent in the system.

But this line of thought evidently failed to strike much response and was carried no farther.

The political argument—opposition to the rise of independent powers within the state—had general premises deeply entrenched in the national consciousness. Everyone, from right to left, believed, with more or fewer qualifications, that sovereignty belonged to the people. It was but one step from this to declare that the people's government, therefore, should not be defied by private institutions; and it was easy to extend this proposition to economic institutions, as well as political.

In their nature as corporations, banks gave rise to one set of objections, springing from their monopoly of financial prerogative through special charter. Indeed, they provided so much the most flagrant instances of abuse of corporate privilege that they were mainly responsible for fixing national attention on the problem.

Their power over the currency was viewed as an especially grave encroachment on the domain of government. The regulation of the currency, in the words of Benton, was "one of the highest and most delicate acts of sovereign power . . . precisely equivalent to the power to create currency"; and he considered it "too great a power to be trusted to any banking company whatever, or to any authority but the highest and most responsible which was known to our form of Government." Commercial credit was another matter, "an affair of trade," as Cambreleng put it, "and not of government"; and the logic of this position pointed to the abolition of banks of note issue, on the one hand, and the establishment of free competition among banks of discount and deposit, on the other. The crucial error of the federal government, according to the hard-money advocates, lay in accepting bank notes in the payment of federal dues, by which it thus extended and virtually underwrote the credit of the banks. The remedy was to exclude bank notes from government payments.

The behavior of banks in practice, moreover, violated the national faith in popular rule. The most powerful argument against Biddle's Bank was always its calm assumption of independence. "The Bank of the United States," Jackson charged, "is in itself a Government which has gradually increased in strength from the day of its establishment. The question between it and the people has become one of power." Biddle's conduct, in 1834, in refusing to allow a House committee to investigate the Bank records or examine the

Bank officers, was simply the climax of his oft-expressed theory of the Bank's independence. "This powerful corporation, and those who defend it," as Taney said, without much exaggeration, "seem to regard it as an independent sovereignty, and to have forgotten that it owes any duties to the People, or is bound by any laws but its own will."

But Biddle was simply exhibiting on a larger scale habits long established in banking experience. William Graham Sumner concisely summed up the pretensions of the banks:—

> *The bankers had methods of doing things which were customary and conventional, but . . . contrary both to ordinary morality and to law as applied to similar matters outside of banks. . . . The banks also disregarded law so habitually that it became a commonplace that law could not bind them. . . . We search almost in vain through the law reports for any decisions on the rights or authority of the State over banks or the duties of banks to the State. It may be said that no attempts were made to test or enforce the right of the State against banks, and that, as a matter of practice, it had none. The banks were almost irresponsible. Such decisions as bear at all on the authority of the State over banks proceed from the attempts of the banks to resist the exercise of any authority whatever.*

Such a situation obviously could not be long borne. As Theophilus Fisk put it, "Either the State is sovereign, or the Banks are."

The social argument—the battle against domination by "the rich and powerful"—represented the culmination of the hard-money doctrine. The economic and political arguments, though capable of standing by themselves, were ultimately directed at conditions preliminary to the question: who shall rule in the state? The recurrent economic crises were evil, not only in themselves, but because they facilitated a redistribution of wealth that built up the moneyed aristocracy. The irresponsible political sovereignties were evil, not only in themselves, but because they provided the aristocracy with instruments of power and places of refuge.

The Bank War compelled people to speculate once again about the conflict of class. "There are but two parties," exclaimed Thomas Hart Benton, giving the period its keynote; "there never has been but two parties . . . founded in the radical question, whether *People,* or *Property,* shall govern? Democracy implies a government by the people. . . . Aristocracy implies a government of the rich . . . and in these words are contained the sum of party distinction."

The paper banking system was considered to play a leading role in this everlasting struggle. Men living by the issue and circulation of paper money produced nothing; they added nothing to the national income; yet, they flourished and grew wealthy. Their prosperity, it was argued, must be stolen from the proceeds of productive labor—in other words, from the honest but defenseless "humble members of society"; and Gouge extensively annotated the modes of plunder.

The system was further important in the strategy of the warfare. Taney described the big Bank as "the centre, and the citadel of the moneyed power." "A national bank," declared the Massachusetts Democratic convention of 1837, "is the bulwark of the aristocracy; its outpost, and its rallying point. It is the bond of union for those who hold that Government should rest on property." To a lesser degree all banks acted as strongholds of conservatism. They provided the funds and often the initiative for combat. Their lawyers, lobbyists and newspapers were eternally active. Politicians would gather in their board rooms and consult their presidents and accept gifts of stock. More than any other kind of corporate enterprise, banks boldly intervened in politics when they felt their interests menaced.

The hard-money policy attacked both the techniques of plunder and the general strategy of warfare. By doing away with paper money, it proposed to restrict the steady transfer of wealth from the farmer and laborer to the business community. By limiting banks to commercial credit and denying them control over the currency, it proposed to lessen their influence and power. By reducing the proportion of paper money, it proposed to moderate the business cycle, and order the economy to the advantage of the worker rather than the speculator. It was a coherent policy, based on the best economic thought of the day, and formulated on a higher intellectual level than the alternatives of the opposition.

By origin and interest, it was a policy which appealed mainly to the submerged classes of the East and to the farmers of the South rather than to the frontier. Historians have too long been misled by the tableau of Jackson, the wild backwoodsman, erupting into the White House. In fact, the hard-money doctrine, which was not at all a frontier doctrine, was the controlling policy of the administration from the winter of 1833 on; and for some time it had been the secret goal of a small group led by Jackson, Taney, Benton and Kendall, and passively encouraged by Van Buren. From the removal of the deposits to the end of Van Buren's presidency in 1840 this clique of radical Democrats sought to carry out the policy in its full implications. As soon as the hard-money program was divorced from the glamour of the Hero of New Orleans and had to rest on its inherent appeal, it did very badly in the West.

Andrew Jackson ably summed up its broad aims. "The planter, the farmer, the mechanic, and the laborer," he wrote, "all know that their success depends upon their own industry and economy, and that they must not expect to become suddenly rich by the fruits of their toil." These classes "form the great body of the people of the United States; they are the bone and sinew of the country." Yet "they are in constant danger of losing their fair influence in the Government." Why? "The mischief springs from the power which the money interest derives from a paper currency, which they are able to control, from the multitude of corporations with exclusive privileges which they have succeeded in obtaining in the different States." His warning to his people was solemn. "Unless you become more watchful . . . you will in the end find that the most important powers of Government have been given or bartered away, and the control over your dearest interests has passed into the hands of these corporations."

Taney and Benton worked out the details of the immediate hard-money measures. They proposed to increase the metallic basis of the currency in two directions: by the restoration of gold to circulation, and by the suppression of small notes. The first measure had been for many years close to Benton's heart. Gold had long been undervalued, at the ratio of 15 to 1, with the result that no gold eagles and only a scattering of other gold coins had been minted since 1805, and most of these rapidly left the country. Benton argued that, if the gold were not thus expelled, the amount of specie derivable from foreign commerce, added to the amount obtained from American mines, could supply all financial needs without recourse to small notes or "shinplasters." In June 1834 his bill to revise the valuation to 16 to 1 passed Congress. As an expression of the strictly economic intentions of the hard-money policy, it made a broad appeal to all men of good will, winning the support of John Quincy Adams, Webster and Calhoun. Only diehards like Clay and Horace Binney opposed it.

The change in the coinage ratio was one of Benton's greatest triumphs. He exulted in the new flow of gold to the government mints. "This is the money the Constitution provides," he would say, "and I will not have anything to do with any other kind." Or, in another mood, "What! Do you want a coroner's jury to sit and say, 'Old Bullion died of shinplasters?'" Old Bullion was the name his hard-money fixation had won him, among his friends, at least; his enemies called him sarcastically the Gold Humbug. For a time, foes of the hard-money policy sought to ridicule Benton's reform out of existence. Gilt counters were circulated, with grotesque figures and caustic inscriptions—the "whole hog" and the "better currency." But no one dared argue directly that this infusion of specie would not improve the health of the economy.

The effects of revaluation were immediate. Levi Woodbury reported in December 1836 that more gold had been coined in the twelve months preceding than in the first sixteen years of the mint's existence, and more in the two and a half years since revaluation than in the thirty-one before. In October 1833 there had been only thirty million dollars of specie in the country, of which twenty-six million was in banks. In December 1836 there was seventy-three million dollars, of which only forty-five million was in banks.[23]

Yet the revival of gold would hardly be enough without measures to suppress small notes. This proposal had the sanction, not only of the theory of Adam Smith (and of Nicholas Biddle), but of the

---

[23] It is hard to assess the hard-money claim that specie could have altogether displaced small notes. Gouge calculated in 1841 that "barely by detaining in the country such amounts of gold and silver as come to us in the present course of trade, we should, in ten or twelve years, have a perfectly sound circulating medium." Whether or not 100 percent displacement was possible, or desirable, an increase in the proportion of specie was badly needed.

example of Great Britain, which had established a £5 minimum in 1829. Most economically literate conservatives acknowledged the theoretical advantages of suppression;[24] and Congress and the Treasury, drawing on their authority to define the kind of money receivable in federal payments, could exert real, if limited, influence on the issues of state banks. A joint resolution of 1816 had made all notes from specie-paying banks acceptable in tax payments. In a Treasury circular of April 1835, all notes under $5 were banned, and banks holding government deposits were forbidden to issue such notes. In February 1836 a similar circular banned notes under $10, and a congressional act of April 1836 prohibited notes under $20 after March 3, 1837, and required immediate convertibility for all notes. The conditions imposed on the deposit banks controlled their stock transactions, as well as their note issue, calling for weekly statements and ordering that they should always be open for examination. Declared Secretary Woodbury, "All mystery on the subject of banking should cease."

But these regulations had little effect on the general banking situation. Only by deliberately rousing public opinion within the states could the administration hope to abolish small notes. In some states tattered shinplasters circulated with face values of 12½ or even 6¼ cents. In December 1834 Jackson appealed to the states to follow the national example. Pennsylvania, Maryland and Virginia already had legislation against small bills. In 1835 Maine, Connecticut and New York outlawed notes below $5, while North Carolina, Georgia, Alabama, Ohio, Indiana and Missouri also passed restrictive measures.

But the administration's campaign came too late. The wise counsels of the hard-money advocates were drowned out by the roar of the nation's greatest boom in years. The Bank of the United States alone enlarged its loans an average of two and a half million dollars a month and its paper circulation by a total of ten million dollars between December 1834, and July 1835. Smaller banks rushed to fol-

---

[24] Some conservatives would argue of shinplasters, however, like a Massachusetts committee in 1840, "They float as free as the snow flakes, and every hand is held out to catch as much as it can of the beneficial shower. If they were found to be unsafe or inconvenient, they would instantly be rejected."

low, increasing the amount of paper money from eighty-two million dollars on January 1, 1835, to one hundred and eight million, a year later, and one hundred and twenty million by December 1, 1836.

Wages climbed, opportunity seemed limitless and riches appeared to lie everywhere. A popular tract of 1836—*The Book of Wealth; in Which It Is Proved from the Bible, that It Is the Duty of Every Man to Become Rich*—suggests the temper of the day. Designed to allay any religious misgivings about joining at the trough, the book earnestly declared one thing to be certain: "no man can be obedient to God's will as revealed in the Bible, without, as the general result, becoming wealthy."

The administration watched the speculative mania with profound alarm. In the *Globe* Frank Blair repeatedly voiced the deep anxieties of the hard-money circle. "We have again and again warned the community," he wrote in the spring of 1835, "of the infatuation which had seized them since the panic, to embark in every species of extravagant speculation." A month later: "this state of things cannot last. . . . A reaction is as certain to take place as the sun is to continue its diurnal course." After a year of similiar remarks: "The only remedy is to be found in banking less and trading less."

Jackson, in the early months of 1836, lifted his voice in conversation against "the mad career" in which the nation was rushing to ruin. Benton declared angrily in the Senate: "I did not join in putting down the Bank of the United States, to put up a wilderness of local banks. I did not join in putting down the paper currency of a national bank, to put up a national paper currency of a thousand local banks. I did not strike Caesar," he concluded in magnificent wrath, "to make Anthony master of Rome. . . . The present bloat in the paper system cannot continue. . . . The revulsion will come, as surely as it did in 1819–1820." When Secretary Woodbury made his report in December 1836, he had to predict that the inflation would "produce much distress, embarrassment, and ruin, before this specie can be duly equalized, the excesses of paper sufficiently curtailed, and the exorbitant discounts gradually lessened."

A basic cause of the inflation was land speculation, and the administration had already moved to plug up this great hole in the national economy. The receivability of bank notes in payment for the public lands had practically converted the national domain into a fund for the redemption of the notes, providing in effect a capital for seven or eight hundred institutions to bank on, and filling the Treasury with more or less worthless paper. Benton had pointed out in detail how land sales passed on to the government the job of underwriting the whole banking system. Speculators would borrow five, ten, twenty, fifty thousand dollars in paper from banks on the condition of using it on the frontier. They would then pay the notes to government land offices in exchange for land, which served as security for additional loans; meanwhile, the notes circulated freely as land-office money, some never returning to the original bank for redemption, the rest only after a long interval. This racket not only subsidized the banking interest—land sales had risen from four million dollars a year to five million a quarter—but it also, in Benton's words, irretrievably entangled "the federal Government with the ups and downs of the whole paper system, and all the fluctuations, convulsions, and disasters, to which it was subject."

Benton introduced a resolution requiring that the public lands be paid for in specie. Webster, with his usual policy of supporting sound money except when concrete measures were proposed which might secure it, led the attack on this measure, and a combination of Whigs and conservative Democrats killed it in the Senate. But after adjournment Jackson had Benton draw up an executive order embodying his idea, and the famous "Specie Circular" was issued.

The business community grew furious over this latest evidence of executive despotism. When Congress reassembled in December, the Whigs demanded the repeal of the Circular and the reopening of the land offices to wildcat money, and the Democrats split wide under the pressure. One wing, led by William Cabell Rives of Virginia and N. P. Tallmadge of New York, emerged as defenders of the state banks. Benton vainly urged the imminence of a financial explosion which would leave the Treasury holding the bag; but his efforts won him little more than denunciation as "that most miserable Jacobin of the woods of Missouri, who, with an impudence and insolence unparalleled, has attempted to overthrow the commercial and financial relations and institutions of this country." The final vote disclosed a tiny group of five men, led by Benton and Silas Wright, upholding the hard-money position. The bill passed the House and went to the

President on the day before adjournment. Firm to the end, the old General returned it with his veto.

Jackson thus had to overrule Congress to sustain the hard-money policy. But the Specie Circular furnished the only tense financial issue in the last years of his administration. After the panic session the great scenes of battle began to shift to the states. Here, in places inaccessible to the long arm and grim energy of General Jackson, little bands of devoted Jacksonians fought to stem the rush for bank and corporate charters, unfolding the potentialities of the Jacksonian program, enriching the techniques and amplifying the intellectual resources.

Above all, these local battles called forth the common people in cities, towns and country—the poor day laborer, the industrious mechanic, the hard-handed farmer—the "humble members of society" everywhere. They listened for hours on hot summer days to dry expositions of financial policy. They crowded in bare and unheated halls on cold winter nights to hear about the evils of banking. They read, and thumbed, and passed along tracts and speeches attacking the paper system. They saw the dizzy climb of prices, wages lagging behind, raged silently at discounted bank notes, and wondered at the behavior of Democratic politicians pledged against voting for incorporations. They talked among themselves, with shrewdness and good sense and alarm. . . . Their discontent was real and widespread. It found its leaders, and the experience of these years prepared them for one great final drive on the national scene.

Bray Hammond

APPRAISAL OF SCHLESINGER'S
AGE OF JACKSON

Mr. Schlesinger's book is important and abounds in excellences: it deals with a significant period, it is comprehensive in its interest, and it is entertainingly written. Mr. Schlesinger has a fine talent for peopling an epoch vividly. But his book is marred by two faults. One is a Manichaean naiveté with respect to the nobility of all things Jacksonian and the sordidness of all things opposed. The other is a fumbling treatment of economic matters and particularly of the Bank of the United States.

Mr. Schlesinger's vocabulary purrs over his friends. The landscapes at the Hermitage and Kinderhook smile in a fashion not noticeable where Whigs and Federalists live. The Jacksonian leaders have a "pervading insight," their wrath is "magnificent," one or another of them is "handsome," "grave," "masterly," "erudite," "thoughtful," "quiet," "intelligent," "brilliant," etc., etc., and the old hero himself is touchingly fond of children. The opposition is a sorry outfit. They are Bank "lackeys," they "roar" and "snarl," they deal in "hullabaloo," they are "phony," they have "fantasies," they work "backstairs," their best minds are "opaque," and one gets the impression that Mr. Schlesinger never thinks of them as loving little children at all. Jackson's trick of evading awkward questions by simulating an apoplectic rage that filled his visitors with fear lest the aged president burst a blood vessel on their account is described with affectionate amusement and admiration. The immense services of Hamilton to his country are disregarded. The reader is allowed to look at Van Buren only through high-powered magnifying glasses. Marshall and Story are written down with casual finality, and Taney is promoted as if no dissent existed; Webster is about the only member of Mr. Schlesinger's flock of goats whose defense he bothers to notice.

This review of Schlesinger's *The Age of Jackson* is reprinted from *The Journal of Economic History*, 6 (May 1946), 79–84, by permission of the New York University Press.

The Bank war is properly very important in Mr. Schlesinger's account, and yet he does not make the Bank of the United States a clearly functioning financial institution nor Nicholas Biddle a central banker with specific monetary policies and programs that can be appraised. Instead he makes the Bank a dim sort of moneyed monstrosity and Biddle a vague, sinister figure, "drunk with power," whose career is a darkened background for Jackson's gleaming achievements. This makes poor history. The Bank of the United States was a central bank and should be discussed as such. But Mr. Schlesinger never uses the term, never mentions the purposes for which the Bank was set up, and never but casually speaks of its functions as public in their nature. He says it was "privately controlled"; but so was the Bank of England and so was practically every other similar institution till recent times. He speaks of the Bank's "profitable relations with the government" as if they were one-sided. He even says the Bank "allowed the government to appoint" five directors—a preposterous statement that may be intended for sarcasm but will be taken by most readers at face value. One might as well assert that the Treasury, for example, or any other government department "allows" the President and Congress to say who shall be at its head; for it was by authority of an act of Congress creating the Bank that the government directors were appointed by the President, with confirmation by the Senate.

That the Bank was a public institution formed at the instance of the government and for its convenience, that under Biddle's management it performed its depository services efficiently, furnished a sound and uniform currency, and regulated the state banks, and that the state banks and their borrowers resented its restraint upon credit —these are facts that the Jacksonians liked to ignore. It is less excusable to ignore them now, for they are facts that Gallatin, Dunbar, Catterall, Dewey, and other scholars, on the basis of known information, long ago put outside the field of intelligent controversy. Mr. Schlesinger does not wholly ignore them, but he mentions them in an offhand way as if they had no special significance. "In destroying the Bank," he says, "Jackson had removed a valuable brake on credit expansion; and in sponsoring the system of deposit in state banks he had accelerated the tendencies toward inflation." Mr. Schlesinger glides over startling facts like these, unstartled; and recognizes no need to reconcile them with his general picture of the Bank as an outlaw institution, obscurely dangerous because it "had too much power."

As to the reality of this power, "there could be no question," he says; and he goes clear out on the limb to say that the Bank "enjoyed a virtual monopoly of the currency and practically complete control over credit and the price level." This is sheer romance. Mr. Schlesinger contradicts himself to indulge in it, for he often speaks elsewhere of the currency issues of the local banks, clearly implying thereby that no "monopoly" existed. In reality, of course, the Bank furnished about a quarter of the total paper circulation. As for "practically complete control over credit," the Bank had nothing of the sort, nor has any central bank ever achieved it, even though it should. As for "practically complete" control of the price level, the idea is ridiculous; it would be hard to surpass its utter detachment from the findings of price analysts and historians, to say nothing of common sense. But Mr. Schlesinger leaves the solid earth frequently, in little things as well as big. For example, he speaks of the Bank's "alacrity in opening new offices" in 1831 and 1832 while renewal of the charter was pending, as conclusive evidence, in Taney's words, of its determination to fasten itself on the country. R. C. H. Catterall found "not a grain of evidence" to support such charges, and no one has produced any since. Far from showing "alacrity" in opening new offices, the Bank established none after 1830, in which year it established the last four of the twenty-nine it had in all; of these, all but ten had been set up during the Bank's initial organization in 1817.

Mr. Schlesinger's failure to make proper use of the work of scholars who have written authoritatively on the Bank seems to me inexplicable. I found reference to Mr. Catterall on only one point of fact, and the whole body of Catterall's judicious and thorough work is neglected for a superficial presentation scarcely above the level of Mr. Marquis James's unpenetrating account in his *Life of Jackson*. I had rather Mr. Schlesinger had shown no knowledge of Catterall whatever; for then he would have spared a reviewer the painful effort to understand how he could revive Benton's pomposities about the branch drafts without remarking Catterall's disposal of the question fifty years ago. The same is true of Dewey, who confirmed Catterall, and of Gallatin, whose unimpeachable contemporary testimony clearly indicates the public nature of the Bank, Biddle's good performance before Jackson's attack, the want of justification for that attack, and the degeneration of Biddle after his failure to withstand the attack.

Mr. Schlesinger makes much of the distinction that although the Jacksonians were understood to be opposed to all banks, they really opposed only the note-issue function and not the deposit function. He devotes an appendix to this point and seems to consider it creditable to the Jacksonians, as if it showed how well they understood banking. The opposite is what it shows. For the differences between note and deposit liabilities are only those of form, and one is as capable of mischief as the other. When Mr. Schlesinger quotes Gallatin to show that banking in the United States was universally understood to mean note issue, he should quote the same authority to the effect that there was not "the slightest difference" between note and deposit liabilities—and incidentally he should enjoy making Webster contradict himself by saying not only that note issue was the essential function of banking but also that it was "not an indispensable ingredient" of banking. Mr. Schlesinger has loyally picked up the Jacksonian confusion on this matter. The actual result of the program he praises was to free both the note and deposit functions from regulation—a blunder that the National Bank Act in 1863 and the Federal Reserve Act fifty years later both purposed to undo.

Mr. Schlesinger properly emphasizes the fact that Jacksonian Democracy reflected eastern as well as frontier influences, but it seems to me that he errs in associating the eastern influence with labor alone and not with business enterprise. There was no more important factor in the Jacksonian movement than the democratization of business, which ceased thenceforth to be the *métier* of a predominantly mercantile, exclusive group, or commercial aristocracy, as it was in the days of Hamilton, and became an interest of the common man. This process of democratization went hand in hand with the rise of laissez faire. Mr. Schlesinger appears to see no break in the business tradition, and makes Hamilton represent it as much in 1840 as he did in 1790. But to identify business enterprise of 1840 with business enterprise of 1790, it is necessary to slur over too much—for example, the appeal of Jackson's politics to money-makers like Alexander Hamilton's own son, who was one of Jackson's supporters and advisers, and like Henshaw, who frankly wanted the United States

Bank overthrown so that he and his friends might have room for a big bank of their own. It is also necessary to slur over the more general fact that the speculation which mounted to the panic of 1837 was a great popular phenomenon and reflected the current interests of Americans no less than did the labor and utopian movements of the time. Authentic and American as the latter were, they still were typical not of American behavior as a whole but rather of the idealistic rebellion of minorities against the rising spirit of free enterprise. For a brief period all the diverse dissatisfactions with the old order of things united behind the picturesque intransigence of Andrew Jackson, with this new, un-Hamiltonian spirit of free enterprise prominent and powerful among them. The honeymoon was brief, and in 1840 enterprise eloped with the Whigs. But while it was supporting Jackson, it had separated the corporate form of organization from monopoly and put forth the promise that anyone could be a capitalist, an investor, or a speculator; and it had made banking a form of business "free" and open to all. Business had become the citadel of rugged individualism, and American conservatism had become rooted not so much in Wall Street as in the breasts of rural capitalists and village entrepreneurs—to the recurring embarrassment of liberal and radical causes ever since.

In Hamilton's day business had been strongly federal, but it was now beginning to see advantages in states' rights—a ground of opposition to the Bank that it seems to me Mr. Schlesinger neglects. The states'-rights argument had vigorously survived the Supreme Court's vindication of the Bank's constitutionality, thanks partly to strongly held principle, no doubt, but much more to selfish interest. Hence, in destroying the Bank, Mr. Schlesinger's hard-money heros played directly into the hands of the state banks and of the speculators they abominated. The local banks always called the regulatory measures of the Bank of the United States "coercion" and "oppression," and it was notorious that they wanted it out of the way. In state after state, as its end neared, the legislatures were jammed with charter applications. Benton's words, quoted by Mr. Schlesinger, sound pathetic: "I did not join in putting down the Bank of the United States to put up a wilderness of local banks." He might disavow the purpose but not the deed.

The situation in the United States, with a rapidly growing and acquisitive population pressing to exploit immense resources, was one where the public interest required an extremely powerful restraint upon inflation. The Bank under the direction of Nicholas Biddle was applying that restraint. Jackson, since he abhorred speculation, should have corrected and fostered the Bank. Instead he identified it with the evil it was contending against, a bank being simply a bank to him, destroyed it, and delivered the country to the excesses of a disordered currency and unregulated credit expansion. I do not find fault with him for attacking economic privilege; I find fault with him for *thinking* he was attacking it when in fact he was attacking a semi-governmental institution that restrained speculation. His action was calamitous for a people who were entering a fierce and trampling struggle for conversion of the virgin earth into private property and erection of still more property upon it—a lasting struggle in which the objects of Jacksonian concern have had the most to suffer. Nor should I be fond enough to believe that a central bank or any other governmental instrumentality could have prevented that struggle; but it might have tempered it. And it is significant that today the party interests to which Mr. Schlesinger is allegiant turn to central banking as a first means of accomplishing their social aims. To suggest that the Jacksonians might have sought to nationalize the Bank of the United States as the Bank of England and the Bank of France have recently been would be historically fantastic, but one may question the sagacity of those who went so far in the opposite direction as to destroy the central bank just when it began to be needed most. That action may be excused but cannot properly be praised.

Mr. Schlesinger's book will be widely read; and because its documentation is profuse it will be considered authoritative by most of its readers. I do not think it should be so considered. It represents the age of Jackson as one of triumphant liberalism when it was as much or more an age of triumphant exploitation; it fosters a simplistic notion of continuing problems of human welfare; and it thickens the myths around a political leader who had more capacity for action than for accomplishment.

More Recent Analyses

Jean Alexander Wilburn
THE SUPPORTERS OF THE BANK

Professor Wilburn wrote her path-breaking book, Biddle's Bank: The Crucial
Years, *while studying at Columbia University. In the following selection, she
raises some important questions about traditional historical interpretations
concerning sectional support and opposition to the Bank bill in 1832.*

Congressional Support

It will be recalled that the charter of the Second United States Bank
was to expire in 1836. Hence the question of whether to recharter it
need not have arisen as early as 1832. Clay, Webster, and many
others, including the Bank's own lobbyists in Washington, advised
Biddle to proceed at once with a request for a renewal of the charter
of the Bank. Biddle concurred and the bill for recharter was
presented to Congress in January of 1832.

Opinions differ as to why Biddle finally decided, after considerable deliberation, to introduce a memorial requesting the Bank's
recharter as early as January 1832. According to Thomas Payne
Govan, whose statements are well documented, Biddle, Henry Clay,
and most informed political observers believed Jackson was sure to
win reelection in the fall of 1832, and the decision to apply for recharter was based solely on what was thought to be the wisest
policy for the Bank. There was a faint hope that Jackson might sign
the new charter if presented to him prior to the election, but the
conviction was held that he would not do so if he won reelection
without having accepted or rejected the renewal. By raising the
issue before the campaign, Biddle thought the candidates for Congress would be forced to express themselves with respect to the

Reprinted by permission of the publisher, from Jean Alexander Wilburn, *Biddle's
Bank: The Crucial Years* (New York: Columbia University Press, 1967), pp. 5–19,
118–135.

recharter if Jackson vetoed the bill. It was believed that the people wanted both Jackson and the Bank. The possibility existed, then, that two-thirds of the congressmen to be elected in November of 1832 would be forced to commit themselves to vote for the recharter.[1]

It was not only the pro-Bank men but also the Bank's enemies who believed it stood in high popular favor.[2] The vote in both Senate and House on whether to recharter the Bank supported their position. The bill passed the Senate 28–20[3] and the House by 107–85.[4] Jackson then vetoed it in July 1832. The bill was returned to the Senate immediately, but a two-thirds majority could not be mustered to override the veto. The Bank was then made a campaign issue, and Clay was resoundingly defeated.

Prior to Jackson's veto in July of 1832 the Bank was not caught up in politics as extensively as afterward. At the Baltimore convention of May 1832, at which Van Buren was nominated for vice-president and Jackson chosen unanimously to succeed himself, there was no agreement on an address to the electorate. The state delegations were advised to "make such a report or address to their constituents as they might think proper."[5] The New York Address, published three weeks before Jackson vetoed the bill for recharter, made states' rights the major issue between the parties. The Bank issue was not treated prominently.

The vote of 1832 on whether to recharter the Bank will be the first vote presented, since it had the advantage of being cast before the veto and therefore before the Bank became a major political issue. (See Map 1, and Table 1.)

It is surprising in view of commonly held beliefs to find that the West favored the Bank. Equally surprising are the diametrically opposed positions in New England. Vermont, Massachusetts, Connect-

---

[1] Thomas Payne Govan, *Nicholas Biddle, Nationalist and Public Banker, 1786–1844* (Chicago: University of Chicago Press, 1959), p. 172.
[2] Hezekiah Niles, *The Weekly Register* (Baltimore, 1813–1841), January 9, 1832. Representative Wayne is quoted as stating in the House that the subject of the Bank had been brought before the House at that time to bring odium on those who should oppose it.
[3] *Abridgement of the Debates of Congress*, 11:753.
[4] *Register of Debates in Congress*, 8:1074.
[5] Lee Benson, *The Concept of Jacksonian Democracy; New York as a Test Case* (Princeton: Princeton University Press, 1961), p. 51, quoted from the *Albany Argus*, June 26, 1832, pp. 1–2.

United States House and Senate Vote, 1832

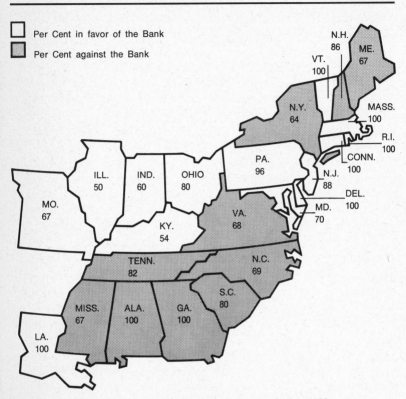

MAP 1. United States House and Senate Vote on the Bank Issue, 1832.

icut, and Rhode Island were all 100 percent in favor of the Bank, yet New Hampshire and Maine stood almost as forcefully against it by 86 and 67 percent respectively. New York, anti-Bank, but adjacent to vigorously pro-Bank middle states, is significant especially when the large number of votes of that state is considered. That the South was heavily anti-Bank runs true to most interpretations, but the complete support of Louisiana has never been singled out for comment. This gains in importance when it is seen that two years later Louisiana would again support the Bank with a 100 percent vote in its favor.

TABLE 1
United States House and Senate Vote, 1832

	House		Senate	
	For	Against	For	Against
Maine	1	6	2	0
New Hampshire	0	5	1	1
Vermont	3	0	2	0
Connecticut	6	0	2	0
Massachusetts	12	0	2	0
Rhode Island	2	0	2	0
New York	12	19	0	2
New Jersey	6	0	1	1
Pennsylvania	24	1	2	0
Delaware	1	0	2	0
Maryland	5	3	2	0
Kentucky	6	5	1	1
Mississippi	0	1	1	1
Alabama	0	3	0	2
Georgia	0	6	0	2
Virginia	6	11	0	2
North Carolina	4	7	0	2
South Carolina	2	6	0	2
Tennessee	2	7	0	2
Louisiana	3	0	2	0
Ohio	10	3	2	0
Illinois			1	1
Indiana	1	2	2	0
Missouri	1	0	1	1

It might be rewarding to look at another interpretation of the vote of 1832.

In 1902 Ralph Catterall wrote what is considered the basic history of the Second United States Bank. It is included in most bibliographies of subsequent writers on the Bank and is authoritatively quoted by them. After mentioning the size of both the House and Senate vote, Catterall proceeded to analyze only the Senate vote. He wrote:

> *The vote in the Senate is significant of the position of various parts of the Union on the question. All the New England senators voted aye excepting*

Hill of New Hampshire; of the senators from the middle states only three were opposed, those from New York and one from New Jersey. In the South and Southwest only three were favorable, those from Louisiana and one from Mississippi. All the Western states were favorable excepting Kentucky, Illinois, and Missouri, which divided their votes. The determined opposition was from the South and Southwest *(italics mine).*[6]

When Catterall said, "All the New England senators voted aye excepting Hill of New Hampshire," the meaning of this statement for all intents and purposes is that New England was 100 percent pro-Bank. Isaac Hill's opposition should be regarded not as representative of the section of the country so much as a quirk attributable to his own personality. He is described thus: "He was frail and lame, an abusive editorial writer, an acrid partisan, ..."[7] "He had the rancorous malignity of those men who have been in a contest with persons who have treated them from above downwards."[8]

The rhetorical implication of Catterall's statement about the middle states is that they were pro-Bank. There is no highlighting of the decisive role New York played. Nor has he drawn the sharp contrast between Louisiana and the adjacent territory. Everything is oriented towards his generalization: "The determined opposition was from the South and Southwest."

Through failure to analyze the House vote the problem is oversimplified and a generalization easily come by. Only when the vote of each house is considered are we alerted to the strength of the New York opposition, the split in New England, and Louisiana's singular role. Examination of these areas might have led subsequent writers to significantly different interpretations. One of the most recent writers on the Jacksonian era, G. G. Van Deusen, said, "Really formidable opposition came only from the West and Southwest."[9] To support his statement Van Deusen gave as reference Catterall's analysis of the senatorial vote. It should be noted that Catterall's regions, *South* and Southwest, here became *West* and Southwest.

Another aspect of Catterall's analysis has led to confusion: Ex-

---

[6] Ralph C. H. Catterall, *The Second Bank of the United States* (Chicago: University of Chicago Press, 1903), p. 235.

[7] Bray Hammond, *Banks and Politics in America* (Princeton: Princeton University Press, 1957), p. 331.

[8] Ibid., as quoted from William G. Sumner, *Andrew Jackson* (Boston, 1882), p. 186.

[9] G. G. Van Deusen, *The Jacksonian Era* (New York: Harper & Bros., 1959), p. 65.

actly which states he included in the Southwest is not clear. He must have included more than just Mississippi and Louisiana since three of four senators voted pro-Bank in these states. Tennessee must have been considered as belonging to the Southwest because Catterall did not include it among the western states. Mississippi, Louisiana, and Tennessee taken together as the Southwest showed three votes against the Bank and three votes pro-Bank. Hence he must have included in the Southwest Alabama and perhaps Georgia along with Mississippi, Louisiana, and Tennessee. The "determined opposition" came, then, from Tennessee and from states which today are included in the South, viz., Virginia, North and South Carolina, Georgia, and Alabama. It is doubtful that Tennessee, Jackson's home state, should be given a "regional" interpretation. Hence the regional opposition to which Catterall referred would today be called "southern opposition."

That he referred to it as the "South and Southwest" is unfortunate on two counts. First, it kept him from drawing the generalization that except for Jackson's home state, the Southwest and West gave strong support to the Bank. Had he viewed the Southwest as Tennessee, Mississippi, and Louisiana, this is the conclusion to which he must have come. Second, as was pointed out earlier, his conclusion that the *South* and Southwest presented the determined opposition has developed into the belief that the *West* and Southwest presented the really formidable opposition—just the contrary to the true state of affairs.

There is one final distortion in Catterall's analysis which resulted from the peculiar nature of what is reflected by the senatorial vote.

It is surprising that about one half of the senators who voted against the Bank were actually men who were known to be, or had expressed themselves to have been, in favor of the Bank.[10] Indeed, some had actively fought for the Bank. How was it, then, that they voted against the institution? Very simply, these men felt it more important to support Jackson *at this time,* just prior to the election, than to hurt his chances of reelection by placing him in the position of having to veto or sign a bill on the Bank. If the bill for recharter

[10] Letter of Thomas Cadwalader to Nicholas Biddle, November 12, 1831, The Papers of Nicholas Biddle (Manuscripts Division, Library of Congress, Washington, D.C.). Cited hereafter as NBP.

failed in Congress, no comment from Jackson would be required. They really wanted the whole issue of the renewal to be brought up in the following session of Congress after the election in the fall was over. But failing this, the least they could do was to keep it from passing Congress then.

There are many letters in the Biddle Manuscripts to support this point of view, and the following is typical:

Thomas Cadwalader to Biddle[11]

(Private)   *Barnard's—Wash.*
My dear Sir,   *21.Dec.1831*

I yesterday reported my arrival. I have had this morning a long and frank conversation with Mr. McLane.[12] *He says* positively[13] *that the President will reject the Bill, if the matter is agitated this Session. He (the President) and those about him would regard the movement, before the election, as an act of hostility, or as founded on the idea that his opinions would bend to personal views, and that his fears would induce him to truckle. Mr. McLane is sure that under such circumstances he would apply his veto, even if certain that he would thereby lose the Election. The question he says cannot now be started without being regarded as a party one, and the influence of the government would be thrown upon it so that we should lose a large number of votes which under other circumstances we should gain—the rejection not being considered as a final one—as the question may be renewed at the next session, or a subsequent one, the Veto once given the President would never swerve, and that two-thirds would be required on any subsequent trial. Accordingly to the Secretary's view of it, therefore, we are now to see whether we can rely on two-thirds under the circumstances averted to, namely the operation of party feeling, and Government influence and to that inquiry I devote myself. Mr. McLane seems to have canvassed the Senate thoroughly, and we have gone over the names together. He gives us—Maine, Massachusetts, Rhode Island, Connecticut and Vermont—two each.*

and New Hampshire making	11
New Jersey 2.—but if this session, strike off Dickerson—say then	1
. . . . *Maryland (if* this Session, *we lose* Smith!!! *for* certain),	1

*N. Carolina—Mangum—(our friend) would vote
      with the party if brought on
      now—Brown against us—*
S. Carolina Hayne dead against the Bank—*Miller*

---

[11] *Correspondence of Nicholas Biddle,* ed. Reginald C. McGrane (Boston: Houghton Mifflin Co., 1919), pp. 147–148.
[12] Secretary of the Treasury under Jackson.
[13] All italicized passages in this letter are italicized in the original.

> *against us* now. *Georgia Forsyth—on*
> *our side but for this Session would*
> *be adverse. Kentucky (Clay)* 1
> *Tennessee—Grundy would work for us strongly* bye and bye,
> *But now would be contra. Ohio and Louisiana* 4
> ....
> *Alabama—Moore* con. *King—in favor, but would go with*
> *party if* now *to vote.*[14]
> *Missouri—(Buckner)* 1
> ....

This letter not only represents the point of view of the pro-Bank democrats as to the inadvisability of raising the Bank issue in this session but also shows McLane's first estimate of the Senate's vote with seven pro-Bank members expected to vote against the Bank. This estimate was by no means final, however. For the next few days Cadwalader devoted himself to consultations with Secretary Mc-Lane, Congressman McDuffie, and General Smith (United States Senator from Maryland), a staunch supporter of the Bank and a Democrat, estimating and reestimating to determine as accurately as possible how each member of the Senate and House would vote *if the issue were to be brought up during that session.* These men in turn had pro- and anti-Bank congressmen poll their delegates as to their anticipated votes. Cadwalader sifted, refined, and weighed these reports until he was satisfied that he could accurately and confidently report to Biddle exactly how each man would cast his vote.

One need not depend solely on the Biddle Manuscripts for this information. For example, in Cole's *Whig Party in the South* the Mangum Manuscripts are quoted to show why Mangum of North Carolina voted against the Bank even though he was pro-Bank. Congressmen were not the only ones to take this position. John A. Quitman, governor of Mississippi, made the position quite clear. In the summer of 1832, when the question of rechartering the Bank absorbed and agitated the country, the friends of the Bank in Mississippi proposed to waive all other issues and nominate an electoral ticket solely with reference to that question. They announced the

---

[14] King had promised to make his debate in the Senate in favor of the Bank, yet ultimately voted against the Bank. See Ingersoll to Biddle, March 1, 1932, NBP.

names of several men who, as to other leading questions, held different views. Quitman was nominated and he wrote the following letter:

To James Cook

Monmouth, Aug. 28, 1832

On my return from the eastern section of the state, I read in your pa-per of the 10th inst. an editorial suggestion of the names of several citi-zens as electors for President and Vice-President of the United States, who are known to be in favor of a renewal of the charter of the Bank of the United States, with a request that the individuals named should sig-nify to you their acceptance or rejection of the proposed nomination. My name having been suggested, I conceive it a duty to state that, al-though I have long considered the Bank of the United States a valuable institution, well calculated to promote the general good by its tendency to lessen the price of exchange, and to produce and preserve a uniform and sound paper currency throughout the Union, and would be pleased to see its charter renewed . . . yet, I do not consider the question of re-chartering it the only[15] *or most important one* which is likely to be involved in the election of the first and second officers of the govern-ment. . . .[16]

Then there were important statesmen such as George Dallas, senator from Pennsylvania at the time, who voted pro-Bank in 1832 but after the veto declared that Jackson was more important than the Bank.[17] We also know from Bassett that "while many politicians nearer home sent assurances of support, James Buchanan, in St. Petersburg, sent in his submission." He was in favor of the Bank, but after the veto he would support his leader.[18]

But we are primarily interested here in those senators who voted against the Bank before the veto but who are known actually to have favored the institution. Below is a list of all senators who voted against the institution with an asterisk next to their names if they were supporters of the Bank.[19]

---

15 Italicized words are in italics in the original letter.
16 J. F. H. Claiborne, *Life and Correspondence of John A. Quitman*, 2 vols. (New York: Harper & Bros., 1860), 1:130–131.
17 John Spencer Bassett, *The Life of Andrew Jackson*, 2 vols. (New York: Double-day, Page and Co., 1911), 2:620.
18 Ibid., p. 621.
19 We are not entirely dependent on the Biddle Papers for this information, although it is probable that the information in the Papers is trustworthy, since it came from members of Jackson's Cabinet or his Kitchen Cabinet who would have no motive

Wm. R. King*	Alabama
Gabriel Moore	Alabama
Geo. M. Troupe	Georgia
John Forsythe*	Georgia
Elias K. Kane*	Illinois
Geo. M. Bibb	Kentucky
Thos. H. Benton	Missouri
Powhatan Ellis*	Mississippi
Isaac Hill	New Hampshire
Mahlon Dickerson*	New Jersey
Chas. Dudley	New York
Wm. Marcy	New York
Bedford Brown*	North Carolina
E. P. Mangum*	North Carolina
Robert Hayne	South Carolina
S. D. Miller*	South Carolina
H. L. White	Tennessee
Felix Grundy*	Tennessee
L. W. Tazewell	Virginia
John Tyler	Virginia

Of twenty senators, nine voted contrary to their feelings about the Bank. Is it correct, then, to say as Catterall did, that an analysis of the senatorial vote indicates how the various sections of the country felt about the Bank at the time? Since there are only two senators per state, a change in one vote means a 50 percent change in the generalization we can make about a particular state. If we analyze the senators in favor of the Bank on this basis,[20] the resulting generalization is that New York and Virginia opposed the Bank, for these are the only two states in which both senators were genuinely opposed to the Bank. Nine of fourteen in the South and Southwest were in favor of it and seventeen of twenty-six, in the South and West. We cannot then say that "the determined opposi-

for exaggerating. However, see Milton Sydney Heath, *Constructive Liberalism* (Boston: Harvard University Press, 1954), p. 167, on Forsythe, and Arthur Charles Cole, *The Whig Party in the South* (Washington: American Historical Association, 1913), p. 26, on Magnum.

[20] There is no indication that any senator known to be against the Bank actually voted in favor of it.

tion was from the South and Southwest." In fact we must conclude that the South, Southwest, and West favored the Bank, a generalization which will appear nearer the truth in subsequent chapters.

Whatever bias was introduced by Catterall into his analysis of the 1832 vote has been greatly reduced by our inclusion of the House of Representatives. We have counted a senatorial vote no more heavily than a representative's vote. Since there were 192 votes cast from the House and 48 from the Senate, the error involved is now considerably less. Furthermore, when the House vote is analyzed in the Biddle Manuscripts as to how it is anticipated the representatives will vote, there is closer agreement between the representatives' real sentiments and their voting behavior than existed in the Senate.

After the election of 1832 there began a series of vindictive incidents between Jackson and Biddle finally resulting in the removal of the government deposits by Jackson and a contraction of the money supply by Biddle.

In 1834 Polk of Tennessee succeeded in getting the issue of the Bank referred to the House Ways and Means Committee. The Committee offered a resolution on April 4th that the "Bank ought not to be rechartered." On this issue the vote stood at 134 against the Bank and 82 in favor. Although we are not concerned with events after 1832, it is interesting to compare this later vote with that of 1832. (See Map 2, and Table 2.)

Contrary, again, to what one would expect, the far western frontier states have grown more favorably disposed toward the Bank than before. The only western state consistently against the Bank was Tennessee, Jackson's home state. As was previously mentioned, Louisiana continued full support. The New England split was more intensified, with Rhode Island undecided. The South remained about as intensely anti-Bank as before. The turnabout in Indiana, Ohio, New Jersey, and Maryland is very dramatic. Pennsylvania should really be included in this category; being the home of the Bank, and passing from 96 percent favorable to 52 percent favorable constitutes a comparable change.

When both votes are considered, it appears that consistent support came from Louisiana, Missouri, Kentucky, Delaware, Connecticut, Massachusetts, and Vermont. Consistent anti-Bank states were Ten-

United States House of Representatives Vote, 1834

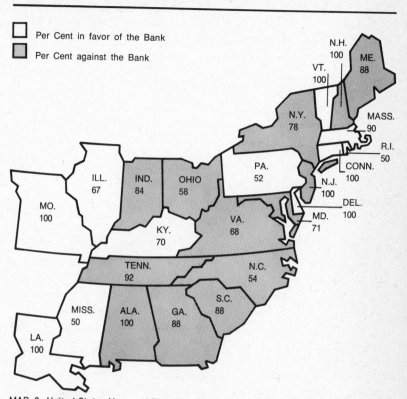

MAP 2. United States House of Representatives Vote on the Bank Issue, 1834.

nessee, Alabama, Georgia, South Carolina, North Carolina, Virginia, New York, New Hampshire, and Maine. A neat generalization about either of these groups is hard to come by. Perhaps there is none. It may be that Louisiana had completely different reasons from those of Connecticut for its complete support of the Bank. The problem has always been attacked at the national level. No systematic work has been done to discern the attitude toward the Bank at the state level.

Conclusion

Our inquiry to determine the identity and extent of the support for the Second Bank of the United States has led us to a state

TABLE 2
United States House of Representatives Vote, 1834

State	For	Against	State	For	Against
Maine	1	7	Mississippi	1	1
New Hampshire	0	4	Virginia	6	13
Vermont	5	0	South Carolina	1	7
Connecticut	6	0	Tennessee	1	12
Massachusetts	9	1	North Carolina	6	7
Rhode Island	1	1	Georgia	1	7
New York	7	29	Alabama	0	4
New Jersey	0	5	Louisiana	2	0
Pennsylvania	12	11	Ohio	8	11
Delaware	1	0	Illinois	2	1
Maryland	2	5	Indiana	1	5
Kentucky	7	3	Missouri	2	0

by state analysis of the attitudes of the state banks, the national and state legislatures, and the populace in general. The investigation has been based in large part on material which ought to spell out with the greatest clarity, if any evidence can, the reasons why people supported or failed to support the Bank— that is, petitions to Congress. As we have seen, the Jacksonian politicians against the Bank were a well-organized group spreading a strong net of influence throughout the Union. Despite efforts from Washington, however, they were able to raise no state bank memorials against the Bank and only eight anti-Bank citizens' memorials. In contrast to this, the Bank's supporters forwarded to Congress 118 citizens' memorials and about seventy state bank memorials.

We have found that Nicholas Biddle was correct when he said, "state banks in the main are friendly." Specifically, only in Georgia, Connecticut, and New York was there positive evidence of hostility. A majority of state banks in some states of the South, such as North Carolina and Alabama, gave strong support to the Bank as did both the Southwest states of Louisiana and Mississippi. Since Virginia gave some support, we can claim that state banks in the South and Southwest for the most part supported the Bank. New England, contrary to expectations, showed the banks of Vermont and New Hampshire behind the Bank, but the support of Massachusetts was both qualitatively and quantitatively weak. The banks of the Middle states all supported the Second Bank except for those in New York. There, the Mechanics' and Farmers' Bank together with the other banks Olcott controlled "arrayed a powerful force against the Bank." Aside from Olcott's interests, the influence exerted against the Bank by the state banks was insignificant. In Connecticut, for example, several officers of banks along with a few citizens signed an anti-Bank memorial. But this was the extent of their effectiveness, for the Connecticut legislature voted unanimously for the Second Bank.

What can we conclude, in summary, about the attitude of the people in these different areas? Only a handful of anti-Bank memorials was signed, hence it is impossible to call the populace hostile. However, from the evidence of pro-Bank memorials it *is* possible to see that the most enthusiastic efforts to support the Bank came from the West. Actually, popular support for the Bank can be claimed for more areas than just the West. Writing a memorial and securing hundreds and sometimes thousands of names to it is a very positive act, requiring energy inspired by strong feeling. Especially was this the case with regard to the Second Bank. The popular President Jackson had come out against the Bank in his annual messages to Congress in 1829 and 1830, so his position with respect to the institution was well known to the people. What percentage of pro-Bank citizens would have had the courage to affix their names to memorials diametrically opposed to the views of their admired President? Yet about 118 pro-Bank memorials were recorded as having been presented to Congress. In contrast, even with the President behind them, only eight memorials against the Bank were organized and forwarded to Congress. The least, then, that we have a right to claim is that there was stronger pro-Bank than anti-Bank feeling among the people of the United States at that time. Furthermore, the geographic distribution of the supporting memorials was fairly widespread—New Hampshire, Vermont, Massachusetts, Connecticut, New York, Pennsylvania, Maryland, some southern states, and the West. New York was not represented solely by the merchants in the City and the citizens of the far western section. Albany, Herkimer, Jefferson, Otsego, and Oneida Counties, among others, sent in memorials.

Now we return to the question originally raised in Chapter 1: how could the "Bank War" have been waged so fiercely and for so long with just a tiny band of supporters consisting of stockholders of the Bank, its employees, and a few prominent statesmen confronting such a mighty array of the Bank's enemies? Actually we can claim that in 1832, at the most crucial period in the Bank's history, the Bank was supported by most state legislatures, by a majority in both Houses of the United States Congress, by an impressive number of state banks, and by more direct expressions of pro-Bank than anti-Bank feeling among the people at large.

But now we have succeeded only in reversing the question originally posed, for now a mighty array of supporters faces a small minority opposed to the Bank. Having placed ourselves in this awkward position we are bound to say something about the causes of the Bank's destruction. We cannot take refuge behind the agrarian people of the frontier areas or the numerous state banks. Can we perhaps blame the "eastern mechanic?" But we have Root's convincing statement in the New York Senate to the contrary, as well as several pro-Bank memorials from Massachusetts and Philadelphia signed specifically by mechanics. A Massachusetts memorial is captioned "Manufacturers and Mechanics," and one from Philadelphia reads specifically "Manufacturers, Mechanics, Merchants and Others." John Quitman, writing a letter from New York City where he was visiting in July 1831, says that "the working interest" along with manufacturers and other groups inclined toward Clay and the American System.[21] The American System meant support of the Bank, high tariffs, and internal improvements.

Was it the "business man's dislike of the federal Bank's restraints upon bank credit?" If so, we must read as meaningless the eloquent pleas for a branch Bank in Albany to relieve the distress of the businessman left in the hands of the state banks,

---

[21] J. F. H. Claiborne, *Life and Correspondence of John A. Quitman,* 2 vols. (New York: Harper and Brothers, 1860), I:108.

and ignore the countless number of businessmen's signatures on memorials from New York City, Boston, Philadelphia, and elsewhere. We would also have to disregard the belief reflected in many memorials that the agrarian, manufacturing, and other economic interests fluctuated together and were dependent in common on the Bank for their expansion and well-being. Very few business houses in New York City seem to have sided with Jackson against the Bank.[22] Earlier we found that the merchants in the City had volunteered to circulate a favorable petition and as soon as permission was granted they secured 1,000 names within twenty-four hours.

What, then, did destroy the Second Bank of the United States?

The failure of Congress to recharter the Bank and the consequent destruction of the Bank has been implicit throughout this investigation. Perhaps a more precise way to state this is to say that the Bank was destroyed because Congress failed to raise a two-thirds majority to override the veto. It is to this problem, then, that we must address ourselves. Realizing that there was a majority in both Houses in favor of the Bank, even without counting those Congressmen who voted against the Bank but were really pro-Bank in sentiment, we must try to indicate why the necessary majority could not be mustered.

It is important to understand that the decisive conflict over the Bank was not only between the National Republicans and the Democrats, as is so commonly thought, but was also within the Democratic Party itself. The National Republicans were out-and-out Bank supporters, but the Democratic Party embraced substantial numbers of men on both sides of the Bank question. As has already been pointed out, those who voted against the Bank but were pro-Bank in sentiment cast their votes the way they did because they gave Jackson's reelection priority over the Bank issue. Had they cast their votes in favor of the Bank, the renewal of the charter would have been assured. But party unity came first. Now the idea of "Party first," although a widely recognized principle of political behavior, carries with it a certain opprobrium. The Van Buren and Biddle manuscripts and Niles'

---

[22] George Douglas was apparently one of the few. See Joseph Alfred Scoville, *Old Merchants of New York* (New York: T. R. Knox, 1885), p. 38.

Register, however, provide impressive material which both explains and partly justifies the Jacksonian Democrats' adherence to this principle in 1832.

It will be recalled that Van Buren at that time was our minister to the Court of St. James in England, having been appointed to the post by Jackson after Van Buren had resigned as Secretary of State. In those days it was assumed that appointment to the office of Secretary of State indicated the President's choice of his future successor. Van Buren had discharged his duties as Secretary honorably, and the approval by the Senate of his appointment as minister to England should conventionally have passed that chamber. However, Calhoun, Vice-President of the United States and presiding officer of the Senate, had been rejected in favor of Van Buren as Jackson's successor, and consequently viewed Van Buren as his political archenemy. The vote in the Senate was rigged, 26–26, so Calhoun could have the satisfaction of casting the deciding vote against Van Buren. It then became necessary to recall Van Buren after he had been representing this country for some time. This was an unusually petty act of vindictiveness on Calhoun's part, and it was sanctioned by Webster and Clay, already identified with the cause of the Bank.[23] With the tenuousness of England's respect for the United States, the full humiliation to the country as a whole—but especially of President Jackson and Van Buren—can be imagined.[24] But seldom has an act been so fully revenged. Its repercussions can be seen from the following correspondence.

The day of the Senate vote, January 26, 1832, one of Biddle's lobbyists, Ingersoll, had just arrived in Washington. He wrote Biddle that day saying that the Speaker of the House, who was against the Bank, has nonetheless warned him that nothing is more likely to defeat the Bank issue than bad timing in the presentation of the petition for renewal of its charter.[25] Ingersoll goes

[23] Niles' *Register* of February 25, 1832, quotes the *Richmond Enquirer* as referring to the rejection as "the prostration of the dignity and integrity of the Senate of the United States by the coalition of Clay, Calhoun and Webster."

[24] Even Webster himself said that the rejection of the nomination would be regarded by foreign states as not favorable to the character of our government. See Niles' *Register*, February 4, 1832.

[25] George Dallas of Pennsylvania when presenting to the Senate the Bank's memorial

on to tell Biddle of Van Buren's rejection and describes how various senators voted on the matter.[26]

Voluminous letters were written to Van Buren in England over this incident both by people politically sympathetic with him and by others who differed from him. Among these letters is one from Elijah Hawood, Washington, dated January 30th. He informs Van Buren of his rejection and says that it would have been impossible except for the influence of the Bank operating against him. Certain senators' votes could not have been procured without that influence.[27] But Hawood prophesies that this act will rebound: as a direct result of this,[28] Van Buren will first be Vice-President, and then President. A letter from William Carroll of Nashville to Andrew Jackson says much the same as Hawood. Carroll explains that "two men know him, now, to one, that knew him sixty days ago." He adds that Van Buren will now be supported by the Jacksonians, whereas Calhoun's friends have all disappeared in the last ten days.[29]

From the Van Buren manuscripts we learn that on the same day Hawood's letter was written there was a special meeting called at Tammany Hall in New York City to protest the action of the Senate. Attendance at the meeting cut across both factions of the Democratic Party. A resolution against the Senate's action was signed both by members of the Regency and by others who, like Saul Alley, were not Regency members.[30]

Charles Butler of New York wrote on January 31st to Van Buren saying that the people have been roused against the vote, but that in the end all will be for his good. He tells Van Buren that the most respectable people were at the Tammany meeting.[31]

for renewal of its charter remarked that he had discouraged presentation of the document at that time because "he felt deep solicitude and apprehension, lest, in the progress of the inquiry and in the development of views, under present circumstances it might be drawn into real or imagined conflict with some higher, some more favorite, some more immediate wish or purpose of the American people." See Niles' *Register*, January 9, 1832.

[26] Ingersoll to Biddle, January 26, 1832, NBP.

[27] There is no evidence in the Biddle manuscripts to support this statement.

[28] Hawood to Van Buren, January 30, 1832, Van Buren Manuscripts. Numerous letters predicted this same outcome.

[29] Carroll to Jackson, February 20, 1832, Papers of Andrew Jackson, vol. V, 2nd Series.

[30] January 30, 1832, Van Buren Manuscripts.

[31] Butler to Van Buren, January 31, 1832, Van Buren Manuscripts.

William A. Duer wrote to Colt, Biddle's close advisor, that he is ashamed of the Senate's behavior, even though he differs from Van Buren on many political matters.[32]

On February 4th Ingersoll again wrote Biddle from Washington about this incident. He says that he regrets Van Buren's rejection—this turns Jackson's men against everything that is supported by Webster and Clay, such as the Bank.[33] James Watson Webb, also in Washington to do what he could for the Bank, wrote Biddle a long letter appraising the congressional situation, in which he says much the same thing, adding that the rejection has drawn Jackson Party lines very tight.[34]

Because Webster and Clay symbolized pro-Bank sentiment, Van Buren's rejection had the effect both of unifying Regency and anti-Regency people within the party and of turning some of them against the Bank.

This incident in the Senate is not new to any historian, though the intensity of feeling it aroused, with consequent repercussions on both the Democratic Party and the Bank, has perhaps not been fully appreciated. Niles' *Weekly Register* from January through March of 1832 reflects the relative importance of the issue. Almost every publication refers to the matter giving it prominence as the first or second article on the first page or reporting at great length the Senate debates on the question.[35] The incident further corroborates Marvin Meyers' contention that the "Bank War" forged and gave character to the Jacksonian Party.[36] Actually the effect of the incident was to provide a rationale for the principle of "Party first." It was also another dramatic step towards turning the Bank question, not primarily a political issue, into a matter of party politics. Obviously the whole burden of Congress' failure to override the veto cannot be attributed to the rejection of Van Buren. But it could hardly have failed to influence some of the wavering pro-Bank Democrats. It is interesting to notice that eight of the

[32] Duer to Colt, January 31, 1832, Van Buren Manuscripts.
[33] Ingersoll to Biddle, February 4, 1832, NBP.
[34] Webb to Biddle, February 6, 1832, NBP.
[35] See especially Niles' *Register* of January 21st and 28th, February 4th, 11th, 18th, 25th, and March 17th, 1832.
[36] See Meyers' contention, p. 3.

nine senators referred to earlier[37] as having voted against the Bank but believed to be pro-Bank in sentiment voted for Van Buren's confirmation.[38]

Earlier, when Virginia was under consideration, discussion of additional correspondence from that state was postponed until the rest of the country had been examined. Since these letters offer evidence bearing on the present investigation, now is the appropriate point at which to consider them. On June 14, 1830, Henry Clay wrote to Biddle:

> Unless I am deceived by information received from one of the most intelligent Citizens of Virginia, the plan was laid at Richmond during a visit made to that place by the Secretary of State[39] last autumn, to make the destruction of the Bank the basis of the next Presidential Election. The message of the President, and other indications, are supposed consequences of that plan.[40]

According to McGrane, Van Buren was known to have been in Richmond in the fall of 1829. "Therefore," he suggested, "the question arises, could the Southern politicians have induced or suggested to Van Buren the idea of an attack on the Bank, holding out to the latter the hope of the next Presidential election, while their main idea was to gain time for their own propaganda?"[41]

J. Robertson wrote Biddle from Virginia about a year later:

> You must be very sensible of the deep rooted hostility among the prominent politicians in this State against the Bank of the United States. Every art and device has been employed by them, to infuse into the minds and keep alive, a similar feeling among the people—not by any discussions about the merits of the Bank, or about its constitutionality, but by starting such topics, and repeating such charges and insinuations against the Institution and its management, as are calculated to strengthen and even inflame the prejudices of their adherents. In this work of delusion and mischief, you have probably seen, the Richmond Enquirer take the lead. Besides the Editor's own disingenous [sic] and deceptive observations,

[37] See the Senate vote, p. 189, below.
[38] Niles' *Register*, February 4, 1832.
[39] Martin Van Buren.
[40] Reginald C. McGrane, ed., *Correspondence of Nicholas Biddle* (Boston: Houghton Mifflin Company, 1919), p. 105.
[41] Ibid., p. 105.

he is continually endorsing and dealing out to his readers, the slanderous and calumnious paragraphs and statements of such profligate presses throughout the Union, as are embarked in the same cause. And yet the truth is, he knows nothing about the Bank, or about Banking, and he cares nothing about them. . . . In seeming to attach so much importance to what is said in the Enquirer *about the Bank, I may as well add, that I have good reasons for believing, that its course is approved of in Washington. And I have also equally good reasons for believing, that it is the course which was marked out eighteen months ago to be pursued in certain contingencies.*[42]

We have admittedly stressed that the Jacksonians did not want the Bank raised as an issue before the election. But the above evidence does not contradict this; it is chronology that has entered to confuse us. We have claimed that in *1832* they did not want the issue raised. In the fall of 1829 it was not yet apparent to the politicians how the Bank was gaining in popular favor. To support this point of view, there is a letter from Degrand in Boston dated April 5, 1831, which asks of Biddle: "Shall we also triumph in New York? Is Van Buren frightened at his attack on the Bank?— Has he *now* become aware of its increased and increasing popularity?"[43]

But all that need concern us now is that Virginia and New York were in some sense in league. Indeed, we need not even suppose them to be consciously in league to establish the point that both Virginia and New York were against the Bank and cast their votes that way. The four powerful states at this period, both with respect to the number of Congressional votes and in terms of influence, were New York, Pennsylvania, Massachusetts, and Virginia. It is apparent that both New York and Virginia were working very hard to gain support for their anti-Bank position. Olcott and the Regency, together with the Virginia politicians and the Virginia press, were making their position felt. So was Pennsylvania, as we have seen, but on the opposite side. How significant Massachusetts' apathy now becomes! Pennsylvania and the Bank needed rousing enthusiasm from Massachusetts. To counteract the impact of the Virginia–New York combination, it was important

---

[42] Robertson to Biddle, July 4, 1831, NBP.
[43] Degrand to Biddle, April 5, 1831, NBP.

for Massachusetts not simply to vote in favor of the Bank, but also to bombard Congress with as many memorials from state banks, citizens, and the state legislature, as could be mustered. Had Massachusetts brought such pressure to bear, undoubtedly this would at least have influenced some of the borderline members in Congress.

New York, and especially the Farmers' and Mechanics' Bank, must, however, bear the brunt of the responsibility. When we realize that a two-thirds majority consisted of 32 votes in the Senate and about 128 in the House of which the Bank was assured of 28 and 107 respectively, we see that the New York delegation, with two senators' and nineteen representatives' anti-Bank votes, could almost by itself have swung the needed majority. Ironically enough, had the bill passed both Houses with a somewhat larger majority than it did, there might very well have been no need for an overriding two-thirds majority, for there might not then have been a veto. There are several letters indicating that Jackson had changed his position regarding the action he would take on the Bank bill. Charles F. Mercer, a congressman from Virginia, wrote Biddle on January 27, 1832, that Mr. B.[44] of Tennessee has told him he will vote for renewal of the Bank's charter.[45] But he also has told him that unless the Bank bill passes by a considerable majority, General Jackson will not approve it. He goes on to tell Mercer that Jackson has said that he has twice stated his objections to renewal. But if the people sustain the Bank by a large majority, so will he.[46] Secretary Livingston and Ingersoll met on February 27th and Livingston asked Ingersoll to find out from Biddle whether he will agree to the President's terms for a new charter.[47] Biddle accepts the terms.[48] When Ingersoll reported this to Livingston, Livingston said, "If such a bill goes to him as he can sign, he will sign it without hesitation."[49]

Thomas Payne Govan, however, rejected the theory that Jackson wavered. His rejection was based on an undated memorandum in

[44] John Bell, a representative in Congress from Tennessee.
[45] He ultimately voted against the Bank.
[46] Mercer to Biddle, January 27, 1832, NBP.
[47] Ingersoll to Biddle, February 23, 1832, NBP.
[48] Biddle to Ingersoll, February 25, 1832, NBP.
[49] Ingersoll to Biddle, March 1, 1832, NBP.

Jackson's handwriting which Govan believed was written in January 1832. The memorandum referred to the Bank as unconstitutional and said that if one is necessary, it must have no concern with corporations.[50]

Thomas Olcott's role is especially significant when we recall that the New York legislature was sufficiently pro-Bank at the time Morehouse first tried to obtain a vote on his resolution against renewal of the Bank's charter to shelve the issue. But Olcott's determined pressure, supported by the Regency, was effective enough first to move a pro-Bank majority to a tie of 55–55 and then to reduce it to an anti-Bank vote of 73–35.

But, if we place some of the responsibility on Olcott, then Nicholas Biddle must also shoulder his share. For he, with the immense power of the United States Bank behind him, was in a position to take a decisive step in Albany which was probably the only means of curtailing Olcott's influence. From 1826 on he had been made aware of Albany's economic needs, and later was specifically cautioned as to the weight of the Farmers' and Mechanics' [Bank] influence. But he chose not to act. Perhaps to a resident of the important city of Philadelphia it appeared impossible for Albany to play such a pivotal role. As Biddle was forewarned, however, he "found it out in the end."

These are just some of the reasons, for surely there are more, as to why the veto could not be overriden. Since it was not the intention of the present undertaking to attempt to explain the demise of the Bank but only to discover its supporters, no further exploration in the direction of the former topic will be attempted. Yet one further comment might be ventured.

Superficially it may appear that once again, in explaining the destruction of the Bank, we have been caught in the political trap. This is only partially true. Actually both politics and economics were involved. The rejection of Van Buren was indeed political. Massachusetts' apathy was not. Rather, it existed as a result of that state's relative economic independence. This was true also of Virginia, New York, and Connecticut, for they all had admirable banking systems of their own.

[50] Thomas P. Govan, *Nicholas Biddle, Nationalist and Public Banker, 1786–1844* (Chicago: University of Chicago Press, 1959), p. 184.

Likewise, those areas most vocal in support of the Bank were primarily motivated by economic dependence on the Bank, lacking both capital and a circulating medium of their own. The "economic motives" of Thomas Olcott have already been discussed.

It is still of interest to ask how the theory of nation wide state bank hostility gained such a strong foothold in men's minds. Anyone writing on the Jacksonian era is likely to read Jabez Hammond's *Political History of New York.* This book is a gold mine of information about the period, Hammond having been an informed contemporary of many prominent men of his day. About 1820 he was a member of the New York Senate from Cherry Valley, Otsego County. It will be remembered that Olcott had control of the banking in Cherry Valley. In addition, Morehouse, who presented the resolution against the Bank in the New York Assembly, was an agent of the Olcott group. Interestingly enough, he too came from Otsego County. Hammond, therefore, was fully exposed to the state banks' hostility and politicking, for he lived in their midst, and Olcott was said to have dealt not just secretly but also openly to gain his ends. It might not be wrong to suggest that Jabez Hammond may have attributed to the nation at large what he saw locally. This is not too far-fetched, given the poor transportation and communication of those days. Men often had to reason from their particular situation to a generalization about distant parts which they had not experienced firsthand. For instance he said, "Was it in human nature, and especially, was it in *bank nature,* . . . to resist this prospect of adding to their gains?"

We found in our investigation that banks could and did resist immediate short-run gains in favor of long-run ones. A comment on this problem is made in the letter from Robinson of Virginia to Biddle, in which he tells Biddle of Girard's statement that as a *banker* he will be better off if the Bank is not rechartered, but not as a merchant.[51] Robinson expresses surprise at Girard's making such a foolish statement. He adds that Girard surely must see that if the demise of the Bank brings in its wake the calamities Girard claims it will, then *both* as a banker and a merchant he will be worse off.

[51] See Robinson's letter, p. 92.

Catterall carried the state bank hostility theory one step further and claimed that the United States Bank had been particularly offensive to the banks of the South and West, and consequently the Bank could count on opposition from most of these corporations.[52] He was quite correct in saying that the Bank had hurt this area badly, but such behavior dated back to the very early years of the Bank. Meanwhile Biddle's generous attitude in later years toward the South and West had altered opinions. But from such statements it can be understood why the theory of widespread state bank opposition came to be so generally accepted by historians.

Another interesting question which we might consider is why the people of the West should have come to be singled out as representing the heart of anti-Bank sentiment. Because the Bank was made a political issue in the election of 1832, some writers have concluded that a vote for Jackson meant a vote against the Bank, and have believed that those areas giving Jackson the heaviest support were the most anti-Bank states. The West, except for Clay's state, Kentucky, greatly favored Jackson. Indeed, Van Buren in his *Autobiography,* a book naturally included in the bibliographies of most writers on the Bank, said of the election results: "The will of the people in regard to the bank had been most clearly expressed on its own appeal and according to the forms of the constitution."[53] Even Andrew Jackson said on September 18, 1833, in a cabinet communication: "Can it now be said that the question of a recharter of the Bank was not decided at the election which ensued?"[54]

There were some very convincing statements made in the United States Senate and House, however, contradicting Jackson and Van Buren. Henry Clay, speaking in the Senate and referring to the presidential campaign of 1832 remarked:

In the canvass which ensued, it was boldly asserted, by the partisans of the President, that he was not opposed to a Bank of the United States. . . .

[52] Ralph C. H. Catterall, *The Second Bank of the United States* (Chicago: University of Chicago Press, 1903), p. 166.
[53] Martin Van Buren, *Autobiography,* ed. by John C. Fitzpatrick, Annual Report of the American Historical Association for the Year 1918, 2 vols. (Washington: United States Government Printing Office, 1920), 2:627.
[54] T. F. Gordon, *The War on the Bank of the United States* (Philadelphia: Key and Biddle, 1834), p. 111.

They maintained, at least wherever those friendly to a National Bank were in the majority, that his re-election would be followed by a recharter of the Bank with proper amendments . . . ; but they, nevertheless, contended, that these objections would be cured, if he was re-elected, and the Bank sustained. I appeal to the whole Senate, to my colleague, to the people of Kentucky, and especially, to the citizens of the city of Louisville, for the correctness of this statement.[55]

William Wilkins, senator from Pennsylvania, referring to the election of President Jackson addressed the Senate thus: "I do not think that result turned upon the question of the recharter of the Bank; nor was it a popular decision of that inquiry. . . . Thousands of voters threw their weight on the side of the successful candidate, who would vote for a National Bank tomorrow."[56]

In the House of Representatives, Moore of Virginia said:

Every gentleman here knows that Jackson would have been elected whether he was for or against the Bank. . . . The chartering of the Bank was not the only question upon which the Presidential election turned; on the contrary, it is probable that more than one half of those who voted for the present Chief Magistrate were, at that time, in favor of rechartering the Bank.[57]

Representative Wise of Virginia exclaimed in the House: "I, for one, once did think that the President would sanction such a charter. . . . On all proper occasions when using my feeble efforts to elect him, I confidently declared this belief to many of the people whom I represent."[58]

In a speech to the House, Representative Chilton Allen remarked:

I deny that the election of General Jackson either proves, or conduces to prove, that the people of the United States are opposed to a National Bank. General Jackson certainly went before the people, at the last election, as a Bank man. . . . Then, Sir, I undertake to say that the Jackson party, in every county and district in the United States, presented General Jackson to the people, . . . as friendly to a United States Bank, properly modified.[59]

[55] Ibid., p. 113.
[56] Ibid., p. 114.
[57] Ibid.
[58] Ibid.

Finally, John Quincy Adams argued for the same point of view. He referred to the House vote of June 1832 on the Bank in which 107 voted in favor of rechartering and 85 against.[60] He pointed out that of those standing for reelection who had participated in this vote, the people returned those representatives in exactly the same proportions as they had voted in 1832, i.e., 51 of the 107 and 41 of the 85. This he found more truly reflected the people's attitude toward the Bank.[61]

We have also seen repeatedly in the Biddle correspondence that many people were pro-Bank but gave Jackson's reelection priority over the Bank. Further, it is quite clear that Jackson was reelected mainly because of his immense personal popularity. Bassett quoted Van Buren as saying that nothing but Jackson's popularity could have carried the people in the contest against the strongly entrenched Bank.[62] John Quincy Adams believed that Jackson's whole strength rested on his personal popularity founded on his military services.[63] On February 6, 1832, James Watson Webb wrote Biddle that he is convinced of the folly of Jackson's friends trying to postpone the Bank question until the following session. Whether Jackson signs or not, Webb declares, it will not produce the slightest change in the prospect of his reelection.[64]

Chilton Allen stated about Jackson: "For the fact is, that his popularity was so overshadowing, that he could have been elected on any side of any question."[65]

These many opinions strongly emphasize that the question before the American people as they saw it was not whether they were voting for or against the Bank, but simply for or against Jackson who was represented to many of them as favoring a modified national bank.

---

[59] Ibid., p. 115.
[60] The vote analyzed on Map 1.
[61] Gordon, p. 116.
[62] John S. Bassett, *The Life of Andrew Jackson,* 2 vols. (New York: Doubleday, Page and Company, 1911), 2:650.
[63] John Quincy Adams, *Memoirs of John Quincy Adams,* ed. by Charles Francis Adams (Philadelphia: J. B. Lippincott & Co., 1874–1877).
[64] Webb to Biddle, February 6, 1832, NBP.
[65] Gordon, p. 115.

As was suggested earlier, another factor contributing to the isolation of the Southwest and West as especially hostile areas was Catterall's error in analyzing only the Senate vote of 1832, the results of which supported his thesis. The impact of his opinion is heightened by his having singled out this area not just once with respect to the people as a whole, but a second time with respect to the state banks.

One of the most significant reasons for the disparity between the conclusions herein reached and those of many earlier writers concerns the period of the Bank's history under consideration. Most writers have chosen to explain the forces that destroyed the Second Bank by examining the whole span of twenty years during which the Bank was in existence. Wherever substantial hostility was observed, regardless of the year in which it occurred, it was charged with the responsibility of destroying the Bank. There has been a failure to distinguish between the long and short run. The present study has been an intensive one of the very short period just prior to the veto of 1832, because this period seemed the most relevant to the problem at hand. The intriguing aspect of the Bank issue concerns events which occurred after the Bank had begun to function properly and the people had had the opportunity of experiencing its benefits. For only after this did the contradiction arise between its great service to the American people and its demise. Before this period the situation was fairly easy to understand. Bad management under Jones, stringent management under Cheves, and the early years of growing mastery of the problem under Biddle led many groups to complain and express hostility toward the institution. That this was their attitude is fully understandable and natural, but not a very challenging situation to interpret. Neither those groups of people whose criticisms were directed at the Bank during its early or middle years, nor events of that period should necessarily be blamed for the Bank's destruction. The time was not yet ripe to judge. Not until the years chosen within the close compass of those discussed herein, after the Bank had matured and been experienced sufficiently long for its effects to be discernible, is it possible to identify those elements which led to its destruction.

Peter Temin
BIDDLE'S INSTITUTION NOT A CENTRAL BANK

Peter Temin had already made important contributions to American economic history before the publication of his innovative The Jacksonian Economy *in 1969. Careful economic analysis and an emphasis on quantitative methods have characterized his writing. The following selection questions previously developed interpretations of the economic effects of Jackson's War on the Bank.*

A New Approach.   [The traditional account of the Bank War] is in error at three main points. First, the boom did not have its origins in the Bank War. It resulted from a combination of large capital imports from England and a change in the Chinese desire for silver which together produced a rapid increase in the quantity of silver in the United States. Banks did not expand their operations because they were treating the government deposits as reserves, to finance speculation, or because the Bank of the United States was no longer restraining them; they expanded because their true—that is, specie—reserves had risen.[1] Second, the Panic of 1837 was not caused by President Jackson's actions. The "destruction" of the Bank of the United States did not produce the crisis because it did not produce the boom. The Specie Circular and the distribution of the surplus also did not have the effects attributed to them. And third, the depression of the early 1840s was neither as serious as historians assume nor the fault of Nicholas Biddle. It was primarily a deflation, as opposed to a decline in production, and it was produced by events over which Biddle had little control.

[1] Macesich noted that the reserves of the banking system had risen rapidly during the boom. This observation is correct, but Macesich's attempts to formulate a new interpretation of the boom were not entirely successful and have not been widely accepted. See George Macesich, "Sources of Monetary Disturbances in the U. S., 1834–1845," *Journal of Economic History* 20 (September 1960): 407–434, and "International Trade and United States Economic Development Revisited," *Journal of Economic History* 21 (September 1961); 384–385; Jeffrey G. Williamson, "International Trade and United States Economic Development: 1827–1843," *Journal of Economic History* 21 (September 1961): 372–383; Douglass C. North, *The Economic Growth of the United States, 1790–1860* (Englewood Cliffs: Prentice-Hall, 1961), pp. 198–202.

These errors have arisen because of the nature of the sources used to compile the traditional account. The most important source, as is usual in historical investigations, has been the opinion of informed contemporaries. There is no doubt that we must rely on the opinions of informed witnesses for an understanding of some aspects of the 1830s, but there is good reason to doubt that we can discover the whole story from their words. Most of these observers were also participants, and their objectivity may be questioned. Nicholas Biddle could not possibly have given a balanced account of Jackson's involvement with the Panic of 1837. Other contemporary observers held ideas about the operation of the economy that we can no longer accept today. Albert Gallatin, for example, former Secretary of the Treasury and dean of the New York banking community, could assert with great finality: "It has always been the opinion of the writer of this essay that a public debt was always an evil to be avoided whenever practicable; hardly ever justifiable except in time of war."[2] And even if the difficulties of personal subjectivity did not exist, the opinions of illustrious contemporaries would still not be a good source. They simply were not sufficiently consistent to provide the raw material for a unified account.

The two opinions most often quoted are those of Nicholas Biddle expressed in an open letter to John Quincy Adams, November 11, 1836, and the 1841 essay of Albert Gallatin from which an opinion was just quoted. Biddle supported one line of argument found in the traditional account by saying: "In my judgment, the main cause of it [the current crisis] is the mismanagement of the revenue—mismanagement in two respects: the mode of executing the distribution law, and the order requiring specie for the public lands." And Gallatin supported a different part of the story by announcing: "Overtrading has been the primary cause of the present crisis in America."[3]

Unfortunately, Biddle did not think much of the opinion expressed by Gallatin, and Gallatin did not agree with Biddle. Biddle noted in his letter that

[2] Gallatin, pp. 28–29.
[3] Nicholas Biddle to J. Q. Adams, Nov. 11, 1836, reprinted in *Niles' Weekly Register* 60 (Baltimore, Dec. 17, 1836): 243–245; Gallatin, p. 26. See also the 1837 comments of Abbot Lawrence, in Hamilton A. Hill, *Memoir of Abbot Lawrence* (Cambridge, 1884), pp. 16–18. Hughes and Rosenberg document the use of the word "overtrading" and the prefix "over-" in the recent literature.

It is said that the country has overtraded—that the banks have over-issued, and that the purchasers of public lands have been very extravagant. I am not struck by the truth or propriety of these complaints. The phrase of overtrading is very convenient but not very intelligible. If it means anything, it means that our dealings with other countries have brought us in debt to those countries. In that case the exchange turns against our country, and is rectified by an exportation of specie or stocks in the first instance—and then by reducing [the ratio of] the imports to the exports. Now the fact is, that at this moment [November 1836], the exchanges are all in favor of this country—that is, you can buy a bill of exchange on a foreign country cheaper than you can send specie to that country.[4]

And as we have already noted, Gallatin said, "[T]he charges against the President for having interfered in the currency resolve themselves into the single fact of having prevented the renewal of the charter of the Bank of the United States." He went on to say,

The direct and immediate effects cannot be correctly ascertained; but they have been greatly exaggerated by party spirit. That he found the currency in a sound and left it in a deplorable state is true; but he cannot certainly be made responsible for the aberrations and misdeeds of the bank [of the United States] under either of its charters. The unforeseen, unexampled accumulation of the public revenue was one of the principal proximate causes of the disasters that ensued. It cannot be ascribed either to the President or to any branch of the government, and its effects might have been the same whether the public deposits were in the State banks, or had been left in the national bank, organized and governed as that was.[5]

These divergent views by well-qualified contemporary observers cannot be reconciled by appeals to opinion alone. Reference must be made to the actual events taking place. Such observations comprise the other main source of data for the traditional account, but they have not been used in any systematic fashion. Each author has chosen a few facts about the monetary system or the banking structure to present, but almost no one has tried to put these data into a systematic framework or tried to make explicit the implications of the cited observations.[6] As Brinley Thomas once said in a different

[4] *Niles'*, 60, 243–245.
[5] Gallatin, pp. 31–32.
[6] Exceptions to this rule are provided by Macesich, 1960, and Jeffrey G. Williamson, *American Growth and the Balance of Payments, 1820–1913: A Study of the Long Swing* (Chapel Hill: University of North Carolina Press, 1964).

context, the empirical data have been used "as a drunk uses lamp-posts: more for support than for illumination."

This can be seen clearly in the treatment of the core of the traditional story of the boom: the nature of the "credit expansion." It is stated that banks used government deposits and notes of other banks as reserves, and that they expanded their activities without references to their true reserves, that is, specie. As Schlesinger phrased it in the passage just cited: "The proportion of paper [that is, bank obligations] to specie lengthened." Phrased another way, the reserve ratio of banks—the inverse of the ratio of obligations to specie—declined. But not one of the historians repeating this story cites any evidence on the reserve ratio of the banking system. One occasionally sees references to the behavior of individual banks and states, but never is there documentation of how the system as a whole behaved.

This gap in our knowledge of the 1830s has been extremely costly. The behavior of individual banks does not necessarily parallel the behavior of the banking system as a whole, and the experience of any single state is not always a good index of the progress of the Union. The story of the 1830s constructed from accounts of individual banks and states is seriously in error, and it can be corrected only by the use of data about the economy as a whole. Incorporated systematically into a coherent theoretical framework, the aggregate data on the 1830s enable us to discriminate between alternate hypotheses and schemes of causation. As a result, we can say both that the traditional account is invalid and that the alternate account to be presented here is supported at many points by the available data.

The Second Bank as a Central Bank. . . . The arguments about the constitutionality of the Second Bank and its supposed control by foreigners (or, alternatively, by a small group of natives as a result of the nonvoting status of foreign stockholders) add little to our understanding of the economic issues in Jackson's opposition. He said in his summary: "We can at least take a stand against all new grants of monopolies and exclusive privileges, against any prostitution of our Government to the advancement of the few at the expense of the many," but the connection between these sentiments and the operation of the Second Bank is open to question. Without attempting to judge the issue of Jackson's ultimate motivation, this economic analysis of his veto message certainly supports the conclusion of Marvin Meyers: "The Bank was called a Monster by Jacksonians. A monster is an unnatural thing, its acts are out of reason, and its threats cannot be estimated in ordinary practical terms. The effort to destroy the Monster Bank and its vicious brood—privileged corporations, paper money—enlisted moral passions in a drama of social justice and self-justification."[7]

Nevertheless, this effort obviously had economic consequences, and it is appropriate to evaluate it as an economic measure. Later chapters will deal with its immediate impact. Here we pose a question of a more long-run nature: Was the Second Bank of the United States a central bank?[8]

There does not seem to be a generally accepted definition of a central bank, but there does seem to be general agreement that a central bank should perform two roles. In normal times, the central bank should act to facilitate commerce and to regulate the markets for money and credit. In times of crisis, the central bank should act to restore confidence by being a "lender of last resort." We consider these in turn.

The first of these functions is somewhat amorphous. There are many things that can be done to make the economy move easily, and it is not clear how many of them a bank needs to perform to become a true central bank. The Second Bank under Biddle did a variety of things that fit this classification. It arranged for payments of the government debt in ways that insulated commerce from these shocks. It arranged for interregional transfers of government funds

---

[7] Meyers, pp. 10–11. The lack of economic coherence in the message informs us about Jackson's advisers as well as about the President himself. "Kendall's authorship of the veto message suggests that its ambiguities in formal ideological statement are beside the point. Kendall did not try to set forth logically consistent doctrine *per se;* rather he probed for the popular mind, as he had learned in Kentucky in the 1820s." Lynn L. Marshall, "The Authorship of Jackson's Bank Veto Message," *Journal of American History* 50 (December 1963): 477.

[8] This question has been posed by many authors, particularly Esther Rogoff Taus, *Central Banking Functions of the United States Treasury, 1789–1941* (New York: Columbia University Press, 1943); Fritz Redlich, *The Molding of American Banking: Men and Ideas* (New York: Hafner Publishing Co., 1951); Smith; and Hammond. The question evaluates the Second Bank by modern, as opposed to contemporary, standards. Obviously, other standards could be used.

without strain on state banks. It tried, on occasion, to neutralize the effects of rapid international specie flows.[9]

Two functions of the Bank may be isolated as having primary importance in this regard. The Second Bank of the United States was chartered at a time when the state banks had suspended specie payments—that is, when they had refused to redeem their notes in specie at par. The government, which had to transfer money from state to state, could not fulfill its obligations, and the Second Bank was chartered to retrieve the government by inducing state banks to resume specie payments. In addition to restoring the redemption of notes at par at their place of issue, the new Bank of the United States also tried to ensure the circulation of notes at par at locations other than the point of issue. As stated above, the Bank moved in this direction by offering to redeem the notes of any of its branches at any other branch.

These efforts, however, were not initially successful. More exactly, they were initially successful, but the establishment of the Second Bank was followed by a crash in which the Bank figured prominently. We have already noted that the normal flow of bank notes was from West and South to the East, and when the Second Bank announced that all notes would be redeemed at all branches, notes from the southern and western branches of the Bank were presented for redemption at the eastern branches. There was no check on the issue of the western and southern branches; their notes returned to other branches, not to them. The managers of these branches did not respond to appeals to restrict their discounts, and the management of the branch at Baltimore took advantage of the general confusion to emulate them. As a result, the liabilities of the Second Bank grew without control.

In the summer of 1818, two years after the establishment of the Second Bank, the directors realized that the Bank was overextended. They rescinded the order making notes of the Bank redeemable at all branches, and they began to curtail the Bank's operations. Within a few months there was a banking panic, leading to severe deflation and depression. Catterall commented that the Second Bank's "Cur-

[9] Redlich, pp. 125–135; Smith, pp. 134–146.

tailments had, indeed, precipitated the panic, for which, however, it was hardly more responsible than was Noah for the flood."[10] The aptness of Catterall's simile may be questioned, but his general reasoning is sound. There was a rapid deflation in England, and there was bound to be some reaction to the shifting of demands after the War of 1812. Nevertheless, the severity of the crisis may not have been inevitable. If there had been no Bank of the United States, or if there had been a better-managed Bank of the United States, the crisis might have been less of a crisis and more of a gradual deflation. The parallel to the deflation after 1839 is striking. In each case, prices in the United States had to fall to bring them into line with prices in England; and in each case, the Bank of the United States was blamed.

But even if the role of the Second Bank is agreed upon, there is still an additional question to be answered. For if the Second Bank could not have avoided expansion in 1817 and 1818—due to institutional constraints or political pressure—then the management of the Bank cannot be held responsible for its role in the panic, even if that role was major. The Secretary of the Treasury in particular must bear a portion of the blame for the Panic of 1819. He persuaded the Bank of the United States to make a bad compact with the state banks in order to induce them to resume specie payments. The Second Bank agreed to act as if it had received government funds on deposit with the state banks, but not to actually receive them for five months. It agreed not to collect balances owed to it by the state banks until it had considerably expanded its business. And it agreed to accept checks on other state banks in payment for these debts. In other words, the Second Bank agreed to conduct its business as if it could collect the debts owed to it without actually collecting them. It could not obtain the government deposits it had to service, and it could collect private debts only by incurring other debts, at first because it had to expand its discounts and then because it was obligated to accept checks of one bank in payment of debts of another.

In addition, the Second Bank was hampered in those efforts it did make to curtail the activities of state banks. The Treasury resisted

[10] Catterall, p. 61.

any pressure on state banks in an effort to maintain specie payments, and state courts and legislatures did likewise in an effort to protect local businessmen. Although the management of the Second Bank was not blameless, the Treasury's pressure on the Bank was as important as the independent actions of the Bank in the expansion leading to the crisis. The cause of the Panic of 1819 was the banking structure that allowed each state to strike out on its own and the financial necessities of the federal government that placed it at the mercy of state banks.[11]

This glimpse of the early history of the Second Bank of the United States is important for several reasons. Whatever the correct view of the period, contemporaries were convinced that the Second Bank was culpable. This is typified in Gouge's often quoted statement about the attempts of the Bank to curtail its activities in 1818: "The Bank was saved and the people were ruined."[12] This hostility never disappeared, even though the Second Bank's management in 1832 bore no relation to the management in 1818. In addition, this episode raises the question of the relationship between the Bank of the United States and the Treasury. It is not clear whether the Bank had the power to work independently of the Treasury, or whether it was simply a means through which the Treasury exerted its influence. To the extent that it was the latter, its role as fiscal agent of the government was more important than its central banking activities.[13]

In any case, the Second Bank began the long process of rebuilding itself and public confidence. The policy of redeeming the Bank notes at any branch was abandoned and replaced by the defensive policy of paying out notes of other banks whenever possible. This policy defended the Bank because the Bank constantly received new supplies of notes of other banks from the government, which had received them in payment of duties or taxes. If the Bank paid with them instead of its own notes, it did not expand its own liabilities, and it ran little risk of depleting its specie reserves.

[11] Leon M. Schur, "The Second Bank of the United States and the Inflation after the War of 1812," *Journal of Political Economy* 68 (April 1960): 118–134; Catterall, pp. 24–26; Hammond, pp. 249–250.
[12] Quoted, for example, in Catterall, p. 61, and Hammond, p. 259.
[13] See Richard H. Timberlake, Jr., "The Specie Standard and Central Banking in the United States before 1860," *Journal of Economic History* 21 (September 1961): 318–341.

The cost of this defense was severe. As the Second Bank was paying out notes of state banks in return for bills discounted, it could not return these notes to the issuing bank for redemption. The Second Bank therefore had no means of control over the state banks.

Nicholas Biddle, when he assumed the presidency of the Second Bank in 1823, set out to restore the original policy of issuing the Bank's own notes. In order for the Second Bank to issue its own notes, it had to return state bank notes to the issuing bank for redemption. If it did not do so, it would accumulate balances of state bank notes—an asset of doubtful liquidity—to offset its highly liquid liability of bank notes. If it did, state banks would be prevented from issuing more notes than they could redeem, and the Second Bank would have established some measure of control over them. As a result of this control, discounts on state bank notes would fall as the expectation of easy redemption increased. People would then use these notes for interregional transfers instead of using only the Second Bank's notes, and the Second Bank could resume its offer to redeem its notes at any branch without fear of inundation in the East.[14]

The effects of this policy appear mostly in the rates of discounts for western bank notes. Using discounts on notes at Philadelphia— the home of the Second Bank—as a guide, we find the following experience. The discounts on New England notes fell continuously, but not very far. With the exception of notes from Maine, New England notes never sold at a discount of more than 5 percent. This narrowed to about 1 percent in the late 1820s, but for reasons that have little to do with the Second Bank. The Second Bank did not do very much business in New England, and the banking system in that region was highly sophisticated. The increasing quality of New England notes was the result of the policies of the Suffolk Bank (to be described shortly), not of the Bank of the United States.

Discounts on relatively poor notes from Middle Atlantic and Southeastern states fell from something over 5 percent in the early 1820s to something under 5 percent a decade later; high-quality notes from these regions sold near par throughout the period. Discounts on notes from western and southwestern banks stayed around 5

---

[14] Catterall, pp. 96–98. Biddle's predecessor, Cheves, had also redeemed state bank notes for specie on a regular basis. Ibid., p. 77.

percent, but notes from Tennessee, Kentucky, and Alabama went from being sold at great discounts—25 percent or more—to being accepted at the rates applicable to neighboring states. Although notes of distant banks did not circulate at par in Philadelphia, there was beginning to be a "national currency" usable without too much difficulty.[15]

We therefore must discriminate between the periods before and after Biddle's accession to the presidency of the Second Bank. During the first period—despite initial attempts to do more—the Second Bank of the United States was merely a large bank. It acted as the government's fiscal agent, but its management was too frightened to take any responsibility for the state of the currency or the economy. Nicholas Biddle acknowledged this responsibility when he became head of the Second Bank in 1823, and the Second Bank acted thereafter to produce a national currency by the symbiotic policies of issuing its own notes and rapidly redeeming the notes of other banks that it received.

There are three points to be noted about this policy. First, it was a deflationary policy. It restricted the volume of notes a bank could issue without depleting its reserves, but that is all it did. It was a substitute for a legal reserve requirement, even though the restrictions on bank activities were not as strict as a legal requirement would have been.[16]

Second, this policy was not unique to the Second Bank. The Suffolk Bank of Boston also redeemed notes as soon as it received them unless banks had agreed to maintain a balance at the Suffolk

[15] Jonathan Elliot, *The Funding System of the United States and Great Britain* (Washington, 1845), pp. 1106–1128 (printed also as U.S. Congress, House Document 15, 28th Congress, 1st Session); Sumner, p. 198; Catterall, pp. 442–444; Van Fenstermaker, pp. 77–95. A list of discounts, however, does not give a true measure of the currency. There were difficulties in dealing with myriad bank notes of varying quality, and the simple problem of obtaining information was formidable. A *Bank Note Reporter and Counterfeit Detector* of 1830 listed the current discount in New York on notes of 500 banks and the names of perhaps twice that number of counterfeit, altered, and spuriously signed notes. William H. Dillistin, *Bank Note Reporters and Counterfeit Detectors, 1826–1866* (New York: American Numismatic Society, 1949), p. 99.

[16] Hammond, p. 277, asserted that a central bank in an expanding economy had to be mostly "negative," that is, deflationary. This assertion seems to be based on Hammond's moralistic view of enterprise (see his comment, p. 275), a view that led him to claim, p. 573, that prices *rose* "persistently though haltingly" under the National Banking Act.

Bank for that purpose. The Suffolk Bank thus did for New England what the Bank of the United States was attempting to do for the rest of the country. The Suffolk Bank was a private bank, which shows that the policy in question was not dependent on government support. The bank redeeming or threatening to redeem notes needed only to have a source of notes to use. The Bank of the United States was the fiscal agent of the government, and it received from the government the notes paid to the government by individuals. The Suffolk Bank was a clearing house for several large Boston banks, and it acquired the notes paid to those banks.[17]

These two banks were specially situated, but all banks received notes of other banks and could present them for redemption. Why could not any bank regulate its fellows? Clearly, only a large bank could be an effective regulator. And more important than mere size was the volume of notes flowing into the bank. The Bank of the United States was particularly well suited to be an effective constraint on other banks—both because of its large size and its position as fiscal agent of the government—but it was by no means the only bank that could adopt the policy.

A problem must be raised at this point. What was to prevent banks, when presented with their notes for redemption by the Second Bank, from presenting to the Second Bank its notes in return? Clearly, nothing. Notes of the Second Bank could be counted as reserves by individual banks fearing the Second Bank's policy of presenting notes for redemption. Therefore, if the Second Bank wanted to affect the ratio of monetary liabilities to *specie* reserves, it had to ensure that the state banks did not have as many of its obligations as it had of theirs. Monetary obligations, of course, included deposits as well as notes, and a bank could cancel a debt to the Second Bank as easily as return its notes. Consequently, the Bank of the United States had to issue its notes and deposits less freely than an ordinary bank would have done—that is, it had to maintain a reserve of bank debts owed to it against its liabilities as well as a reserve of specie. As the balance sheet in Table 2.1 shows, the Second Bank had such a dual

---

[17] See the discussion of the Suffolk Bank in Redlich, I: 67–87, especially 71, where Redlich recognized that the power of the Suffolk Bank derived from its threat to present notes for redemption, even though various institutional forms obviated the use of this power in most cases.

reserve in 1832. It owed state banks $2.0 million, but the state banks owed to the Second Bank $6.1 million—the sum of their balances with the Second Bank and the value of their notes held by the Second Bank.[18]

The third point to be noted about the policy of rapid note redemption is that it was not discretionary. The Second Bank could police the state banks, but if it did so, it gave up the discretionary power to either increase or decrease the volume of money by varying the rate of note redemption. If the Second Bank allowed the supply of money to expand by accumulating a balance of state bank notes, it thereby relaxed its policing function. And since the Second Bank was returning notes to the issuing bank for redemption as fast as possible in ordinary times, there was no way for it to induce more contraction in other banks by this means.[19] If the Bank of the United States wished to preserve its policing function, therefore, it could affect the supply of money only in the same ways open to other banks. Because it was a large bank, it would have a large impact on the supply of money, but this impact would not differ from the impact of any other large bank. And only if the Bank of the United States was willing to lose its creditor status vis-à-vis other banks and consequently its opportunity to police them, could it expand the currency.[20]

In fact, the Bank of the United States in normal times assumed the role of policing the state banks rather than controlling the volume of money. In terms of modern institutions, it assumed a role performed by the Comptroller of the Currency in the late nineteenth century and now jointly by the Comptroller, the Federal Reserve, and the Federal Deposit Insurance Corporation.[21] As such, it was an important administrative agency of the government, but not a central bank.

Now let us turn to the question of the Second Bank's actions in

[18] This was a typical condition. U. S. Congress, Senate Document 128, 25th Congress, 2nd Session (1838), pp. 208–211.
[19] There were daily settlements in the major cities. Govan, pp. 85–86.
[20] Biddle's attempts to introduce a small amount of discretion into this function must be placed in this context. His minor indulgence of state banks in April 1825—cited by Hammond, p. 308—must be contrasted with his severity in October of that year, to be described below.
[21] Lester V. Chandler, *The Economics of Money and Banking,* 4th ed. (New York: Harper and Row, 1964), pp. 144, 179–180. The Comptroller still regulates all national banks in accordance with informal agreements between it and the other regulators. Ibid., p. 591.

crises. A central bank is supposed to act in crises as well as in normal times—a central bank's role in crisis being probably its most important defining characteristic. The essence of a crisis was the withdrawal of trust in the banking system by the public, and they all followed the same pattern. People became unwilling to hold bank obligations, fearing that banks would default on them. They attempted to exchange their bank notes or deposits for specie, exerting pressure on the banks, which did not have specie reserves equal to their liabilities. In order to get more specie—or some asset that would have replaced specie in the minds of the public—the banks called in their loans, hoping they would be paid at least partially in coin. Their debtors found it hard to pay off these loans in a time of stress, and the strain on them intensified the general lack of confidence in the monetary structure. More people demanded specie for bank notes or deposits, and the crisis deepened.

A central bank would have short-circuited this procedure by lending to the beleaguered banks. It would have supplied specie to the banks if it had specie, or—if it did not have specie—its notes might have done as well. In either case, the banks would not have had to call in loans to get the means to redeem their notes or deposits, and they would not have encouraged the general distrust. When people saw that the banks could pay off their obligations, they would once again have been willing to hold these obligations, and the crisis would have subsided. Because a central bank lends to banks when the banks cannot borrow elsewhere, it is called a "lender of last resort."

In the time between Biddle's accession to the presidency of the Second Bank in 1823 and Jackson's veto of the recharter bill in 1832, there was only one crisis serious enough to need a lender of last resort. This was the crisis of 1825, and the actions of the Bank in this crisis have been cited by investigators trying to show it was a central bank.

The literature does not assign a cause to the small expansion that led to the crisis of 1825, but it was part of a world-wide movement in 1824–1825. The Secretary of the Treasury moved to relieve the stringency existing in the money market in late 1824 by early repayment of government debt falling due January 1, 1825. This action did relieve the market, but as the expansion resulted in a panic the following year, the wisdom of this action may be questioned. Nevertheless, there can be no doubt that the Treasury was performing a central banking function.[22]

According to Redlich, a modern supporter of the Second Bank, Biddle realized the severity of the situation in April 1825, and started to prepare for a crisis. The Second Bank sold government securities and in other ways increased its reserves. When the expected crisis came in July 1825, Biddle was in a position to help the banking community. Redlich stated: "There can be no doubt that for some critical weeks in 1825 Biddle acted as the lender of last resort, thereby fulfilling a true central banking function." But Redlich added that the Bank was careful not to fall into debt to the state banks and that it was willing to sell government securities.[23]

These qualifications are very important. Biddle apparently was not willing to forego even temporarily the Second Bank's role as regulator of state banks in favor of the central banking function. The lender of last resort thus had to restrict its loans so as not to become a net debtor. The willingness to sell government securities also worked against the Bank's main policy. In a crisis, the central bank should act to bring money into circulation, enabling debts to be settled without a cumulative banking contraction. Selling government securities withdrew money from circulation and acted to encourage the crisis. Redlich defended the Second Bank's policy on the grounds that government securities were bought from hoards—as opposed to funds active in commerce—and that banks were not sensitive to their reserve position in any case.[24] This defense is not convincing. First, it is hard to believe that *all* purchases of government securities were made from hoards, and the actions of the Secretary of the Treasury in prepaying part of the public debt assumed just the opposite; namely, that at least some of the money acquired would be spent and not hoarded. Second, although banks did not use reserve ratios as modern banks do, nevertheless they were sensitive

[22] Taus, pp. 30–31; Margaret G. Myers, *The New York Money Market* (New York: Columbia University Press, 1931), I: 160–161.
[23] Redlich, I: 135–136.
[24] Ibid., p. 137.

to their reserve position. To use another inference, it is only in this case that the Second Bank's pressure against bank reserves through its presentation of notes for redemption has any meaning.

The other principal defender of the Second Bank as a central bank, Bray Hammond, recounted that the Bank was the agent in the government's repayment of seven million dollars of the public debt in October 1825. Since the Second Bank made this payment by extending its own obligations—that is, since it paid with its own notes and checks—it became indebted to the state banks. To correct this situation the Bank sold its holdings of government bonds, carrying on the policy for four weeks until it was secure.[25] The Second Bank was engaging in deflationary actions at exactly the time when inflationary movements were needed. It was withdrawing money from circulation to strengthen its reserves at a time when it should have been putting money into circulation to ease the crisis. Even if some of the Bank's new reserves came from hoards, the effect of its sales was still deflationary.

The result of all this was that "a sharp drop occurred in the total of Bank credit outstanding in November 1825, just when the business community would have been most grateful for an expansive policy." We may paraphrase the comment with which W. B. Smith followed this observation by saying that Biddle *and his supporters* have erred in exaggerating the helpfulness of the Second Bank in this emergency.[26]

The Bank of the United States, therefore, gets a higher rating on its aspirations to be a central bank than on its accomplishments. It helped to regulate the banking sector, but it was hampered by this regulatory function in its attempts to alleviate crises. It was unwilling to abandon temporarily its control over state banks in order to support them in the crisis of 1825, and it consequently never functioned as a lender of last resort. Nevertheless, the Second Bank was prob-

---

[25] Hammond, p. 310. See also Catterall, p. 107, and Smith, p. 139. Smith, like Redlich, said only that the Second Bank was in danger of falling into debt to the state banks. Biddle's account of the sales can be found in U. S. Congress, House Report 460, 22nd Congress, 1st Session (1832), pp. 434–435. He said the Second Bank was actually in debt to the state banks.

[26] Smith, p. 140. The Treasury's repayment of the public debt, of course, did serve to alleviate the crisis, to the extent that it was not offset by the Second Bank's actions.

ably as close to being a central bank as any bank of its day, and this judgment should not be interpreted to mean that there was no room for improvement. The veto of the Bank foreclosed this possibility, and it is lamented on these grounds by the supporters of the Bank.[27]

But even if the Second Bank had been a true central bank, would that have been desirable? It seems heretical to challenge this underlying assumption in most discussions, but there are a few points to be raised. It is assumed that a central bank would have acted to eliminate or at least reduce the severity of business fluctuations, but a recent study of the actions of the Federal Reserve in 1929–1933 casts some doubt on the reliability of this prediction.[28] In addition, it is taken for granted that business fluctuations were bad. . . . The depression of the early 1840s was not nearly as bad as has been thought. If the depression did not produce massive unemployment and loss of income, then it is quite possible that the costs of preventing it could have been greater than the costs of the depression. In particular, if the only way to avoid crises was to reduce sharply the rate of economic growth, the economy was probably better off with crises than without them.

This is not to suggest that all central banks are bad and that all economies in all times would be better off without them. It is, instead, a mild caveat to the use of modern standards to evaluate historical events. Central banks are modern institutions, and they operate today in a context very different from that of the nineteenth century. We like to think that the knowledge we have accumulated and the theories that we have formulated would have been of some use to our predecessors, but it does not necessarily follow that modern institutions controlled by men unfamiliar with modern ideas would have been of value. In fact, it is hard to see how any bank managed by men of the early nineteenth century could have fulfilled the role of a modern central bank, for the simple reason that this role is the product of late nineteenth and twentieth century ideas. Nicholas Biddle sometimes talked like a modern central banker, but it would have been

[27] Smith, p. 254; Hammond, p. 346.
[28] Milton Friedman and Anna Jacobson Schwartz, *A Monetary History of the United States, 1867–1960* (Princeton: Princeton University Press, 1963). Chapter 7 published separately as *The Great Contraction.*

a superhuman effort for him to have taken the Second Bank far enough out of its contemporary setting to make it into a true central bank.[29]

[29] It is worth noting that the Second Bank's founders and supporters generally did not support it on central banking grounds. See Timberlake, 1961, on this point, and Frank Whitson Fetter, *Development of British Monetary Orthodoxy, 1797–1875* (Cambridge: Harvard University Press, 1965), for an analysis of the Bank of England at this time.

Suggestions for Additional Reading

Three brief studies published in recent years contribute substantially to our understanding of the Bank War. The most general of these is Robert V. Remini, *Andrew Jackson and the Bank War, A Study in the Growth of Presidential Power* (New York, 1967). Objective, carefully researched, and acceptably written, it provides the best, brief summary of the controversy available. The subtitle correctly indicates its emphasis. Selections from the other two works are reproduced in this volume. They are Jean Alexander Wilburn's *Biddle's Bank, The Crucial Years* (New York, 1967) and Peter Temin's *The Jacksonian Economy* (New York, 1969). Both deserve to be read in full. Both plow new ground, providing fresh interpretations and first rate examples of modern methods of historical research and analysis. Wilburn's quantitative investigation throws important new light on contemporary attitudes toward the bank and Temin's economic analysis casts serious doubt on a number of commonly accepted explanations for the economic fluctuations of the time.

Other relatively recent studies well worth examination include Frank O. Gatell's *The Jacksonians and the Money Power*, as well as a number of journal contributions. Among the latter may be listed Jacob Meerman, "The Climax of the Bank War: Biddle's Contraction, 1833–1834," *Journal of Political Economy* 71 (August 1963): 378–388; Harry N. Scheiber, "The Pet Banks in Jacksonian Politics and Finance, 1833–1841," *Journal of Economic History* 23 (June 1963): 196–214; Lynn L. Marshall, "The Authorship of Jackson's Bank Veto Message," *Journal of American History* 50 (December 1963): 466–477; and Leon M. Schur, "Second Bank of the United States and the Inflation After the War of 1812," *Journal of Political Economy* 68 (April 1960): 118–134. Valuable articles have also appeared by two authors whose work has, in part at least, come under critical scrutiny by Peter Temin (see above). Thus alerted the reader must draw his own conclusions. The articles are: Richard H. Timberlake, Jr., "The Specie Standard and Central Banking in the United States before 1860," *Journal of Economic History* 21 (September 1961): 318–341, and "The Specie Circular and the Sales of Public Lands: A Comment," *Journal of Economic History* 25 (September 1965): 414–416; and George Macesich, "Sources of Monetary Disturbances in the United States, 1834–

1845," *Journal of Economic History* 20 (September 1960): 407–434, and "International Trade and United States Economic Development Revisited," *Journal of Economic History* 21 (September 1961): 384–385.

Two classic studies provide almost indispensable background reading on the history of the second Bank: Ralph C. H. Catterall, *The Second Bank of the United States* (Chicago, 1903) and Bray Hammond, *Banks and Politics in America from the Revolution to the Civil War* (Princeton, 1957). These standard works are valuable despite certain shortcomings: Catterall's unconscious bias in favor of the Bank and Hammond's focus on certain pet interpretations such as the importance of Biddle as a central banker.

Of the general histories of banking in the United States, among the most useful are Paul Studenski and Herman E. Krooss, *Financial History of the United States* (New York, 1952) and W. J. Shultz and M. B. Caine, *Financial Development of the United States* (New York, 1937). On the history of banking theories, consult Lloyd W. Mints, *A History of Banking Theory* (Chicago, 1945) and Sister M. Grace Madeleine, *Money and Banking Theories of Jacksonian Democracy* (Phila., 1943). Standard works emphasizing economic aspects of the Bank are Fritz Redlich, *The Moulding of American Banking: Men and Ideas*, 2 vols. (New York, 1951); Walter B. Smith, *Economic Aspects of the Second Bank of the United States* (Cambridge, 1953) and Esther R. Taus, *Central Banking Functions of the United States Treasury* (New York, 1943). Among the general interpretations of the Jacksonian period especially interesting are John William Ward, *Andrew Jackson: Symbol for an Age* (Princeton, 1961) and Marvin Meyers, *The Jacksonian Persuasion: Politics and Belief* (Stanford, 1957).

Considerable light on the Bank War is shed by the biographies which have been written about those playing an important role in the contest. On Jackson himself, Robert V. Remini is responsible for a handy, relatively recent study entitled *Andrew Jackson* (New York, 1966). Valuable older and more detailed works are John S. Bassett, *The Life of Andrew Jackson* (New York, 1928) and Marquis James, *The Life of Andrew Jackson* (Garden City, N.Y., 1938). Thomas Govan's *Nicholas Biddle* (Chicago, 1959) provides a detailed, indispensable biography of the Bank's president. To imitate a statement once made concerning George Bancroft's *History*, it may be said that on almost every page Govan votes for Biddle and against Jackson. Useful biographies of other contemporaries are William M. Chambers, *Old Bullion Benton, Senator from the New West* (Boston, 1956); Elbert B. Smith, *Magnificent Missourian: The Life of Thomas Hart Benton* (Phila., 1958); Carl Swisher, *Roger B. Taney* (New York, 1936); Charles Wiltse, *John C. Calhoun, Nullifier* (New York, 1949); Glyndon G. Van Dusen, *The Life of Henry Clay* (Boston, 1937); and Richard N. Current, *Daniel Webster and the Rise of National Conservatism* (Boston, 1955).

For the historiography of the Jackson era, the student can do no better than to consult Alfred A. Cave, *Jacksonian Democracy and the Historians* (Gainsville, Fla., 1964). A good brief bibliography of the contemporary source materials available on the struggle over recharter may be found in Wilburn (see above), pages 137–139. Especially useful is the *Register of Debates* in Congress, volume viii. The student who wishes to get his own view of the contemporary controversy over the veto message should read for July and August 1832, the rival Washington newspapers, *The Globe* and *The Intelligencer.* Both reprint editorials from all over the country and both are available on films.